GW00854198

# THE FREE, THE UNFREE AND THE EXCLUDED

# The Free, the Unfree and the Excluded

A treatise on the conditions of liberty

PHILLIP COLE
*Centre for Practical Philosophy*
*Middlesex University*

**Ashgate**
Aldershot • Brookfield USA • Singapore • Sydney

Published by
Ashgate Publishing Ltd
Gower House
Croft Road
Aldershot
Hants GU11 3HR
England

Ashgate Publishing Company
Old Post Road
Brookfield
Vermont 05036
USA

**British Library Cataloguing in Publication Data**
Cole, Phillip
  The free, the unfree and the excluded : a treatise on the
  conditions of liberty. - (Avebury series in philosophy)
  1. Autonomy (Philosophy) 2. Liberty 3. Social control 4. Social
  justice
  I. Title
  123.5

**Library of Congress Catalog Card Number:** 98-71968

ISBN 1 85628 954 0

Printed in Great Britain by The Ipswich Book Company, Suffolk

# Contents

# Acknowledgements

This book began life as a PhD thesis, awarded by the University of Keele, and thanks is due to Dr Brian Smart who supervised that process. Parts of it have also been tested in classes and research seminars at various institutions, and so thanks are due to colleagues and students at Staffordshire University and Middlesex University for their critical and supportive feedback over the years. Finally, thanks to Dr Roshi Naidoo, who lived through both stages of its life with the utmost patience, and whose own work and intellect have set me standards and principles I can only hope this work can live up to.

Some sections of the book have been adapted from previously published essays. Chapter 3 develops arguments first published as "Social Liberty and the Physically Disabled", *Journal of Applied Philosophy*, Volume 4 Number 1, 1987, pp.29-39. Chapter 6 draws on "Liberalism and Welfare: the Limits of Compensation", *Liberalism and the New Europe*, eds. B. Brecher and O. Fleischmann (Avebury, Aldershot, 1993).

# Introduction

This book develops a particular theory of freedom, and explores the relationships between this view of freedom and issues of social justice. Often, the idea of freedom has a negative role to play in relation to the idea of social justice -- its function is to limit the scope of social justice, to set boundaries around programmes of social justice in order to preserve 'individual liberty'. This is usually stated in terms of a conflict between state authority and individual liberty, such that state action is often, if not always, a threat to that liberty: and as programmes of social justice are most often state-provided, such programmes themselves encroach upon the sphere of freedom. Undoubtedly, the idea of freedom does have a legitimately negative role to play here, but the claim explored in this book is that it also has a positive role to play which is *prima facie* equally important. Rather than simply acting as a negative side-constraint upon programmes of social justice, freedom is also a positive goal that programmes of social justice must pursue. Therefore the idea of freedom contributes substantial content to the theory of social justice, rather than simply drawing boundaries around it.

There is a specific family of issues of social justice which, it is claimed, can be best understood as problems of freedom. These issues can be characterized as a particular form of deprivation, best understood as exclusion, where particular groups are excluded from full participation within society's institutions and practices. The claim is that full participation is constitutive of freedom, and that therefore exclusion from participation is a violation of freedom. Seeing these issues of exclusion as problems of freedom leads to a distinctive approach to how they should be understood within the context of social justice, and a distinctive view of what social justice demands in these cases. Therefore the book examines the relationship between freedom and social justice both in theory and practice, and the way in which that relationship has been specified in liberal theories. The practical problem being addressed is the exclusion of certain groups from particular institutions and practices, and the strategies of social justice which can best tackle this form of deprivation.

The theory of freedom developed is impure. It is argued that freedom has positive as well as negative aspects and conditions -- that

1

people require both the space and power to be free; one without the other is insufficient as a guarantee of liberty. Neither the space nor the power needed for liberty can be preserved in a purely negative way. Freedom can only be ensured by taking positive steps. Without such a framework of empowerment, any space preserved by the purely negative framework not merely remains empty, it collapses in upon itself. It must therefore be part of any programme of social justice to create, preserve and protect the positive conditions of freedom.

The theory of freedom is radically impure in that while freedom requires both negative and positive conditions, and requires some balance between the two, no single such balance that will be right for all people under all circumstances is identified. People differ, and the conditions they require for freedom differ. There can be no *apriori* priority laid down for either aspect of liberty, positive or negative: this priority cannot be decided at the level of theory, only at the level of practice. This impure theory contrasts with purer negative or positive theories in this respect. These purer theories do not simplistically identify only positive or only negative aspects or conditions of freedom -- most theories of liberty do identify both sorts of condition as important. However, they *do* proclaim the priority of one kind of condition over the other, such that when there is a clash between the two, it is allegedly theoretically transparent which ought to prevail. Another consequence of such priority is that the absence of the secondary type of condition does not constitute a violation of freedom. In contrast, the impure theory of freedom claims that, where there is a clash, which kind of condition ought to prevail can only be decided in the particular circumstances of the situation, not at the abstract level of theory; and that the absence of either type of condition can constitute a violation of liberty. As a consequence, the impure theory describes a distinctive relationship between freedom and ability, a relationship which is both simpler and more politically satisfying than that relationship as described in purer theories.

A distinction has been made between the negative and positive *aspects* and *conditions* of freedom. By the negative and positive aspects of liberty it is to be understood that the free person (1) is not prevented from doing *x* (negative; non-interference), and (2) is able to do *x* (positive; power) -- they must have both the *space* and the *power* to act. By the negative and positive conditions of liberty is meant those conditions which must be in place if the negative and positive aspects are to be guarantied: these conditions are negative and positive in the sense that some such conditions are characterized by an *absence* of certain factors, while other such conditions are characterized by the *presence* of certain factors. What the impure theory crucially recognizes is that both negative and positive conditions *each* contribute to *both* the negative and positive aspects of liberty; and that the undermining of either negative *or* positive conditions of freedom can destroy *both* the negative and positive aspects.

The connection between freedom and social justice is made through establishing the conditions for freedom: what must fill the space and constitute the power of the free person is choice and the power to enact choice; but that choice must have a certain quality -- that is, it must be *autonomous* choice. The free person is an autonomous chooser and doer. Therefore there are three types of condition for freedom: first, the negative condition of being left alone to act out choices; second, the positive condition of being able to make choices about which action to take; third, the positive condition of being able to act out choices. These three types of condition can be summarized as:

(1)    The Non-interference Condition: being left alone to choose which plan of life one wishes to pursue.
(2)    The Autonomy Condition: the capacity to make rational choices concerning the best options to pursue.
(3)    The Power Condition: the powers and resources needed in order to pursue those chosen options.

The programme of social justice aims to ensure the positive conditions that underlie freedom, the Autonomy Condition and the Power Condition. It can ensure the Autonomy Condition be putting in place the kind of education and access to information needed in order to make autonomous choices, as well as those levels of welfare required to ensure that people are in a condition to make such choices. It can ensure the Power Condition by enabling all to have access to the powers and resources they need to act out their choices in practice.

Therefore the impure theory of freedom places positive demands upon social justice. Part of the programme of social justice is concerned with the conditions needed to be an active chooser, doer and participator in the community: that is, an actively participating member. Social injustice arises when people are deprived of that opportunity, when they are excluded from the community, when their membership is rendered empty. Therefore programmes of social justice cannot be restricted to compensating people for the effects of exclusion, but must aim at the ending of that exclusion. People are excluded from active participation in the community, not by their nature, but by alterable social, political, cultural and economic practices.

3

In those cases where it is considered that those practices can be altered, so that people can become active participants, then the failure to alter those practices is both a violation of liberty *and* a social injustice. It is a violation of liberty because it constitutes the failure to provide the positive conditions for freedom to which all members of the community are entitled. It is a social injustice because it deprives people of the equal opportunity to be active participants in their own community, an opportunity to which all are equally entitled.

And so the close connection between freedom and social justice can be seen. There are some issues of freedom that are also issues of social justice; that is, those issues of freedom that rest on the provision of the positive conditions of liberty. Therefore there are some issues of social justice that are also issues of freedom. This book focusses on those issues. This is not to claim that all issues of freedom are issues of social justice; nor is it to claim that the sole aim of a theory of social justice is to ensure the conditions of freedom. The claim is only that it is at least part of the concern of social justice that the conditions of freedom be enjoyed equally by all.

At heart, the approach taken in this book is based on the notion of *entitlement*: it is, in an important sense, an entitlement theory. The fundamental assumption underlying the arguments is that all people are of equal moral and political weight: all should receive equal consideration when it comes to ethical or political questions. This principle of the moral equality of persons is one that anything recognizable as a liberal political theory would share. However, the approach taken here is to draw strong consequences from that principle, stronger than most liberal theories would be prepared to accept. It is argued that, in virtue of their moral and political equality, all people are, *prima facie*, entitled to the equal value of their membership of the community; and this *prima facie* entitlement to equal membership gives rise to an equal entitlement to what is required to ground such membership, to be an actively participating member. The entitlement is *prima facie* in that it can be over-ridden, but very strong grounds are needed to justify any such move. The entitlement to the equal opportunity to be active participants in the community is therefore grounded in the fact of membership of that community. While most (if not all) liberal theories do hold the principle of moral equality of persons, and therefore that all carry equal moral and political weight, they do not hold that all are entitled to the equal value of membership of the community; or if they do, the grounds needed to over-ride that *prima facie* entitlement are set at too low a level. The critique of this gap within liberal theories between the principle of

4

moral equality and the commitment to the equal value of membership constitutes the negative aspect of the book. It develops criticisms of theories of freedom that recognize the need only for negative conditions of liberty; or which, if they do recognize the need for both kinds of condition, give theoretical priority to the negative. This priority cannot be justified, either in theory or practice.

There are also criticisms of views of social justice that claim that freedom in a negative sense takes priority over the aims and goals of social justice: that is, theories that see freedom purely in terms of a negative side-constraint, rather than as one of the positive goals of programmes of welfare. Such a view restricts programmes of welfare to after-the-event compensation strategies, which aim to compensate people for their exclusion from the community, or the loss of the value of their freedom. This priority of the negative cannot be justified. If this is correct, it means that there are no good theoretical reasons why the community should not pursue the goal of the equal value of membership for all, whatever positive demands that places upon the community. The community, or its agencies, must act to create, maintain, and protect the conditions of active membership, such that all have an equal opportunity to be active choosers, doers and participators at all levels of society.

## Chapter Outlines

### Part 1: Groundwork

### Chapter 1: Methods and Assumptions
This chapter outlines the approach taken to political philosophy. The approach is not neutral: the book engages in the clarification of political concepts, such as freedom, autonomy and justice; but it aims to clarify them in a normative way. While alternative definitions may be simpler and clearer than the definitions offered here, the argument is that those definitions are morally inadequate. For example, "freedom is the absence of coercion" is admirably clear and concise as a definition, but is morally inadequate if meant to be complete and all-inclusive. Definitions of the concepts in political philosophy are *essentially* normative: firstly, because they define values; and secondly, because it is impossible to lay down correct rules for the use of these terms that are morally or politically neutral. There is no neutral high ground available for the political philosopher.

Definitions of political concepts are also essentially *incomplete*. Freedom, equality, power, etc., can take many different forms in practice, such that no single definition can capture them all. Therefore, while any such definition of freedom can capture *some* aspects of freedom, it would be over-ambitious to claim that it has captured freedom in its entirety: it may enable us to articulate some problems of freedom, but it may be inadequate to deal with other families of such problems. Therefore the discourse of freedom must be open-ended, allowing room for other definitions of freedom which, while incompatible with the definition favoured in this book, do not necessarily contradict it.

*Chapter 2: The Impure Theory of Freedom*
This chapter outlines the impure theory of freedom and its connections with the idea of social justice. The impure theory of freedom recognizes the necessity of both positive and negative conditions of freedom, of both the space and power to be free; and it places no *a priori* priority on either kind of condition.

The chapter also outlines a close rival theory: impure negative theory. Both theories recognize, as any theory of freedom must, that some cases of the inability to act are violations of the freedom to act, but they differ over which cases of inability count. Impure negative theory recognizes the need for both negative and positive conditions for the freedom to act, but still gives priority to the negative conditions by arguing that it is only interference with these negative conditions that constitutes violation of freedom. Those who lack the positive conditions for freedom are not unfree, they are merely unable. Impure negative theory therefore argues that only cases of the absence of the negative conditions of freedom are issues of freedom; absence of the positive conditions constitutes some other kind of issue. In this chapter, it is argued that impure theory is superior to impure negative theory in its conception of unfreedom.

*Part 2: Issues of Freedom*

*Chapter 3: Freedom and Ability*
In this chapter, the example of the physically disabled is examined to show how the impure theory of freedom enables us to deal with problems of exclusion and marginalization. The situation of the disabled is characterized as an issue of freedom: their exclusion from certain social institutions and practices is a violation of their liberty.

It is argued that alternative theories of freedom fail to do justice to the exclusion of the disabled from active participation in the community, by taking it that it is inalterable. Rather, this exclusion is not merely the result of natural disability, but also of alterable social, political and economic practices: while such groups are disabled by their nature, they are unabled by alterable social practices. Therefore the failure to alter those social practices is a violation of their freedom, a violation which is concealed by the rival theories of freedom.

## Chapter 4: Freedom and Autonomy
This chapter articulates the three types of condition for freedom: the Non-Interference Condition, the Autonomy Condition, and the Power Condition; and it focusses in particular on the Autonomy Condition. If freedom is constituted by both the space and power to act, then one aspect of freedom must be concerned not merely with the space to choose to act in a particular way, nor the power to enact those choices in particular ways, but also the quality of those choices: they must be *autonomous* choices. This chapter develops this concern with the quality of the will, and argues that this is a legitimate concern for a theory of social justice.

## Part 3: Issues of Justice

## Chapter 5: Freedom and Neutrality
The notion of an active community, acting to ensure the autonomy of its members, raises the danger of an over-active state, deciding what sort of lives people must lead, and imposing a particular conception of the valuable life upon people. To avoid this danger, it might be argued, the community must remain neutral on the question of the valuable life, and the best way to do this is to insist on the priority of the negative interpretation of freedom as a side-constraint. Therefore, even though the more positive aspect of the theory of freedom may be coherent, there are still good reasons to give a negative non-interference principle of freedom priority.

In this chapter it is argued that such an objection is mistaken. The most valuable form of neutrality is neutrality *between persons* -- that persons are regarded as having equal moral weight. But this neutrality between persons does not entail neutrality on the question of what makes life valuable: instead, that question must be answered if the equal value of life chances is to be secured: an anarchic anything-goes principle according to which the negative non-interference principle is strictly adhered to, is not regarded as a coherent option.

## Chapter 6: Freedom and Equality

It might still be objected that the danger of the over-active state is still more serious than the danger of the under-active citizen: the inequality of life chances is not such a serious injustice that such an intensive programme of social justice is called for.

In this chapter it is argued that the inequality of life chances undermines membership and therefore violates freedom, and that this inequality *is* sufficiently serious to justify the kind of programme of social justice envisaged here, that seeks to ground the equality of active membership for all. The argument is based on two grounds:

(1) Inequality of economic and social position leads to inequalities along many other dimensions, including health and longevity. These values are distributed according to economic and social position. The fact that someone has more of a material resource than another may not seem that serious an injustice; but the fact that someone, because of their enjoyment of those greater resources, also enjoys a longer and healthier life than that other, is a serious injustice. For example, the opportunity to give birth to a living, healthy child is not distributed equally; nor is it distributed randomly -- it is distributed according to social and economic position.

(2) Social and economic position cannot be separated from political position: from the value of membership. The value of participative membership is destroyed by inequality of resources. This unequal membership is morally indefensible. And as the free agent is characterized as the equally active choose, doer and participator in the community -- as the active citizen -- then such inequality destroys freedom.

Therefore a commitment to rough equality of resources is justifiable both in terms of arguments from justice and freedom.

## Chapter 7: Freedom and Welfare

The programme of social justice called for by the impure theory of freedom, and the characterization of the free agent as an equally active chooser, doer and participator in their community, has a particular shape. It must move beyond the compensatory, backward-looking theories of social justice that dominate liberal political theory

Rather, this chapter argues for an approach to social justice that aims to include and enable all members of the community, in the name of equal liberty. It is argued that the kind of welfare provision that actually dominates in liberal-capitalist states does little to secure the equal worth of liberty. By failing to tackle the causes of exclusion, such systems of welfare allow the positive conditions of freedom to be destroyed, and therefore allow the value of membership of the community itself to be destroyed.

Exclusion from the major institutions and practices of our society is the destruction of freedom; it is a social injustice for that reason. And so exclusion is a particular type of issue of social justice, one which calls, not merely for compensation, but for positive steps to restore or create and protect the conditions of liberty -- one which calls for something best understood as liberation.

# Part 1
# Groundwork

# 1 Methods and Assumptions

## Section 1.1 -- The Nature of Political Theories

Political philosophy is concerned with political theories, and political theories are concerned with political values and their application to the world. Different political theories can be characterized by making a list of their political values. But this may not be that useful, because different theories may have exactly the same list of values -- so in what sense can they be different theories? The answer is that different theories place those values in a different order of priority -- they have different agendas. Therefore, if a political theory is to be characterized, its values must be placed in an order of priority. However, this may still not be that useful: a neat list of values in a cardinal order may not be practically possible -- theories are more complex than this. Rather, theories should be seen as *patterns*, rather than lists, of values, each consigning different weights to those values -- it is their extra weight within the pattern that gives certain values priority over others. It is helpful to imagine political theories as three-dimensional models, with values arranged close or distant from one another. What characterizes a political theory is the way in which it arranges those values: some will lie close to the centre, or close to each other; others may be in the margins or at a distance from each other. A stable political theory *can* contain values that clash with each other, but maintain its stability by keeping those values at a distance from each other, or mediating them through some other value. If this three-dimensional metaphor is accurate, then political theories are highly complex systems of values.

This book is concerned with the value of freedom, and it specifically addresses the value of freedom as found within contemporary liberal theories. The variety and complexity of liberal thought presents an immediate problem [1]. The focus on the value of liberty is not meant to suggest that liberty is the only political value on the liberal agenda, nor even that it necessarily comes at the top of the liberal agenda -- in fact, the value that most characterizes liberal theory is that of moral equality, the equal moral value of persons. However, any liberal theory certainly gives prominent place to the value of liberty, and it does play a central role in anything recognizable as a liberal theory.

Other values one could expect to find in a liberal theory are these: pluralism, welfare, social justice, equality [2], neutrality, democracy,

13

public order, limited government, private property. Some liberal theories no doubt include other values, or omit some of these: some may omit the value of equality, or democracy, or social justice. Even where different theories have roughly the same list of values, they combine them in different patterns and give them different weights -- some may place the greatest weight on private property, others on limited government, or on liberty, or on neutrality [3].

Another source of variation is that different values will clash within different theories. For example, some may feel that a commitment to the value of equality clashes with the commitment to neutrality, and they would have a point. Others might claim that the value of social justice clashes with the values of limited government and private property, and again they would have a point: social justice may demand the redistribution of wealth, and that may entail the need for a more extensive state, and may also require the violation or over-riding of private property rights. But this is only a serious problem if the values of private property or limited government in the theory carry a weight comparable to that of the value of social justice.

Similarly, different values can be seen as complimenting each other: some may tie the value of liberty close to the value of private property, while others may argue that the value of private property actually undermines the value of liberty. Understood in terms of the three-dimensional model of political theories, each value has attracting and repelling forces, which pull some values close together while pushing others way. These clashes or attractions depend upon how each value is characterized: each value may be given a different characterization within different theories. This is why different values, such as freedom and equality, can be held both to clash with each other and complement each other in different theories; it depends how freedom and equality are characterized.

Part of the project of this book is a critique of contemporary liberal theory's treatment of freedom and social justice and the relationship between these two values. The complexity of political theories, especially liberal theories, renders that project perilous. It is critical, but critical of what? Of liberal theory, but which particular version? Faced with that variety and complexity, one has no choice but to identify certain strands which run through liberal thought: of a certain conception of liberty as predominantly negative; of a certain conception of social justice as predominantly compensatory; of a conception of neutrality which rules out appeal to the idea of the valuable or good life. One cannot claim that these strands run through *all* possible versions of liberal theory, but they are sufficiently common to act as the ground of criticism of such figures as Robert Nozick and John Rawls. But what must be avoided is a reductionist picture of liberal theory, which characterizes it as a single-value theory, or as a theory which necessarily privileges one particular value over others.

## Section 1.2 -- Freedom and Equality

The focus of this book falls upon the values of liberty and social justice and the relationship between them: the claim is that the specification of that relationship found in contemporary liberal thought means that programmes of social justice would in fact fall far short of securing the conditions of liberty. This claim, of course, depends upon particular characterizations of the values of freedom and social justice, which will be supplied in chapter 2; but it also requires a qualification. The overall goal of a theory of social justice is to ensure that the conditions needed for a particular conception of the valuable or good life are in place and accessible to all people entitled to that life, whatever that conception of the valuable life and whatever the grounds of entitlement. Therefore such strategies aim to secure a whole pattern of values. The value of freedom must therefore be kept in context: it is not the only goal of a theory of social justice, and may not be the most important goal. The claim being made here is simply that it should be at least *one* of the central goals of any theory of social justice.

The theory of social justice described in chapter 2 is egalitarian: it assumes that all members of the community are entitled to the equal value of that membership, and that the task of social justice is therefore to ensure that all members of the community have equal access to the conditions that provide the foundation for the value of membership. Membership comprises being an equally active chooser, doer and participator in the community. This egalitarian principle has its source in the moral equality of persons, that all persons are morally and politically equal, and should therefore receive equal consideration when it comes to moral and political issues. Therefore the whole project rests upon an assumption of a principle of the moral equality of persons. This principle will, however, remain an assumption, and the only defence offered of it here is that it is the central political intuition of modern political theory, and that it plays a central role in the liberal political tradition. Amy Gutmann claims that what distinguishes modern political theory from ancient or classical theories is the commitment to individualism, and that the belief in human equality has its source in this individualism. An assumption of human equality is

15

the "unifying theme of liberalism..." (Gutmann, 1980, p.18), although "...no single postulate of human equality is to be found in classical liberal theory" (Ibid.). She identifies two equality assumptions within the classical liberal tradition: firstly, an assumption of the equality of passions, typified by Hobbes, Bentham and John Stuart Mill; and secondly, an assumption of the equality of rationality, typified by Locke and Kant (Ibid., chapter 1, especially pp.18-20). The equality assumption is widely appealed to by contemporary liberal theorists. For example, John Gray describes it as a principle "that confers on all men the same moral status and denies the relevance to legal or political order of differences in moral worth among human beings" (Gray, 1986, p.x). Antony Flew describes it as a principle of respect for persons "as choosers and doers of their own ends" (Flew, 1981, p.43), and says that it is "sometimes seen as a secular version of something believed to be common to the three great traditions of Mosaic theism, Judaism, Christianity, and Islam as popularly presented as teaching the Brotherhood of Man under the Fatherhood of God, with the apparent consequence that all human souls are of equal value in the eyes of their Creator" (Ibid., p.21). And Bruce Ackerman describes the "liberal assertion of equality" (Ackerman, 1980, p.67), which states: "1. I am a person with a conception of the good. 2. Simply by being such a person, I'm at least as good as you are" (Ibid.). Will Kymlicka takes the "duty to treat people with equal consideration" (Kymlicka, 1990, p.34) as a basic principle upon which political theories can be critically assessed. For example, what is attractive about utilitarianism as a moral theory is its "deepest principle" (Ibid., p.36), that is: "Each person has an equal moral standing, each person matters as much as any other..." (Ibid., p.37); and what is unattractive about it is its failure to adequately deliver that principle in practice (Ibid., pp.35-47). He takes seriously Ronald Dworkin's view, that every plausible political theory is based upon equality as the ultimate political value (Ibid., p.4) [4]:

> A theory is egalitarian in this sense if it accepts that the interests of each member of the community matter, and matter equally. Put another way, egalitarian theories require that the government treat its citizens with equal consideration; each citizen is entitled to equal concern and respect. This more basic notion of equality is found in Nozick's libertarianism as much as in Marx's communism. (Ibid., p.4)

16

However, while this ideal of moral equality, of treating persons as equals, is taken as fundamental in liberal political theory, there is also the problem that: "The idea of moral equality is too abstract for us to be able to deduce anything very specific from it" (Ibid., p.43). And: "The idea of moral equality, while fundamental, is too abstract to serve as a premiss from which we deduce a theory of justice" (Ibid., p.44). With that caution in mind, it has to be clear how the principle of moral equality can be used in political argument: "Each theory of justice is not *deduced from* the ideal of equality, but rather *aspires to* it, and each theory can be judged by how well it succeeds in that aspiration" (Ibid., p.44).

Therefore while, in one sense, it is difficult to ground such a notion of moral equality, it also seems intuitively indispensable. Michael Walzer recognizes both these aspects when he identifies two questions: (1) in what respects are we equal?; and (2) by virtue of what characteristics are we equal? (Walzer, 1983, p.xii). While he attempts to answer the first question, he says he does not know the answer to the second. However:

The answer has to do with our recognition of one another as human beings, members of the same species, and what we recognize are bodies and minds and feelings and hopes and maybe even souls. For the purposes of this book, I assume the recognition. We are different and we are also manifestly alike. (Ibid., p.xii)

According to the position being developed here, moral equality gives rise to the *prima facie* entitlement to the equal value of membership of the community: unless there are very strong grounds to justify inequality, all members of the community are equally entitled to the benefits and burdens that arise from that community. Again, Walzer recognizes the importance of membership:

Membership is important because of what the members of a political community owe one another and to no one else, or to no one else in the same degree. And the first thing they owe is the communal provision of security and welfare. (Ibid., p.64)

This means that the theory is egalitarian at another level, in that it aims at the rough equality of outcomes: the moral equality of persons can only be guarantied by the equal value of membership of the community, and this can only be guarantied by equal distribution of the

17

resources needed to be actively participating members of that community. The entitlement to the equal opportunity to be active choosers, doers and participators in the community is grounded in the fact of membership. Social injustice, therefore, consists of the *exclusion* of certain groups from that opportunity. Therefore the exclusion of groups such as the physically disabled from certain institutions and practices undermines their equal membership of the community, and therefore constitutes a *prima facie* injustice. Unless some compelling reason can be found to justify the exclusion of such groups from these institutions and practices, then this exclusion is a social injustice. It is assumed that no such justifying reason can be found in these cases, and therefore the fact of injustice is established.

The connection with the theory of liberty is made through the conception of the free person as an equally active chooser, doer and participator in the community -- a chooser and doer of their own ends, and a participator in the choosing and doing of the ends of the community of which they are a member. The free person is, therefore, not *independent* of the community, but is embedded within it; respect for their freedom requires their full inclusion as members of the community. The free person has a range of options from which to choose, and those options need to be embedded within a community in order to be meaningful -- positionless people lack genuinely meaningful options. The exclusion of people from membership of the community deprives them of the opportunity to make genuinely meaningful choices, and this is to deprive them of their autonomy. The autonomy of the agent does not only rest upon their powers of rational decision-making, their self-understanding, it also rests upon the nature of the community.

The freedom of the agent therefore rests upon the opportunity to be an active member of the community. Freedom is not the absence of social context, it is the presence of a certain form of social context, a context that ensures the conditions of freedom. Therefore the theory of freedom must be concerned with the social context for action, and therefore must make positive connections with the question of social justice. The freedom and equality of members of the community are therefore intimately connected: anything that undermines their membership of the community must injure their freedom; and anything that undermines their freedom injures their membership.

Liberty and an egalitarian theory of social justice are, therefore, not opposed to each other -- the theory of liberty developed here requires an egalitarian theory. This connection is worth stating, because freedom and equality of outcome are often portrayed as values which necessarily clash -- more freedom means less equality, more equality means less freedom. But this equation is naive, over-simplistic, and politically damaging for those who find themselves lacking that aspect of equality which is important for liberty.

In this context, equality and freedom do not clash. Instead, the claim is that people should have equal access to the resources, opportunities and powers they need in order to be equally choosing, doing and participating members of the community; that an important constitutive element of their freedom is to be able to choose, do, and participate in the community; and that an important element of their equality is their freedom to choose and do and participate. Lack of access to those resources, opportunities and powers undermines both freedom and equality. That is why the central concern of this book is the destruction of the freedom of certain marginalized groups in the community, and why the focus falls upon the problem of their access to resources, opportunities and powers -- a problem of social justice, but a problem of freedom too.

## Section 1.3 -- The Method

The importance of 'method' in political philosophy can be seen in F.A.Hayek's claim that there is no such thing as social justice (Hayek, 1973-1979, Volume 2, pp.62-65). For Hayek, political justice is real and effective, and so is political injustice. But talk of social justice is based upon a linguistic error -- the concept is a powerful mirage enforced by a misuse of language:

> We are, of course, not wrong in perceiving that the effects of the processes of a free society on the fates of the different individuals are not distributed according to some recognizable principle of justice. Where we go wrong is in concluding from this that they are unjust and that someone is to be blamed for this. In a free society in which the position of the different individuals and groups is not the result of anybody's design... the differences in reward simply cannot meaningfully be described as just or unjust. (Ibid., pp.69-70)

To be told that free market processes cannot give rise to social injustices seems extraordinary. Those processes do seem to give rise to injustices which are not to do with the breach of some explicit and acknowledged political or legal rule about how people should be treated by other people or by institutions, indeed not to do with the violation of rules at all. Instead, these injustices arise from inequalities of wealth and power, inequalities which mean that the opportunities for some are drawn suffocatingly tight, rendered empty or meaningless in the face of endless poverty and deprivation, in the face of an unceasing struggle to survive. No rules are being broken here: but something terrible is taking place. Faced with this reality, to be told that market forces cannot give rise to social injustice may seem trite and pedantic: the central concern of political philosophy must be with what happens to people, not with what happens to words.

However, this response is very unphilosophical: political philosophy must be concerned with what happens to words, because what happens to people can only be described by using words, and it matters which words are used. And so large parts of this book are concerned with words like 'freedom', 'power' and 'justice', and concerned with how they should be used. However, there is a question of emphasis: some versions of political philosophy have been primarily concerned with laying down rules for the correct treatment of words, and only secondarily, if at all, with laying down rules for the correct treatment of people. It was this 'linguistic turn' that led to the declaration that political philosophy was dead [5]; and it was a return to an interest in how people ought to be treated, partially inspired by writers like John Rawls, Robert Nozick and Ronald Dworkin, which led to the revival of something that can rightly be described as *political* philosophy, rather than merely the philosophy of political language: people are concerned with political reality once more, with what actually happens and ought to happen to people.

As David Miller points out, the linguistic turn in political philosophy is difficult to pin down (Miller, 1976, p.2): this may be because one implication of the linguistic turn is that there is no such thing as *political* philosophy -- and so it would be odd if any of these thinkers actually produced any political philosophical work. However, Miller is still sufficiently concerned with the linguistic turn that he attacks it, as the approach still lingers. Although few writers adopt the linguistic approach as a whole in political philosophy, they still occasionally adopt it as a tactic; they try to solve disputes by appealing to the 'grammar' of a concept, or to 'ordinary language', or to the 'traditional understanding' of a concept to be found in classic texts. Hayek's dismissal of the idea of social justice as a linguistic mistake is a dramatic example of the appeal to 'grammar' by a writer who does not take the linguistic approach seriously elsewhere in his work.

Of course, there must be a concern with words, but that is not all there should be, and that is not what should take precedence over other issues. Alan Brown distinguishes four ways of doing political philosophy: logical or analytical analysis of the meaning and function of concepts; the question of method, of determining what considerations are relevant in evaluating different practical options; the metaphysical issue of examining the presuppositions of political discourse; and the question of application, of finding the best way to achieve the goals fixed upon as the good or the right (Brown, 1986, pp.11-12). He comments:

...it does seem possible to answer questions of meaning without relying on answers to our other questions. For this reason (though for others besides) philosophers in recent times have focussed on questions of meaning; for this concern is in a sense purer, more abstract (a mode of thought which is philosophically attractive) and is, in this way, prior to any other. (Ibid., p.12)

However, he goes on to say:

...there is a danger in restricting ourselves to this question: if we do so our enquiries are in themselves pointless. For the whole point of asking such questions is to answer our practical concerns. An adequate practical philosophy must therefore push beyond questions of meaning to consider issues of method, metaphysics and application. Only then will the inquiry have served its function. (Ibid.)

And he points out that: "no-one doing political philosophy limits himself in this way, as a matter of fact, for there is always a suppressed normative content to such inquiries" (Ibid., p.17). It is this last point which is of greatest concern, and which Jean Grimshaw draws attention to in her critique of political philosophy. She says: "There is no 'real' or 'fundamental' meaning of 'justice' or of 'the state' which some process of conceptual analysis, all by itself, can discover" (Grimshaw, 1986, p.28). And: "Meanings are not just *given*; they are not timeless things which have a 'logic' which can be investigated by a process of dehistoricised conceptual analysis" (Ibid., p.29). An example of the danger of such an approach is the use of the word 'we' in the treatment of certain moral and political issues: "'We' are assumed to be a community of equals who have simply to make moral decisions" (Ibid., p.32). And she concludes:

The view that philosophy is merely a question of 'techniques' of clear thinking, and that philosophical discussion can be aimed at clarifying concepts without reference to questions of 'fact' or 'value', has an inbuilt tendency to remain uncritical of current or commonsense concepts and beliefs. (Ibid., p.33)

Taking Grimshaw's critique seriously, this book is concerned with words in a particular way. In Part 2, competing definitions of freedom will be examined, and will be criticised for leaving too much out: they account for some cases of freedom but not all. But the claim is not that these definitions are wrong: they are right, within their self-defined limits. The phenomena they capture within those limits *are* instances of freedom, and for the reasons they say they are. However, it is a mistake to claim that, once a definition of freedom has been offered, whatever falls outside of those definitional limits cannot possibly be an instance of freedom. It may well be an instance of freedom, but of a different sort to the type characterized in the definition. And so the classic definition of freedom as the absence of coercion, where coercion is intentional interference by other agents, is right within its own limits: that is to say, it captures a particular family of issues of freedom; but there are other issues of freedom which it fails to capture, and which remain issues of freedom for all that.

One problem is that in an ever-changing world, new forms of freedom and unfreedom are going to emerge: this problem will be returned to below. Perhaps more importantly, the problem is that definitions necessarily limit themselves -- they cannot be endlessly open, or else they cannot be definitions at all; and they must be self-consistent -- an inconsistent definition is, again, no definition at all. But not all forms of freedom are going to be consistent with each other -- there are many ways of being free, and people cannot be free in all ways at once. Therefore it is unlikely that all forms of freedom can be squeezed into any single definition without significant loss. There are always going to be forms of freedom and ways of being free which fall outside the limits of the single definition, but which remain forms of freedom, despite all the attempts of the definitional legislator to define them in some other terms. Therefore, while definitions of freedom must limit themselves, the discourse of freedom must be open-ended, and not base itself on any single definition. We must beware of approaching the idea of freedom like the blind men approached the elephant, each touching part and assuming that to be the whole.

It might be replied that there is some central core or common element which all forms of freedom must share in order to be forms of *freedom*. But this is doubtful: there may be no essence of freedom which can be captured in a single definition. There may be a feature that all forms of freedom share -- but that shared feature may, in the end, be so vague, so diffuse, so general, that it would be ridiculous to claim that it was the *essence* of freedom; it may tell us nothing particularly interesting about freedom. As David Miller puts it: "...this common meaning may be so vague that it masks the significance which the term has for any of the groups who use it..." (Miller, 1976, p.3). In that case, if the task is to find out why freedom is important, sifting out that shared feature will not help; rather, the various forms and patterns freedom takes in the community should be explored, and the task becomes to discover why those forms and patterns are important in people's lives.

This raises problems for a method. For example, it puts claims of neutrality in political philosophy at risk. In a sense, it would be odd for political philosophers to claim to be neutral: they are talking about political *values*, and how can values be neutral? But some political philosophers do claim that they have offered a definition of a value which is indisputably the correct definition whichever way you look at it, even though they do not claim to apply that value to the world in a neutral way [6]. So at the level of practice -- actual descriptions of the social and political world in terms of a political theory -- there cannot be neutrality: such descriptions are made from a particular political or moral perspective, and so must have a particular political or moral point to them.

However, the claim is that neutrality can be achieved at the level of theory: the basic terms of those descriptions, words like 'freedom' and their definitions, can be neutral between rival perspectives of the world -- otherwise there could be no meaningful dispute between competing descriptions. There must be agreement on a shared definition of 'freedom' before there can be disagreement over whether a particular person is free [7]. The discourse of political philosophy is not concerned with particular people at particular moments, but with the basic terms used in a description of political and social reality: it will be a meta-discourse over and above those descriptions, which seeks to define and clarify the terms used in political disputes, but which does not *enter* those disputes. The claim is, therefore, that definitions which are objective, neutral between rival political and moral perspectives, that are not 'essentially contestable', can be arrived at. (The opposing claim is, of course, that all definitions of political terms *are* essentially contestable [8].)

The position taken in this book is that this sort of neutrality is illusory. When there is a dispute in political philosophy over whether a person is free, the disagreement is rarely over their material circumstances; rather, the dispute is over whether those material conditions are necessary or sufficient to ensure that they are free. This dispute cannot be settled by the definitional legislator who rises above the ideological dispute to offer down 'neutral' definitions to the disputants. The definitional legislator who draws boundaries around the concept of freedom has to insist that anything that falls outside those boundaries cannot be freedom evaluable. But a defence of those limits must itself be deeply *political*, because the legislator has to insist that certain constraints which fall upon people do not violate their freedom, simply because they fall outside of her proposed definitional boundaries. She therefore must insist that the victim of those constraints cannot complain about their situation in terms of freedom or unfreedom, but in some other terms -- and this is to impose a form of silence upon certain groups in society. Whether or not the constraints are a violation of freedom determines what the victims of those constraints can say about their situation, and determines the response of the community to those constraints. For example, if the community is one which takes freedom more seriously than other values, then the refusal to see those constraints in terms of freedom means that the community will take them less seriously than it otherwise would, and place the problems faced by the groups suffering those constraints further down the political agenda. And so while the definitional legislator may genuinely want to stay out of the ideological battle, her defence of particular definitional boundaries is necessarily deeply political, and is the defence of particular political or moral practices. This makes it not merely difficult, but conceptually impossible for the political philosopher to rise above political debate and occupy the high ground of meta-discourse. As a consequence, the approach taken in this book does not attempt to be neutral at the level of theory or practice. The definitions of political terms developed here are designed to lead to a particular conclusion -- that the exclusion of groups like the physically disabled from society's institutions and practices is a moral violation of their freedom.

Arguments from the philosophy of science show why the definitional high ground is so illusory. The philosopher of science is well aware of the dangers of declaring that "All swans are white": there may be a black swan lurking in some corner of the world violating

24

those definitional boundaries. And it would be no good to then declare that "All swans are white or black"; for even if all the corners of the world are searched for swans, systematic breeding or the course of evolution may produce swans of many colours in the future. The same problem ought to haunt the political philosopher. Freedom appears in the world in many different forms, and some of those forms must change over time, as society itself changes and becomes more complex. Freedom is not something that exists over and above or beyond actual social practices -- it is situated in societies, in practices; the more complex the society, the more complex the possible forms of freedom and unfreedom. Our political language may fail to keep pace with such changes. David Miller points out that linguistic analysis of political concepts runs the risk of "temporal parochialism" (Miller, 1976, p.3). And William Connolly talks of a "lag between inherited terms of discourse and changing constellations of social life..." (Connolly, 1983, p.220). He says of the concept of power:

> It may be that the reach of the traditional language of power, coming from an era in which the web of social institutions was less tightly drawn, is now insufficient to characterize the conditions in which we live. (Ibid., p.219)

It is "necessary to *revise* the language of power to fit more closely the circumstances in which we now live" (Ibid., p.220). If that is true of the concept of power, it may also be true of the concept of freedom. While the drive for precision and simplicity is a powerful one in political philosophy, where talk of power or freedom is complex and ambiguous it may be because the social reality of power and freedom is complex and ambiguous, and a drive for precision and simplicity may obscure that reality, rather than make it clearer.

These problems mean that there is unlikely to be any set of necessary and sufficient conditions that capture all there is to say about freedom or all the forms in which freedom can appear or disappear in a changing social context. Any definition of freedom will be essentially *incomplete*, as there will always be some component of freedom or pattern of freedom which falls outside its limits. A definition is correct within its own limits, but incorrect if meant to cover all possible forms of freedom. And so the definition of freedom offered in Part 2 of this book makes no claim to capture all there is to say about freedom, or to displace any other definition in the field. What it does is capture a particular family of issues of freedom, issues that other definitions of liberty exclude. What is hoped is that it will enrich the open-ended discourse of liberty, and enable more to be said about freedom and unfreedom than could be said before, so that what is happening to certain marginalized groups within society can be better articulated.

## Section 1.4 -- Conclusion

Political theories have been characterized as highly complex systems of values, which cannot be represented by simple cardinal listings of values. Taking this into account, the critique of liberal theory and its understanding of the values of freedom and social justice and the relationship between them is recognized as a highly complex task. The method to be used acknowledges this complexity by recognizing that freedom can appear in many different forms, and cannot be captured within the limits of any single definition. Particular definitions of freedom are not, however, wrong -- they are correct within their self-defined limits, and do capture particular families of issues of freedom. Therefore while particular definitions of freedom must be closed, the discourse of freedom must be open-ended and responsive to changing social, political, economic and cultural forms. The definition of liberty to be developed in Part 2 is therefore designed to capture a particular family of issues of freedom, rather than encompass everything that freedom can possibly be, or everything that could possibly destroy it.

The idea of neutrality in political discourse has also been rejected. The defence of particular definitions of political terms cannot be neutral, but is deeply political; it is in effect the defence of particular political practices. The approach taken here therefore does not attempt to be neutral either at the level of theory or practice. The definitions of political terms developed here are designed to produce a particular conclusion -- that the exclusion of certain social groups from society's institutions and practices is a moral violation of their liberty.

## Notes

[1]     For example, John A. Hall is reluctant to call Milton Friedman and those who follow him in espousing capitalism as a necessary condition of liberalism as liberal at all -- rather they are neo-conservatives (see Hall, 1988, p.36 and note 7). John Gray calls those who are reluctant to follow Hayek and other free market theorists revisionary 'liberals' (see Gray, 1986, pp.26-27). Ralf Dahrendorf is contemptuous of liberals like Hayek: "I despise that negative attitude which calls itself liberal, and is in fact little more than the defence of vested interests of the haves..." (Dahrendorf,

1979, p.38 and see pp.91-92). Joseph Raz comments: "It is probably true to say that no political cause, no one vision of society nor any political principle has commanded the respect of all liberals in any given generation, let alone through the centuries" (Raz, 1986, p.1).

[2]    Social justice and equality are listed as separate values, because not all theories of social justice aim at equality; and, just as important, even where a theory of social justice does aim at equality, that does not necessarily exhaust all of its goals -- it may aim at other values too.

[3]    For example, Robert Nozick leaves out the value of equality (see Nozick, 1974, pp.233-235); John Gray claims that classical liberal theory is agnostic on the value of democracy (Gray, 1986, p.74); Ronald Dworkin leaves out the value of the worthwhile life (see Dworkin, 1978, p.127).
Nozick places greatest weight on the value of private property (see especially Chapter 7, Section I, of Nozick, 1974); Gray on limited government (1986, pp.73-74); and Dworkin sees equality of respect and concern as the "constitutive political morality" of liberalism (1978, p.127).

[4]    See Dworkin (1977) pp.179-83; Dworkin (1986) pp.296-301; Dworkin (1987) pp.7-8.

[5]    See Peter Laslett's introduction to Laslett, ed. (1956). There he pronounces that: "For the moment, anyway, political philosophy is dead" (p.vii). As for the culprits, he says: "The Logical Positivists did it. It was Russell and Wittgenstein, Ayer and Ryle who convinced the philosophers that they must withdraw unto themselves for a time, and re-examine their logical and linguistic apparatus. And the result of this re-examination has been radical indeed. It called into question the logical status of all ethical statements, and set up rigourous criteria of intelligibility which at one time threatened to reduce the traditional ethical systems to assemblages of nonsense. Since political philosophy is, or was, an extension of ethics, the question has been raised whether political philosophy is possible at all." (p.ix).
See T.D.Weldon, "Political Principles", in the same edition, for a stark statement of the linguistic/positivistic approach. And see Sir Isaiah Berlin, "Does Political Theory Still Exist?" in Laslett and Runciman, eds. (1962).

[6]    For example, Felix Oppenheim claims: "I believe that the concept of constraints on freedom can be defined...using only descriptive terms. This definition captures the core meaning of 'unfreedom' in ordinary language, abstracting only from negative valuational overtones. This way, moral philosophers and political scientists...with different moral convictions can nevertheless agree as to whether a given situation is to be characterized as one of unfreedom." (Oppenheim, 1985, p.305).

[7]    Felix Oppenheim says: "Meaningful disagreement about the value of freedom depends on agreement on that about which one disagrees" (Oppenheim, 1961, p.9).

[8]    For such a dispute see Miller (1983), Oppenheim (1985), and Miller (1985). For a rejection of Oppenheim's approach see Connolly (1983)

pp.140-141. The idea of "essential contestability" is first described in W.B.Gallie (1955/56). The following articles are just some that have appeared about the idea, although I suspect that what they debate is not what Gallie originally meant: McIntyre (1973); Cane (1973); Gray (1983); Swanton (1985).

# 2 The Impure Theory of Freedom

## Section 2.1 -- Dimensions of Liberty

This book sets out to investigate the value of liberty, and to investigate its relationship with the value of social justice and the family of other values it implies, such as equality and welfare. Often in liberal theory, freedom is opposed to equality and welfare, and therefore to social justice -- programmes of social justice are seen as limited by the value of liberty: where the pursuit of equality and welfare through programmes of social justice encroaches upon the value of liberty, then such programmes are illegitimate. Freedom, therefore, has had a predominantly negative role to play in relation to social justice, in drawing boundaries to its legitimate activity.

Such approaches see issues of freedom and issues of social justice, welfare and equality as utterly distinct, having little or no connection with each other, apart from the negative one described above. What follows from this approach is that inequality of wealth cannot be an issue of freedom: the poor person is as free as the rich person, despite the fact that the former can do very little while the latter can do a great deal -- they are equally free to do as much as the other. Inequality of wealth is a problem of social justice, not of liberty, and the two must not be confused. John Rawls articulates this position by making a distinction between liberty and the worth of liberty:

> The inability to take advantage of one's rights and opportunities as a result of poverty and ignorance, and a lack of means generally, is sometimes counted among the constraints definitive of liberty. I shall not, however, say this, but rather I shall think of these things as affecting the worth of liberty, the value to individuals of the rights that the first principle defines... Thus liberty and the worth of liberty are distinguished as follows: liberty is represented by the complete system of the liberties of equal citizenship, while the worth of liberty to persons and groups is proportional to their capacity to advance their ends within the framework the system defines. Freedom as equal liberty is the same for all; the question of compensating for a lesser than equal liberty does not arise. But the worth of liberty is

not the same for everyone. Some have greater authority and wealth, and therefore greater means to achieve their aims. (Rawls, 1972, p.204)

Such a position, although it does explicitly exclude issues of welfare and inequality -- such as poverty, deprivation, ill health and disablement -- from the discourse of freedom, does not *necessarily* lessen their importance. That importance depends upon the priority of liberty within the theory. However, liberty does have a central role to play in liberal theories, and therefore the exclusion of such issues from the discourse of freedom *does*, in fact, lead to their marginalization within the theory. The position taken in this book is that these *are* issues of freedom, and therefore that any discourse of liberty must make room for them. This is not to confuse the value of freedom with welfare or equality, or to deny that they are logically distinct. It is to claim that they are practically entangled, so that at least some issues of freedom are issues of social justice, and at least some issues of welfare and equality are also issues of freedom.

The family of practical problems focussed on can be characterized as problems of a particular kind of social deprivation, understood as the exclusion of certain groups from full participation within society's institutions and practices: for example, the exclusion of the physically disabled from the workplace. Within liberal theory, these problems of exclusion are certainly recognized as issues of social justice, but they are seldom seen as issues of freedom. It will be argued here that they *must* be seen as issues of freedom -- otherwise we shall fail to see what sort of problems of social justice they are. In other words, the exclusion of these issues from freedom-talk leads to a distorted and misleading understanding of them within the theory of social justice. It is only by recognizing that liberty is at stake here that a correct view of what social justice demands in these cases can be arrived at.

The discussion of these issues requires a particular view of freedom and of social justice. The view of freedom is fully outlined in Part 2 of the book, and the view of social justice fully outlined in Part 3. However, a certain amount of groundwork must be done before the full implications of those views become clear, and that is the task of this chapter. Throughout, this book will be critical of views of freedom that place priority on the negative conditions of freedom, on non-interference by others and by the state. This negative view of freedom has grown from a concern with state power and the political repression that a powerful state can impose upon its citizens: this concern to protect the individual from interference from the state obviously leads to a concern with the negative conditions of freedom, and this is undeniably a valid and valuable view. However, it is also a severely limited view, which, while articulating a particular family of issues of freedom, excludes other equally important families. The next section of this chapter examines these limitations more closely.

## Section 2.2 -- The Idea of Freedom

In the debate over the ideas of positive and negative liberty, the fact that the idea of negative liberty is highly complex and is indeed divided into two main approaches is often overlooked. Richard Flathman (Flathman, 1987, p.30) characterizes the two possible approaches as Pure and Impure Negative theory. According to the Pure Negative theory ($N$), absence of external interference is a sufficient condition for freedom. According to the Impure Negative theory ($IN$), absence of external interference is necessary but not sufficient -- an additional necessary condition for freedom to do anything is the possession of the *ability* or *power* to do it. Together these conditions -- the *absence* of external interference and the *presence* of the ability or power to act -- are sufficient to ensure freedom. One requires both the space *and* power to be free.

According to Flathman, $IN$ has been the main position in traditional liberal thought, certainly since and including Hobbes; and it is $IN$ that is usually assumed in liberal political texts about other issues. Although Flathman is more concerned to attack positive theories of freedom, he does initially attack the pure theory, $N$: it allows that a person unable to do $x$ through the lack of power or ability is still free to do it; and that simple movement, like falling off a log, would count as free movement. Flathman finds both claims unacceptable.

The view that the absence of external interference is both necessary and sufficient for freedom means that, as long as equal non-interference is ensured, all members of the community are equally free, even though some may be able to do very little compared with others. For example, it allows that a person confined to a wheelchair who finds themself unable to use a local library because of lack of disabled access remains as free to use it as anybody else. If the problem being examined is the exclusion of certain groups within the community from particular institutions and practices within it, then $N$ only allows certain of those exclusions to be articulated in terms of freedom-talk. The exclusion of the disabled from public facilities through lack of disabled access is not such an exclusion, which means that disabled groups have to articulate their situation in some other terms. As pointed out in the previous chapter this can have serious practical consequences for them, as it will determine how their situation is understood and prioritized by the community. Certain groups, then, are doubly excluded: excluded from institutions and practices, and excluded at the level of theory itself. The pure negative theory therefore excludes a whole family of issues of liberty from the range of freedom-talk. Despite the fact that the theory includes the disabled in the category of freedom, in that they enjoy equal freedom with all other members of the community, they are in effect excluded from the theory, in that they cannot articulate their situation and the distinctive problems of exclusion they face in terms of freedom-talk. The way in which they are excluded from the theory will be examined more closely in the next chapter, but at this stage it can be seen that the problem of exclusion is a problem both at the level of practice *and* theory.

Flathman does not abandon the negative theory of freedom, but rather defends a version of it that appeals to both negative and positive conditions for freedom, which he describes as impure negative theory. And indeed, with its emphasis on the two necessary conditions for freedom, the absence of interference and the presence of power, impure theory does seem to combine the best aspects of both positive and negative theories of freedom while avoiding their worst absurdities. For example, according to this position the absence of external interference is not *sufficient* for freedom -- so that simply ensuring that someone is left alone is not enough to guarantee their freedom: the homeless beggar may receive little interference from others or the state, but their lack of ability or power means that they do not enjoy equal freedom with other members of the community. Similarly it can be said that the presence of power is not sufficient for freedom -- empowering someone does not necessarily make them free; one can empower people to achieve goals and activities that one has chosen for them. For example, military training can involve empowering conscript soldiers to fulfil goals and activities, but those soldiers have not chosen those goals and activities themselves. According to impure theory, neither the beggar nor the conscript soldier are free: we are not forced to decide which of them is the best exemplar of true freedom, because neither of them possesses sufficient conditions for liberty.

This picture of freedom, with its mixture of positive and negative conditions, is attractive. It avoids rigidity and allows flexibility --

instead of declaring *a priori* that one type of condition of freedom, negative or positive, is necessarily going to have priority over the other, it allows that each situation must be examined in order to judge which condition it would be best to prioritize overall. As Sir Isaiah Berlin argues, to insist on the rigid priority of one kind of condition over the other is dogmatic, and potentially destructive of the very freedom it is supposed to protect (Berlin, 1969, p.xlv-xlvi).

However, it should be noted that Flathman describes an impure *negative* theory, which suggests that he places priority on the negative conditions of freedom at the cost of the positive, and it will be argued that this approach does not solve the problems of exclusion described above. The position developed in this book is a 'purely' impure theory of freedom, which does not prioritize either kind of condition in any way: which kind of condition must be protected or created depends upon the circumstances -- sometimes giving priority to negative conditions may best protect the overall freedom of the agent concerned, but in other circumstances it may be that prioritizing the positive conditions will best achieve this goal.

Flathman's approach (*IN*), with its emphasis on negative conditions, produces some puzzles which the purely impure theory (*I*) avoids, puzzles that perpetuate the problem of exclusion. According to *IN*, a person can be:

(1)    free to do *x*; or
(2)    unfree to do *x*; or
(3)    unable to do *x*.

The person unable to do *x* is neither free nor unfree to do it: the question of her freedom is not at stake -- she is not *freedom evaluable*. Flathman states: "Capacity for action is a condition of the predication of either freedom or unfreedom" (Flathman, 1987, p.86). The ability to do *x* is, therefore, a necessary condition for freedom evaluation, and must extend through both (1) and (2), but not through (3). But the *inability* must extend through both (2) and (3), because the person who is unfree to do *x* is obviously unable to do it in some sense. Therefore the agent in (2) is able to do *x* and unable to do it at the same time.

This particular implication of *IN* is not puzzling at all: under (2) the agent has the *capacity* to do *x* (possesses the relevant powers and abilities), but is prevented from using that capacity by external interference -- in that sense she has the *ability* to do it but is prevented from using that ability. Under (3) the agent lacks the capacity to do *x* (she does not possess the relevant powers and abilities) -- and so she is unable to do it in a much more basic sense. There are, therefore, two levels of inability, and freedom evaluation begins at level (2). The person at level (3) is simply not freedom evaluable; her situation cannot be characterized in terms of freedom-talk -- the problems and difficulties she faces have to be articulated in some other way.

Much can be said in favour of this scheme: it makes freedom-talk in political philosophy clear and simple. There is an important distinction to be made between the person who is unable to do $x$ because others prevent her, and the person who is unable to do $x$ because she lacks the needed resources; and that distinction is well captured by reserving freedom evaluation for the former. Therefore those who are able to do $x$ and are not prevented from doing so are *free* to do it; those who are able to do $x$ but are prevented from using that ability are *unfree* to do it; and those who lack the needed resources are *neither-free-nor-unfree* to do it. However, the theory does nothing to address the problem of the double-exclusion of certain groups at the level of theory and practice -- indeed, the approach re-inforces the exclusion of groups like the disabled from freedom-talk.

This reflects the similar problem with pure negative theory ($N$) already described: that $N$ does not permit the expression of a range of anxieties concerning the situation of certain groups within the community in terms of their freedom or lack of it: e.g., the physically disabled. The person confined to a wheelchair with no access to the local library is as free to use that library as anybody else, according to $N$. The point is that $IN$ is little or no improvement here. According to this position, those who are unable to act, through physical disablement for example, are not freedom evaluable, and therefore freedom-talk is inapplicable to their situation. While $N$'s response to their situation was that they are as free as anybody else to use the library, $IN$'s response is that they are not free to use it, but they are not unfree to use it either -- this is to leave them neither here nor there.

However, it must be noted that it may be open to the holder of $IN$ to discuss issues like that of the exclusion of the disabled from facilities as a matter of urgency. Flathman says:

> ...if $B$'s interventions genuinely *disable* $A$, genuinely *destroy* $A$'s capacity for action, then we should say that $A$ is no longer freedom-evaluable (in the respects in question), not that she is unfree. Putting the matter in this way worsens the charge against $B$ at the same time that it instructs the rest of us as to how we

should, and should not, think about and relate to *A*. (Flathman, 1987, p.226)

And so freedom evaluability is itself valuable, and the destruction of one person's freedom evaluability by the actions of another is an urgent issue. But this expansion of the boundaries of freedom-talk by the introduction of the idea of freedom-evaluability evaluability does not approach the problems of exclusion which are our concern here. The sort of case Flathman describes only allows talk about those situations in which a person's freedom evaluability is destroyed by the interventions of another agent (and in section 2.3 it will become clear that this must be *deliberate* intervention). This means that unless it is believed that the disabled person's lack of ability is due to the deliberate interventions of some other agent, they are not even freedom-evaluable evaluable, and remain outside the boundaries of freedom-talk.

The problem, then, is that *IN* recognizes two ways in which an agent can lack freedom: through external interference, or through lack of the needed powers or resources. However, only the first type of lack counts as unfreedom and therefore as freedom evaluable. Those who lack freedom because of the absence of the needed powers or resources must articulate their lack of liberty in terms other than freedom-talk. *IN* is in the position of recognizing a variety of ways in which people can lack freedom, but of declaring that some of these ways are not *issues* of freedom at all. This is, at the very least, odd.

The impure theory of freedom (*I*) would seem to be in a better position here, in that it both recognizes a variety of ways in which people can lack freedom -- because of the absence of either negative or positive conditions -- *and* allows that any of these ways are potentially issues of freedom. Freedom is lacking in both the case of external interference and in the case of the lack of needed resources: but in the first case the *negative* conditions for freedom are missing, and in the second case the *positive* conditions of freedom are missing. These are both, therefore, issues of freedom although they are different sorts of issues of freedom. For *I*, any lack of freedom is *prima facie* an *issue* of freedom, a potential subject of freedom-talk, the subject of a particular kind of political concern and anxiety. This means that the distinctive problems of exclusion faced by the physically disabled are potentially issues of freedom, and therefore can be subject to the same kind of political concern and anxiety as other forms of exclusion from institutions and practices in the community.

The theory still recognizes that the two ways in which freedom can be absent are importantly different, but does not conclude from this that their importance differs. It cannot be decided *a priori* which kind of lack of freedom is most urgent, most weighty, most worthy of political anxiety: the particular circumstances have to be examined before this can be discovered. There could be cases where lack of freedom because of the absence of needed resources is far more devastating than lack of the same freedom because of external interference, and of course vice versa. For example, lacking the freedom to drive down a road because the local authority has closed it could be seen as far less important than lacking the freedom to do so because of the lack of resources to gain access to transport at all (because other means of getting from *A* to *B* are available in the first case, while in the second case there are no means of getting from *A* to anywhere!). And, equally, lack of freedom to enter a public facility because of threat of violence from others could be seen as far more urgent than lack of freedom to do so because one cannot afford the entrance fee (because in the first case one is permanently excluded, even if one did save up the entrance fee, and there is probably greater mental distress attached to the threat of violence to one's person). It cannot be decided at the level of theory which kind of lack of freedom is most worthy of concern. The impure theory allows us to say that freedom is lacking in both kinds of case: it is merely lacking in different ways and for different reasons -- and it cannot be decided *a priori* which of these ways is more urgent. If this is right, then both kinds of case clearly are freedom evaluable, because in both kinds of case it can be judged that freedom is absent for certain reasons, and it can be judged how best to combat that lack of freedom, if at all -- and this looks very much like freedom evaluation.

There seems to be no good reason for restricting freedom evaluation to the able: freedom-talk need not be restricted to those cases where freedom is lacking because of interference by others; it can be about any of the many ways in which freedom can be taken away, reduced, undermined or endangered. And the extension of freedom-talk to include these issues does not lead to the collapse of any important distinctions, in particular not the distinction between lacking freedom through interference by others and lacking it because of the absence of needed resources -- because to claim that all these cases are freedom evaluable is not to claim that they must be evaluable in the same way. The impure theory of freedom allows us to evaluate the lack of freedom in a variety of ways.

The differences between the three approaches to freedom examined here, the pure negative (*N*) impure negative (*IN*), and impure theories (*I*), can be summarized as follows:


1. Necessary and sufficient conditions for FREEDOM:
*N*        absence of interference
*IN*       absence of interference *plus* presence of ability
*I*        absence of interference *plus* presence of ability
2. Necessary and sufficient conditions for UNFREEDOM:
*N*        external interference
*IN*       external interference
*I*        external interference *or* absence of ability


## Section 2.3 -- The Intentionality Assumption

The critical path taken so far is simple. Pure negative theory (*N*) is rejected because it involves saying to those unable to act because of the lack of needed powers and resources that they are as free to act as anybody else; and this is effectively to exclude them from freedom-talk because it removes the possibility of them articulating their situation in terms of freedom. Impure negative theory (*IN*) is then introduced, because it allows that those unable to act in a particular way *lack the freedom* to act in that way. However, although it allows that the unable lack freedom, it does not allow that their situation is freedom evaluable. This leads to the exclusion of the unable from freedom-talk just as with *N*, and this is to exclude them from a particular sphere of political concern and anxiety.

This problem was solved by stating that freedom evaluation is relevant in all cases where freedom is lacking, whatever the reasons or causes of its absence. While there are important differences between the different ways in which freedom can be lacking, those differences do not merit restricting freedom evaluation, and therefore freedom-talk, to a particular class of cases. Making this move does not lead to the loss of any of the valuable distinctions between ways of lacking freedom, because it can be insisted that all these cases are freedom evaluable without insisting that they must be evaluable in the same way. And so the impure theory of freedom (*I*) is arrived at, which recognizes that liberty has both negative and positive conditions, and that the absence of either kind of condition can undermine freedom and therefore give rise to issues of freedom.

By reserving freedom evaluation for the presence or absence of negative conditions of freedom, *IN* pushes the positive conditions for being free beyond the boundaries of freedom-talk altogether, while at the same time allowing that there *are* such conditions -- and this seems to be an inconsistency: how can certain conditions be necessary for freedom, and yet at the same time their absence not be an issue of freedom? *I* does not restrict freedom evaluation to either kind of condition, and so places no priority on them. The lack of positive conditions can potentially undermine freedom in ways just as serious as the absence of negative conditions. And therefore issues of poverty and disablement can be issues of freedom: they can be addressed, expressed and articulated in terms of freedom. This is not to claim that they necessarily *are* issues of freedom, or that they are *only* issues of freedom. Instead, it is to claim that certain aspects of the situations of those in poverty or those who are disabled can be articulated in terms of the lack of freedom (which *IN* allows), and that this lack is a relevant issue for freedom-talk (which *IN* denies).

The problem, then, is that *IN* recognizes that people can lack freedom in many different ways, because of external interference or because of lack of needed powers and resources -- the unable are *not* free to do what they are unable to do. But it refuses to extend freedom evaluation to the latter type of case -- the unable are not *unfree* to do what they are unable to do. What reasons could there be for restricting freedom evaluation in this way?

For Richard Flathman, one reason is that freedom-talk must be about agents and their actions: "In the absence of attempted actions, there is nothing of which freedom or unfreedom can be predicated (there is nothing that is 'freedom evaluable')" (Flathman, 1987, p.1). But this has curious implications: if a person was able to do *x*, but never attempted to do so because they knew someone would prevent them, then there would be no attempted action and therefore nothing to be freedom evaluable; for example someone in a prison who never tried to walk out is not, according to this position, unfree to walk out. It could be replied that what is relevant is not an attempted action, but a potential action. At least the person able to do *x* but who never attempts it can *potentially* do it, while in the case of the person unable to do *x* there is not even the potentiality. But this involves a very narrow reading of 'potentiality': the person unable to do *x* because they lack the needed resources can, of course, *potentially* do *x* -- they could do it if they possessed the needed resources.

It may be that the defender of *IN* would accept the implication that the person able to do *x* but who never attempts it because they know they will be prevented from doing so is not unfree to do it; but it seems strange to refuse to see such a situation as an issue of freedom. A second reason for refusing to extend freedom-talk to the unable might be the following. Freedom-talk is about *external* causes of inability -- where the causes of inability are *internal* nothing can be said in terms of freedom. Now, this includes the person in the prison within the boundaries of freedom-talk, as it is an external constraint that prevents them from walking out; and it could include those in poverty, as it could be argued that the causes of their poverty are external. But it certainly excludes the physically disabled, because the causes of their inability are internal. There are two reasons why internal causes of inability are unsuitable subjects for freedom-talk: first, being internal, it is assumed that there is nothing that can be done about them; second, being internal, nobody can be *blamed* for them. However, both these arguments rest on an over-simplistic internal/external distinction, and when that naive distinction is discarded so are the arguments.

What must be examined is the *structure of inability* in the community -- the claim being made about the physically disabled here is not that their physical inability undermines their freedom, but that the way the community structures its institutions and practices undermines their freedom. Many of the actions the disabled are unable to perform are not directly due to their physical disability, but to do with the structure of institutions and practices. If public facilities are built without adequate access, then people without the basic causal power to walk who are confined to wheelchairs will be unable to use them -- but this inability is not caused by their lack of the basic causal power to walk, but by the practice of building design and construction (Cole, 1987). And this is, of course, an external factor, not an internal one -- therefore, even if it is accepted that only external constraints can give rise to issues of freedom, there is no reason why the situation of the physically disabled with respect to access to buildings should not be freedom evaluable. This is *not* to claim that everything there is to say about the situation of the disabled must be expressed in terms of freedom-talk and not in terms of other political values: undoubtedly the value of social justice would be a powerful weapon in any debate about this issue. But at least part of the programme of social justice is to secure the conditions of freedom for all members of the community, and so the situation of the physically disabled with respect to access to institutions and practices is both an issue of freedom and an issue of social justice in ways that are closely connected.

The first argument, that the fact that the cause of inability is internal means that nothing can be done, therefore falls because the location of the *cause* of the inability of the physically disabled to gain access to institutions is not necessarily internal. The immediate inability, the lack of the basic causal power to walk, may be internal, but this now seems utterly irrelevant to assessing whether there is an issue of freedom here. There is a complex pattern of factors that prevents this person from moving from A to B, and they may be enabled to move from A to B by altering any number of those factors. Whether those factors are in some sense internal to the disabled agent or external to them seems of little or no significance -- what matters when it comes to deciding if their freedom is constrained is whether some agency has the power to alter those factors, and whether it in fact *ought* to alter them. Failure to alter them under those circumstances constitutes a moral violation of liberty.

The second argument, that no one can be blamed for these cases, is equally mistaken, in ways that confirm the conclusion that the failure to alter the situation of the physically disabled is a moral violation of their freedom. According to this argument, freedom-talk is essentially to do with moral judgment: it matters whether people are free or unfree -- freedom-talk is not merely descriptive, it expresses a particular concern and anxiety about what is happening to people and what ought to happen to them. The accusation that someone has caused another to be unfree is a moral judgment. So for freedom-talk to be relevant in a particular situation, there must be someone who can be identified as morally responsible for the lack of freedom. This is only possible in cases of deliberate external interference, and so freedom-talk can only be about deliberate external interference with freedom. Freedom evaluation is moral evaluation, and only lack of freedom caused by the deliberate interference of others is morally evaluable. Therefore, as nobody has deliberately interfered with the freedom of the physically disabled in order to exclude them from society, that exclusion cannot be a moral violation of their liberty.

The argument rests on two questionable assumptions. The first is that moral evaluation is essentially to do with attaching blame to people. But situations can be subject to moral evaluation without raising the question of attaching blame to certain persons for causing those situations. The point of the moral evaluation is not to blame anybody for the existence of those situations, but to say that those situations must be prevented or altered. Nobody need be causally responsible for a situation which morally calls for action to put it right [1]. Therefore the fact that no particular agent directly caused the physically disabled to be excluded from society's institutions and practices does not rule out the moral evaluation of their situation -- their situation can still be evaluated as one that ought not to be permitted to continue.

However, there does need to be *some* moral responsibility in the picture for freedom evaluation to be relevant, and the second assumption behind the argument is that people can only be held morally responsible for situations that they intentionally cause. As nobody directly caused the exclusion of the physically disabled, there is nobody that can be held morally responsible for that situation, and therefore freedom evaluation is again ruled out. Flathman says that in freedom-talk people are charged with "responsibility for deliberate interference, not merely with causal influence" (Flathman, 1987, p.324). However, this very strong intentionality assumption is not plausible in general moral-talk: people simply are not held morally responsible only for the situations they deliberately cause; they are often held morally responsible for accidents they cause -- judgments of negligence or recklessness have a strong role to play in the discourse of moral responsibility. Therefore in the general discourse of moral responsibility, Flathman's principle does not hold true. More importantly, someone may have moral responsibility for a situation which they in no sense caused, intentionally or accidentally: moral responsibility for situations simply does not entail causal responsibility for them. There may be a situation which morally demands action to alter it, and in the community the responsibility for that alteration may fall upon specific agencies. For example, the Fire Service is responsible for extinguishing fires, even though they do not start them; doctors are responsible for the health of their patients, even though they do not cause their ailments; the Police Service is responsible for tackling crime, even though they do not cause the crime. This responsibility is such that the failure to act to tackle such situations is seen as a highly serious violation of responsibility, and as deeply immoral. Therefore the idea of moral responsibility is far more complex than the strict intentionality assumption allows for. Of course, Flathman does not mean his intentionality principle, that responsibility requires deliberate interference, to apply to general moral discourse, but only to freedom-talk -- but then the question arises why the strict intentionality principle *should* apply to freedom-talk when it is so obviously incorrect within wider moral discourse. The only argument I have found to justify the principle is outlined in section 3.5, but that argument, it will be shown, is itself seriously flawed.

41

If the strict intentionality assumption is dropped within the discourse of liberty, then the situation of the physically disabled within the community can be assessed in terms of freedom. The community as such can be held as *prima facie* responsible for the exclusion of certain groups from its institutions and practices. For example, it has permitted many of its social facilities to be structured in ways that exclude the physically disabled. Such an argument must, of course, involve judgments about what the community can be reasonably expected to achieve in certain situations given its powers, resources and knowledge -- but in the case of the physically disabled, it does not seem unreasonable to claim that the community could, without undue cost or unreasonable foresight, provide them with access to its facilities. Therefore the community's failure to ensure adequate access can be seen as a moral violation of the freedom of the disabled. In chapter 3 it will be argued that it *must* be seen in this way.

Again, this is not to demand that the situation of the disabled be characterized *only* as an issue of liberty: it is only to say that certain aspects of their situation, those aspects that touch upon their lack of freedom, can and ought to be characterized as issues of freedom -- any programme of social justice must have, as an element, a commitment to ensuring the positive conditions of freedom needed by these groups in order to enjoy equal membership of the community.

The strong intentionality principle, that the only thing that can count as a moral violation of liberty is intentional interference with liberty, often underlies negative theories of freedom, although it is seldom explicitly stated or defended; and it is most often the cause of the rigidity and inflexibility of such theories. As the principle is clearly inapplicable within the wider discourse of moral responsibility, this provides grounds for doubting its relevance within the discourse of responsibility for freedom and constraints upon freedom. Without that principle, freedom evaluation can be extended to the unable, and freedom-talk is now open to anybody who lacks freedom, not simply to those who lack it because of the intentional interference of others. Also, this is not to deny that the lack of freedom through the intentional interference of others is often far more serious than the lack of freedom for other reasons; but equally, it allows that there can be circumstances in which lack of freedom for those other reasons can be far more serious than its lack due to intentional interference.

There is, of course, a deep dispute underlying theories of freedom here, the boundaries of which can be clarified by looking at a debate that took place between David Miller and Felix Oppenheim concerning the issue of what can count as a constraint upon freedom

(Miller, 1983; Felix Oppenheim, 1985; David Miller, 1985). For Miller, for something to be a constraint on freedom, *moral responsibility* must be at stake; for Oppenheim *causal responsibility* will do. Now, it may seem that Miller and Flathman are in agreement, and that the impure theory of freedom developed here is in agreement with Oppenheim -- but the debate is more complex than that. The impure theory fully agrees with Miller that moral responsibility must be at stake -- freedom-talk is *essentially* normative; and so when instances of constraints upon freedom are identified, this is the expression of a particular kind of political anxiety, not merely a description of a state of affairs. The issue here is not whether moral responsibility is at stake, but the extent of that responsibility -- does it extend beyond strict intentionality? And does it extend beyond actions to include omissions? Here Flathman, Miller and Oppenheim each occupy importantly different positions. Flathman adopts the very strict intentionality thesis: a constraint is only a constraint upon freedom if it is intended as such by the agent responsible for it. For Miller, the intentionality condition is weakened by allowing for the possibility of negligence. For Oppenheim, causal responsibility is sufficient (Miller, 1985, p.310; Oppenheim, 1985, pp.306-307). On the actions/omissions question, Oppenheim holds that a constraint upon freedom can only arise through a positive action, and not through failure to act. Miller allows that the failure to act can constitute a violation of freedom (Miller, 1985, pp.310-311). So there are two vital distinctions here: (a) between strong and weak intentionality; and (b) between act and omission. Miller's position, and the position taken in this book, is to opt for the weak intentionality condition, and to claim that omissions, the failure to alter conditions, can violate freedom. But two issues must be emphasized. First, the normative character of freedom-talk is not being rejected -- moral responsibility, not mere causal responsibility, is at stake; the extent of moral responsibility in freedom-talk is being revised, because no good reason has been found to restrict it to cases of strict intentionality. Second, the claim is not that an internal disability, like physical disablement, by itself violates a person's liberty, but that the way the community responds to that inability can give rise to issues of freedom; the location of that inability or of what can be altered to enable the agent seems irrelevant to judgments of freedom.

If the above reasons for rejecting the restriction of freedom evaluation to the negative conditions and aspects of liberty are right, then more detail of the proposed impure theory of freedom emerges: first, it rejects the appeal to an over-simplistic internal/external distinction; second, it rejects the strong intentionality assumption. By discarding these crude and rigid assumptions, it becomes a flexible, politically attractive and dynamic theory of freedom, which can transcend the old muddles and dogmas of purer theories. Given the potential of such a theory, it seems worthwhile philosophically and politically to take a bold step in its direction [2].

## Section 2.4 -- The Issue of Exclusion

The charge that certain approaches to the problem of freedom lead to the double exclusion of certain groups -- both at the level of practice and theory -- faces a major criticism. It could be objected that it rests on a category mistake, of seeing an issue of social justice as an issue of freedom; or that it rests on the characterization of liberal thought as a one-value theory, with freedom as that one value; or at the very least that it rests on the assumption that freedom takes priority over other values in the theory, such that being excluded from freedom-talk has serious consequences. Liberal thought is richer than that, and the issue of the exclusion of groups such as the physically disabled from society's institutions and practices can be dealt with under headings other than freedom -- most appropriately under the heading of social justice. It is therefore misguided to criticise liberal theorists of freedom for failing to address such issues, and there is no need for a re-shaped theory of freedom which would include them. Why should it be considered that the problem of exclusion is an issue of freedom rather than an issue of social justice?

A first reply to the objection is that in fact this exclusion from freedom-talk *does* have enormous practical implications for those in such situations, as they have one channel of protest effectively closed to them, and must find some other channel through which to articulate their difficulties. If an able-bodied person were prevented from entering the library through a barrier being placed in their way, they could complain of a violation of their freedom. The physically disabled person, despite the barriers that block their access, is not permitted to complain in such terms. Freedom *is* a central value in the political culture of western democratic societies, and to be deprived of the discourse of liberty to describe one's obstacles and problems and anxieties is to be silenced to an important degree, despite the fact that one *could* articulate those problems in some other discourse.

A second reply to the objection is that seeing exclusion as an issue of freedom is not to deny that it is an issue of social justice;

rather, it reveals why it is such a serious issue of social justice: it can be characterized as an issue of social justice *of a particular kind* -- that is, one where the positive conditions for freedom are missing or are being undermined. It is an issue of social justice that particularly effects certain groups, such as the disabled, in specific and distinctive ways; and it is an issue of social justice which is not merely an issue of inequality of resources, but a particular consequence of such inequality -- the destruction of the conditions people need in order to be equally free members of the community.

The failure to see the exclusion of the disabled as an issue of freedom leads to it being characterized as a problem of social justice of the wrong kind -- as a problem of compensating certain groups for their unfortunate but inalterable exclusion from society. And so far from committing a category mistake, the characterization of the problem of exclusion as an issue of freedom highlights a deeply disturbing mistake in political theory -- the misrepresentation of the situation of excluded groups, like the disabled, as being unavoidably excluded because of their nature, rather than the nature of society. Far from being simply a problem calling for compensation for unfortunate but unavoidable exclusion, it is an issue that calls for a concerted attack upon the conditions that cause exclusion; such that the failure to tackle them amounts to a violation of the freedom to participate in the community. And if all are equally entitled to participate, then this is a deeply serious freedom violation.

For example, John Rawls explicitly lays aside the problems of those faced with needs which fall outside of what he calls the "normal range" (Rawls, 1978, p.70 note 9). He says: "...it is reasonable to assume that everyone has physical needs and physiological capacities within some normal range." His theory of social justice is explicitly written for "those who are full and active participants in society, and directly or indirectly associated over the course of a while life." It therefore openly excludes those who are excluded from full and active participation in society -- although he suggests that he may be able to "attempt to handle these other cases later." And so far from being able to address the issue of the excluded under the heading of social justice, we find them marginalized here too, precisely because their situation is not seen as an issue of freedom. And so they are excluded at the level of practice and at the level of theory, and are excluded from both the theory of freedom *and* the theory of social justice.

The physically disabled *can* be brought into the theory of social justice, but the way they are included, how their situation is characterized, matters, because this will determine what social justice demands in this case. Problems arise when their exclusion from society is seen as 'natural' -- they are naturally unable to do certain things, and this inability naturally excludes them from participation. If that view is correct, all that can be done is to compensate them for this inalterable exclusion by ensuring that at least their basic needs are met. Therefore, while they have been written into the theory of social justice, this has been done in a limiting and marginalizing way, a way that limits the response to their situation. Carole Pateman emphasizes this temptation to regard some as "natural social exiles" (Pateman, 1988, p.235), to suppose that some are "naturally lacking the capacities for public participation" (Pateman, 1988, p.236).

Here lies the mistake, which will be examined in more detail in chapter 3. The point is that the exclusion of the physically disabled is not due to their 'inalterable' nature, but is due to alterable social, political, economic and cultural practices, such that the failure to alter those practices may constitute a moral violation of the freedom of the disabled to be fully participating choosers, doers and deciders in their own community. The disabled are as entitled to full membership of the community as any other group, and therefore are entitled to the conditions required for that membership.

It is therefore crucially important that the physically disabled, and other excluded groups, are written into the theory of freedom. It is only this that can ensure that such problems are raised within the sphere of social justice in the correct way, demanding a particular kind of response. Freedom may be the same for all -- having the space and power to choose the shape of one's life: but the conditions needed to be free will not be the same for all, because people are different and this difference matters. A universal set of freedom conditions, therefore, cannot be fixed -- this would in effect exclude those who are different, those who do not fit this 'normal' range. Similarly, the aim of social justice may be the same for all: securing the equal chance to be an active chooser, doer and participator in the community. But again the conditions needed for such active participation will not be the same for all; and so the responses to the demands of social justice must not be restricted to a 'normal' range, but must be flexible and diverse, responding to people's differing needs, not to some arbitrarily fixed set of 'basic' needs.

In section 6.7 the tendency of social contract approaches to social justice, of which Rawls' approach is an example, to restrict justice to those who possess the power of active participation in the community will be examined more closely. Three assumptions seem to underlie the approach: (1) that all are equally powerful, free and equal agents;

(2) that society is a rational construct arrived at through free and equal negotiations between such equally powerful agents; and (3) that all such agents share the same basic needs in order to *be* free and equal members of the community. None of these three assumptions are true, and surely nobody has ever seriously claimed them to be. They perhaps best describe the sort of ideal community liberal theory aims at. However, they have certain theoretical consequences for the view of freedom within liberal theory. One such consequence is to see the human agent as essentially or naturally free -- freedom is seen as given. In the state of nature, prior to entering into the state of society, all persons are naturally free, and from this historical point on social organization is a necessary evil which limits natural freedom in favour of other goals. At some stage those goals will be sufficiently achieved so as to rule out further limitations upon natural freedom (this is in essence Rawls' distinction between the general and special conceptions of justice [3]). Freedom is something that all possess prior to entering society: social organization is separate from and alien to individual liberty. This means attention must focus on the conditions of unfreedom rather than on conditions of freedom: because freedom is a natural given, then the focus must be on what can constrain it, rather than on what can create it (Bauman, 1988, p.4).

If such a view of freedom is taken, then social organization is always something that constrains freedom: it can never create it. The only role that society can play in ensuring freedom is therefore negative -- any positive steps taken by the community can only interfere with the 'natural' freedom of its members. The characteristic response to problems of freedom that arises from such a view is interference with freedom of normal adult members of the community is unjustified -- it is to treat them as though they were children.

However, this distinction between the adult citizen and the child conceals a third option, in which people are neither children in need of positive support, nor completely autonomous adult citizens -- instead, they are powerless citizens, excluded from participation in their own society. It is this blindness to this third category that constitutes the criticism of liberal approaches to liberty that will be developed in Part 2. Such approaches to freedom and social justice obscure the reality of the exclusion of certain groups in society. They not only conceal these issues in the margins, they conceal the margins too, by keeping attention upon the body in the text -- the body of the abled person, those who are full and active participants in society -- so that the absence of the other is not even noticed. Two categories are presented: (i) the person subject to interference; (ii) the person free of interference

-- and the liberal assumption is that the second category, because they lack interference, are therefore fully free participants in their community. This is to completely overlook the way in which the absence of powers and resources, the positive conditions of freedom, undermines both the positive *and* negative aspects of freedom. In order to be not-interfered with by the power of others, one needs to be reasonably powerful. So even if one were to maintain a purely negative view, that liberty is to be left alone or not interfered with, if that boundary is to be meaningful, then one is inevitably led to the need for positive powers and resources. Just because no one actively interferes within a boundary, it does not follow that those within the boundary are at liberty to do as they would choose -- what one can do within one's boundary is going to be largely determined by power relationships, even though the power of others is not being *intentionally* used to interfere within one's boundary. That is why, in the end, there is something incoherent about the purely negative view of freedom, and about freedom-talk independent of the idea of power.

The word "power" does not appear in the index to Rawls' *A Theory of Justice*, and it appears very rarely in the text. This is not merely extraordinary, it is also significant -- because it is precisely the underlying disempowerment of the excluded which reveals the limitations of these approaches and the strategies of social justice based upon them. Power is assumed, and where its absence is acknowledged it is seen as an inalterable natural fact, and so something that cannot be altered by political action, but only compensated for. This is the mistake. Therefore it is not merely true that the issue of exclusion is an issue of freedom as well as an issue of social justice -- it is *importantly* true, because it reveals what social justice demands in these cases.


## Section 2.5 -- Social Injustice

Another problem remains. While there may be a point at the level of theory in including the problem of exclusion within the boundaries of freedom-talk, is there any practical point in doing so? Is there any point in applying the approach advocated here to practical problems if people are already making exactly the same demands about poverty, disablement and deprivation, and making them perfectly well without appeal to the value of freedom, but by appeal to the value of social justice alone? This is especially so as it is not being denied that these *are* issues of social justice. There would be little point in establishing a theoretical connection between freedom and social justice if, in the end, it makes no practical difference to actual programmes of social justice.

In fact it does result in a practical difference. The impure theory of freedom draws the values of liberty and social justice intimately together. It makes the positive conditions for freedom *prima facie* as important as the negative conditions, and social justice must be, amongst other things, concerned with maintaining the positive conditions for freedom. The crucial point is that this intimate relationship between freedom and social justice actually transforms the idea of social justice -- it takes on a new shape; the two values interact with each other and, to an important extent, shape each other.

What has to be shown, then, is that:

(1)  the impure theory of freedom does transform the picture of social justice; and
(2)  this picture will give rise to a distinctive account of what social justice demands in practice.

The focus must fall upon what is to count as social *in*justice, because it is this that shapes the response; and so what the impure theory of freedom touches upon and re-shapes is the understanding of social injustice. The issue it brings to the foreground is, as was established in section 2.4, the problem of the exclusion of certain groups from particular institutions and practices. The question then is, why is such exclusion a social injustice, and what ought to be done about it.

The reason why such exclusion constitutes a social injustice has already been established in previous chapters. The principle of the moral equality of persons leads to the position that all should receive equal moral and political consideration. They are therefore entitled to the equal value of their membership of the community, and therefore to what is required as a condition for such membership. The exclusion of groups such as the physically disabled from certain institutions and practices undermines their membership, and therefore constitutes an injustice.

The second question is what ought to be done about such an injustice. Does the approach developed here advocate a distinctive response? Being excluded from active participation in the community does not necessarily lead to exclusion from the material benefits of social cooperation: for example, children are by and large excluded from active participation in society, and yet many children are not consequently materially deprived, because they gain access to material resources through other means. If the focus falls upon adults who are deprived of active participation in society, then the problem becomes that of ensuring that the benefits of social cooperation reach such people so that at least their basic needs are met. The problem can be specified like this: certain groups are not receiving enough of the *output* of social cooperation through existing systems of resource distribution (e.g., the market system) through no fault of their own. Therefore alternative systems (e.g., welfare systems) have to be put in place to ensure that they *do* receive an adequate level of output. Once this is done, such that at least basic needs are met, the problem of social justice has been solved.

However, such a strategy has problematic limits. For example, it does little to tackle the reasons *why* people receive an inadequate level of social output. The problem remains one of lack of power to participate at the other end of the process -- the production of social resources. Exclusion from an adequate share of social *output* arises because certain groups are excluded from contributing an adequate share of social *input*. The strategy of setting up welfare systems to get output to excluded groups does little to tackle this prior problem. To opt for this kind of welfare strategy is, in effect, to accept exclusion from social cooperation as a given, inalterable fact about such groups, which can only be *compensated* for.

As has been argued, exclusion from social cooperation is not an inalterable fact about such groups: their exclusion from society is not due to any fact about them, but due to the way society is structured and organized. To take exclusion as a given, and to limit welfare to compensation for exclusion, is an inadequate response to their situation. Further, it could be argued that one of the basic needs of any member of the community is to be an active doer, chooser and participator in that community. If this is right, then the compensation notion of social justice fails to meet even the basic needs of such groups. Of course, it could be argued that there is no such basic need, but it has to be conceded that people deprived of such active participation are deprived of much else besides -- the dignity, self respect, respect of others, and power and control over one's life, that go with such a role. In that respect the position of the excluded is much the same as that of children: experiencing a near total lack of power and control over the content of their lives. These are social goods, and can be just as scarce as more material social goods -- but they cannot be re-distributed by a welfare system. Indeed, one of the central problems of welfare systems seems to be that dependence upon state-provided benefits makes social goods like these even harder to come by.

The problem, then, is not simply that deprivation of active participation in society deprives a person of access to material social goods: those goods can be distributed by other means. The problem is that there are social goods such as autonomy, power, self respect, that cannot be distributed by other means, but which seem to depend upon active participation in society's institutions and practices. And, more important, active participation is not only the foundation of other social goods, but is a social good itself: it is the power to shape, expand and pursue one's own life plans in a free and creative way, rather than having simply to make the best of whatever options happen to be left open to one; and it is the power to contribute to the shaping of the community itself, rather than having to fit within the mould that society has left for one, however narrow and constraining it turns out to be.

It should now be clear how the issues of freedom and social justice meet. That someone is deprived of the conditions of active participation in the community is an issue both of freedom and of social justice -- they are not distinct problems. The welfare strategy of compensation is inadequate and incomplete precisely because it fails to realise that a crucial aspect of the problem of exclusion is that the freedom of the excluded is destroyed. A broader understanding of the problem of exclusion is demanded, and leads to the demand for strategies of social justice that take the idea of welfare beyond compensation, towards empowerment and liberation. It also, it will be argued in Part 3, moves strategies of social justice away from any concept of 'basic' needs. This is, hopefully, a sufficiently distinctive departure from what is normally said about freedom and social justice within liberal theory, that it makes a significant difference both at the theoretical *and* practical levels. At the theoretical level, we have arrived at a distinctive view of what social injustice consists in. At the practical level, we have arrived at a distinctive view of what social justice therefore demands.

This raises a range of complex questions for the theory and practice of social welfare which will be examined more fully in Part 3. For now, it has been argued that the problem of exclusion from social institutions and practices is an issue of social justice and of freedom. It is an injustice because, amongst other things, it diminishes or destroys the freedom of the excluded. Any responses must therefore aim at ensuring and maintaining the freedom of such groups: freedom understood in a richer sense than mere non-interference; freedom understood in the sense of being able be an active chooser, doer and participator in one's community.

## Section 2.6 -- Conclusion

In this chapter, it has been argued that the problem of exclusion from particular social institutions and practices faced by certain groups in the community has been inadequately dealt with by liberal theories of freedom and social justice. Traditional liberal approaches to freedom, characterized by the pure and impure negative views, do not allow the situation of the excluded to be articulated in terms of liberty, by failing to allow that exclusion violates liberty. In response, a 'purely' impure theory of freedom is suggested, that recognizes both negative and positive aspects of freedom, and negative and positive conditions for freedom. It allows that anything that undermines the positive conditions for freedom can be a violation of liberty. As exclusion from social institutions and practices does undermine the positive conditions of freedom of the excluded, and as this exclusion cannot be seen as something they deserve in any sense, then their exclusion is, in fact, a violation of their liberty.

This understanding shapes a particular response within the theory of social justice, in that social *injustice* is now to be understood as the exclusion of groups like the physically disabled from certain institutions and practices and the consequent undermining of their equal membership of the community. The response to this exclusion now cannot simply be compensation for its effects -- it must be a positive programme aiming to restore or create the positive conditions of participation.

It has been argued that the traditional liberal approach to these issues leads to the double exclusion of certain groups: exclusion at the level of practice *and* at the level of theory. Certain groups are not only excluded from active participation in society, they are excluded from articulating their situation in terms of the theory of freedom; and have their situation misrepresented in terms of the theory of social justice. Part 2 of the book will establish in further detail how these groups are excluded from the theory of freedom, and will establish the detail of the impure theory of freedom. Part 3 will demonstrate how the problem of exclusion must then be understood in terms of social justice, and what response the theory of social justice must then make to that problem.

# Notes

[1]     For example, see Miller (1983): "...we are entitled to say that the collectivity has restricted freedom in advance of identifying the particular agents responsible; indeed there may be no point in naming names, since (if the restriction on freedom is unjustifiable) our object in making the judgment may be less to blame or punish specific individuals than to argue for a change in the institutional set up," p.81.

[2]     I have found elements for such an impure theory of freedom in writers including Berlin (1969); Benn (1967) and (1975/76); Connolly (1987); and Young (1986). I have taken points and insights from all of these writers. But the approach to freedom implicit in much of their work has not been spelt out. That I have tried to do here, although I wouldn't claim that any of the above would necessarily agree with what I have said. Some of them, for example Berlin, still place priority on the negative conditions for freedom, even though what Berlin has to say about the importance of positive liberty has been the central influence upon what I have to say here.

[3]     See Rawls (1972), pp.150-152. For example: "The denial of equal liberty can be defended only if it is necessary to raise the level of civilisation so that in due course these freedoms can be enjoyed," pp.151-152.

# Part 2
# Issues of Freedom

# 3   Freedom and Ability

## Section 3.1 -- The Negative/Positive Contrast

In western political philosophy, debates about freedom have been based around a contrast between negative and positive liberty. At its simplest, the difference amounts to this: negative freedom consists in the *absence* of something, while positive freedom consists in the *presence* of something. As freedom is so closely linked to action [1], then freedom must be of value to agents or those who want to be agents. Therefore, if freedom is an absence, it must be the absence of something that is not conducive to agency; and, if freedom is a presence, then it must be the presence of something that is conducive to agency. According to the negative view, what must be absent is external interference so that the agent is left alone to perform actions. According to the positive view, what must be present is power and control by the agent over their actions, and the desires and beliefs that motivate their actions -- those actions, desires and beliefs do not arise at random, nor are they imposed by others; they are, in some sense, genuinely their own, in some sense authentic.

The contrast can be made clearer if expressed in terms of obstacles to freedom, things that can undermine or constrain freedom. If freedom is, negatively, the absence of something, then what undermines or constrains freedom must be something that is actually present. If, positively, freedom is the presence of something, then what undermines or constrains freedom must be something that is actually absent (Feinberg, 1973, p.13). In other words, constraints on liberty understood in the negative sense must be positive; constraints on liberty understood in the positive sense must be negative.

There are many disputes between the negative and positive positions. At the most extreme is the claim that either negative or positive freedom by itself is sufficient for the agent to be free, and that the opposing concept of freedom is false or incoherent or misguided. The extreme negative position would claim that absence of interference by other agents, of whatever form, is sufficient for the agent to be free. Therefore even though that agent may have no authentic control over their actions, they are free as long as nobody interferes. At the extreme, random movement counts as free movement: any movement is free as long as nothing blocks it.

The extreme positive position would be that as long as the agent has authentic control over their ideas, opinions, beliefs, wants, feelings and actions, then that agent is free even where those actions are severely constrained by external interference. As long as the agent has authentic control within those limits, however narrowly they are drawn, then the agent is free. At the extreme, a person in a prison cell can be free in this sense. The Stoics expressed this view of freedom as knowledge of and reconciliation to the limits of one's actions, however narrow those limits happen to be [2].

There are, then, four possibilities:

(1)     The absence of external interference.
(2)     The presence of external interference.
(3)     The presence of authentic control.
(4)     The absence of authentic control.

The extreme negative position only recognizes condition 1 as sufficient for freedom, and only condition 2 as sufficient for unfreedom; while the extreme positive position recognizes only condition 3 as sufficient for freedom, and only condition 4 as sufficient for unfreedom. The impure theory of freedom described in chapter 2 would recognize both conditions 1 and 3 as necessary conditions for freedom, and both conditions 2 and 4 as each sufficient for unfreedom.

In fact, views of freedom rarely take the two extreme stances, as was seen in chapter 2. More usually, the dispute is about priority: which type of condition is most important, most central to a person's liberty? According to the impure theory of freedom, it is impossible to answer that question *a priori*, at the level of theory: the details of the particular case have to be examined. Sometimes the two kinds of condition will conflict, but ideally they will be in harmony: the free agent will have authentic control over her beliefs, desires and actions, and those beliefs, desires and actions will not be interfered with or blocked by others. In a sense, the two conditions depend upon each other: it is difficult to see how an agent can have authentic control over her beliefs, desires and actions when others are interfering with them; and it is equally difficult to see how an agent can resist interference from others unless she has authentic control over her beliefs, desires and actions. The agent needs both the space *and* power to be free: without that power, the space does not exist; without that space, the power is not hers. As was stated in the introduction, the impure theory recognizes that freedom has both negative and positive *aspects* and *conditions.* The negative and positive aspects of liberty mean that the free person (i) is not prevented from doing $x$ (negative; non-interference), and (ii) is able to do $x$ (positive; power). The negative and positive conditions of liberty are those conditions that must be in place if the negative and positive aspects are to be guarantied. And the crucial point here is that the impure theory recognizes that both negative and positive conditions *each* contribute to *both* the negative and positive aspects of liberty; and that the undermining of either negative *or* positive conditions of freedom can destroy *both* the negative and positive aspects.

The three types of conditions of freedom can be summarised as (1) the Non-interference Condition -- being left alone to act; (2) the Autonomy Condition -- having the capacity to make rational choices about which action to take; and (3) the Power Condition -- having the powers to enact the action chosen. [It is important to note that while, as the argument develops, these are referred to as *conditions* of freedom, they are more strictly *types* of condition; such that while there are only three *types* of condition, there are many different actual conditions that fall into one of the three types.]

The agent who enjoys both the negative and positive conditions of liberty is an autonomous chooser and actor: there is an area of her activity that nobody else controls, and over which she has authentic, positive control (although it is important not to fall into the mistake of seeing this area as a confined space with definite boundaries -- the area of her activity over which she has authentic control must extend beyond anything that could be understood as a 'private' space, into a 'public' space shared with others, where that authentic control is collective. It will be argued below that without that public space, anything that could be understood as 'private' space is unsustainable. A world of purely 'privately' free agents is practically incomprehensible). The idea of the autonomous chooser and doer, then, is where the impure theory of freedom finds its fullest practical expression, and must be explored in detail. The notion of the autonomous chooser is an idea which finds favour with many contemporary liberal writers -- although perhaps the notion of an autonomous *doer* is something that receives less emphasis in that work than here. These ideas of autonomous choice and action will be fully developed in chapter 4. This chapter is concerned to show how the impure theory of freedom enables the problem of the exclusion of certain groups from society's institutions and practices to be fully understood as an issue of freedom, by establishing a distinctive connection between freedom and ability.

# Section 3.2 -- The Alterability and Intentionality Theses

This section establishes a conceptual map of freedom, as understood within terms of the impure theory.

*freedom*:
A is free to do *x* if she has the power to do *x*,
    and
if she is not prevented from using that power by some external obstacle.

By "external obstacle" here is meant anything that can prevent *A* from doing *x*, whether a natural object like a snowdrift, or a social object like the actions of other agents. Now, it may seem that all that is being described here is the *ability* to do *x*, and that freedom to do *x* simply amounts to the ability to do it. But talk of ability here is ambiguous, because there is, of course, a sense in which the agent can enjoy the ability to do *x* and yet be unable to do it. She may have the ability to walk, but be stuck in a snowdrift and so unable to exercise that ability. So there is an important contrast between having the capacity to do *x*, and being able to actually perform *x* at any particular time. By "freedom" it is meant that *A* has both the capacity to do *x* and nothing prevents her from performing *x*.

*unfreedom:*
A is unfree to do *x* if she lacks the power to do it,
    or
if she is prevented from doing it by some external obstacle.

Now, there is a glaring deficiency in this accounts as it stands: for it allows that *A* actually doing *x* is a sufficient condition for the truth of "*A* is free to do *x*", regardless of whether she does it under duress, coercion, hypnosis, or under the influence of drugs or delusions. A solution would be to include the phrase "or *refrain* from *x*" in each clause, so that now it is part of being free to do something that the agent can refrain from it if she chooses: there is a genuine choice being made. A second and even more glaring deficiency lies in the definition's conflation of unfreedom and inability -- surely it cannot be claimed that all cases of inability are also cases of unfreedom. For the moment, unfreedom will be limited to those cases of inability that are alterable; a more subtle limitation will be introduced at a later stage in this section.

With these amendments, the full description of freedom and unfreedom within the impure theory now reads:

*A* is free to do *x* if she has the power to do or refrain from doing *x;* and
if she is not prevented from using that power by some external obstacle.
*A* is unfree to do *x* if
(1) she lacks the power to do it or refrain from it;
  or
(2) she is prevented from doing it or refraining from it by some external obstacle;
AND
(3) there is some other practically possible social order under which neither (1) nor (2) would hold.

The final clause (3) is central to the idea of freedom within the impure theory, and can be entitled the *Alterability Thesis*. This thesis simply states that for an obstruction to violate freedom, rather than simply cause inability to act, it must, in principle, be alterable: there is no point in talking of freedom being violated or constrained if there is nothing, individually or collectively, anybody could have done to prevent or remove that obstacle. Argument has to take place over what will count as an acceptable cost for alteration -- some things may be alterable only at a prohibitive cost to those who have to alter it. But the argument now has a more familiar practical form: the dispute is not about the metaphysics of liberty, but over what counts as alterable and what counts as an acceptable or unacceptable cost for alteration. Unfreedom has, therefore, not been conflated with inability, but has been identified as a particular form of inability (and identifying unfreedom as a particular form of inability is, of course, what *any* theory of freedom must do).

However, the description of freedom and unfreedom given above is still unsatisfactory. On its own, the Alterability Thesis seems to have too wide a scope, for there are many obstacles to actions which are perfectly alterable in a non-controversial sense, and which would not, intuitively, seem to count as issues of freedom. For example, a snowdrift outside someone's door prevents them from leaving, but does not seem to have that moral or political significance central to issues of freedom -- it would be odd to say that its presence was a violation of the agent's freedom. So for the Alterability Thesis to be of use, it needs to be limited to those cases that are genuinely issues of freedom, those issues that genuinely do have that moral or political element to them. Being imprisoned by lock and chain has a moral and political significance; being obstructed by a snow drift does not; and so if the theory includes the latter type of case as an issue of freedom, then it is too flabby, and the Alterability Thesis needs to be altered or supplemented to tighten up the theory.

One way of achieving this is to draw a distinction between natural and social obstacles to action, and to conclude that the Alterability Thesis only applies to social obstacles. The snowdrift is a natural obstacle and so the Alterability Thesis does not apply here, and freedom is therefore not at stake. Similarly, with Helvetius' famous example, that one is not unfree to fly like an eagle, merely unable: the inability to fly is a purely natural limitation, not a social one, and so liberty is not at stake. However, although this natural/social distinction is widely appealed to within political philosophy, its use is rejected here. It is perfectly possible that particular natural obstacles to an agent's ability to act could give rise to issues of freedom.

First, where an obstacle is indisputably a natural one, the issue becomes one of alterability: the point of Helvetius' example of the inability to fly like an eagle may not be that this is in some sense a 'natural' limitation, but that it is in fact inalterable: there is nothing that can be done to enable one to fly like an eagle. The snowdrift outside of the door, although a 'natural' obstacle, is importantly different -- it is alterable. The question is whether the failure to remove it constitutes a moral violation of the agent's liberty, and that question can only be settled by examining the context of the particular situation: at the costs the obstacle imposes upon the agent, at their own powers to remove it, at how seriously it disrupts their life-plans, at the costs for others of removing it, at the responsibilities of others towards the agent. For example, if the agent cannot remove the snowdrift and so remains trapped within the house, and others could remove it at minimal cost, and in fact if the local authority has responsibility for clearing snow, then it may be that there is a moral violation of freedom here.

The question of whether there is an issue of freedom here cannot be settled simply by appeal to a natural/social distinction: such an appeal amounts only to the dogmatic assertion that natural obstacles fall outside the scope of the Alterability Thesis, and therefore outside the scope of freedom-talk, without giving any reason why this should be so. The assumption behind the use of the natural/social distinction often seems to be that natural obstacles are in some sense necessarily inalterable, while social obstacles are necessarily alterable; but of course this is not true at all. Natural obstacles can be overcome:

snowdrifts can be removed, rivers bridged, floods blocked; and some social obstacles may actually be inalterable when costs of alteration are taken into account.

Second, applying a straightforward natural/social distinction is problematic when applied to obstacles to action. It is true that the inability to walk can be a purely natural inability: but that inability only renders the agent unable to use certain public facilities if access for those who cannot use their legs is not provided. Therefore this natural inability to use one's legs is only an obstacle because of the community's failure to provide access: and this is a social obstacle, not a natural one [3].

However, the rejection of the natural/social distinction still leaves the problem of finding a limitation of the Alterability Thesis: without that limit, the thesis looks too flabby to be useful to a theory of freedom. The right limitation is in fact to do with moral responsibility. The simple fact that some obstacle is alterable is not sufficient to show that it gives rise to an issue of freedom -- somebody must be morally responsible for its alteration, such that the failure to alter it amounts to a violation of freedom. Now it is not one's actual inability to do $x$ which constitutes the violation of freedom, but the failure of some agency to alter the situation so that one *can* do $x$, where that agency has moral responsibility for the alteration. This element of the theory of freedom is developed in terms of the Intentionality Thesis.

The purpose of the Intentionality Thesis is, along with the Alterability Thesis, to identify those forms of inability that are to count as cases of unfreedom. The Alterability Thesis states that only forms of inability that are alterable count as cases of unfreedom. The Intentionality Thesis will further limit the class by stating that only those alterable forms of inability which have some connection to human intention count as cases of unfreedom: that feature which prevents $A$ from performing $x$ must both be alterable and be connected in some way to human intentions, if it is to give rise to an issue of freedom. The function of the Intentionality Thesis is to spell out that connection with human intention.

There are at least three possible versions of the thesis:

*IT1*:  $A$ is unfree to do $x$ if she is prevented from doing so or refraining from doing so through the action or omission of some other agent or agents $B$, and $B$ performed that action or omission with the intention of preventing $A$ from doing $x$.

*IT2*:  $A$ is unfree to do $x$ if she is prevented from doing so or refraining from doing so through the action or omission of some other agent or agents *B*, and *B* intended that action or omission, but did not necessarily intend it to prevent *A* from doing or not doing *x*: this is an unintended side-effect.

*IT3*: *A* is unfree to do *x* if she is prevented from doing so because the institutions and practices of the community exclude her from participating in *x*, even though that community did not intend those institutions and practices to exclude *A*, and even where the community did not intend those institutions or practices in any strict sense -- they may be 'spontaneous'.

If "prevents *A* from doing or refraining from *x*" is summarised as *X*, then the differences between the positions can be summarised as follows:

*IT1*: *B* intends **X**.
*IT2*: *B* intends that which causes **X**, but not **X** itself.
*IT3*: *B* does not intend **X** nor that which causes **X**.

It can be seen that all three versions of the thesis tie the causes of unfreedom to human agency, but that the link to human *intention* is weakened in each thesis. In IT1 the obstacle to *A*'s action is intended to be an obstacle to *A*'s action by *B*. In IT2 that which acts as an obstacle to *A*'s action is intended, but is not intended as an obstacle to *A*'s action. In IT3 both that which acts as an obstacle to *A*'s action and the fact that it acts as an obstacle are unintended.

Three stories might illuminate the differences:

*IT1*: *B* has a library built which has a series of stairs built leading to the entrance, which prevent physically disabled people from gaining access to the building. *B* had these stairs built with the specific intention of excluding disabled people. They are intended as an obstacle.

*IT2*: *B* has a library built which has a series of stairs leading to the entrance, which prevent physically disabled people from gaining access to the building. But *B* chose the design because it was architecturally the most attractive, and did not take the access of the physically disabled into account. The stairs were not intended as an obstacle.

*IT3*: *B* has a library built open to all, with disabled access. But it emerges that the disabled rarely, if ever, make use of it. Investigation reveals that the financial situation of the disabled, combined with the difficulties and costs of transport, mean that that the vast majority of the disabled are unable to make use of the library.

The function of the Intentionality Thesis is to limit the Alterability Thesis to those cases which are genuine issues of freedom; it does this by bringing moral responsibility into the theory -- cases of inability are only considered to be genuine issues of freedom where there is somebody who can be held morally responsible for altering the state of affairs which renders people unable. Of the three stories, the first two can certainly be made sense of as issues of freedom. In story 1, *B* clearly intends to constrain freedom, and so is morally responsible for that constraint. In story 2, although *B* did not intend to constrain freedom, the question of negligence arises and so makes room for judgments of moral responsibility -- it may be that *B* ought to have taken the situation of the physically disabled into account and so ought to have provided access. In story 3 it becomes more complex: how can *B* be held morally responsible for the exclusion of the disabled in this case?

In fact, the question of moral responsibility is relevant in story 3, even if that responsibility does not fall upon *B*. The community could be held responsible for ensuring that its members have equal access to its institutions and practices. This means that there is no one specific to *blame* for the exclusion of the disabled, but the question of blame is not always relevant to judgments of moral responsibility, as was established in section 2.3. These two considerations -- the moral responsibility of the community as a whole for its members, and the irrelevance of blame -- leave scope for considerations of moral responsibility under IT3; and this allows that at least some of the issues that arise under IT3, such as story 3, are *prima facie* issues of freedom. And so each of the three versions of the Intentionality Thesis performs the task of identifying specific forms of alterable inability as issues of freedom: the question is, then, which version should be adopted.

The position taken in this book is that the exclusion of groups like the disabled from society's institutions and practices is, in fact, a moral violation of their freedom. The next task is to apply the different conceptual maps of freedom that arise from the different versions of the Intentionality Thesis to the exclusion of the physically disabled, to see which of them if any, allows their situation to be described as an issue of freedom. The claim will be that there *is* one conceptual map that does allow this to be said: the question then will be whether that conceptual map is plausible. It will be argued that it is [4].

The impure theory of freedom will be used to make that case. But first, the alternative theories of freedom will be examined to see what conclusions they reach about the situation of the disabled: the pure negative view, as described by W.A. Parent (Parent, 1974A; and 1974B); an impure negative view offered by Patrick Day (Day, 1977); and a richer liberal view of freedom outlined by S. I. Benn and W. L. Weinstein (Benn and Weinstein, 1971; and 1974), which is also raised by Sir Isaiah Berlin (Berlin, 1969), and which is endorsed and developed by John Gray (Gray, 1984).

While both Parent's and Day's accounts have the explicit conclusion that the physically disabled are not unfree to use public facilities, they do so from different perspectives. For Parent, both the disabled and the able-bodied are equally free to use public facilities, even where the disabled are unable to use them. For Day, the disabled are not free to use such facilities, but they are not unfree either -- they are not freedom evaluable. And, it will be argued, the richer view developed by Benn and Weinstein, Berlin, and Gray, has the same, although implicit, conclusion: that the exclusion of the physically disabled from the community's institutions and practices does not constitute a moral violation of their liberty.

To conclude this section, what follows is a full description of freedom and unfreedom as understood by the impure theory, complete with the Alterability and Intentionality Theses:

*A* is free to do *x* if she has the power to do or refrain from *x*,
and
if she is not prevented from using that power by some external obstacle.
*A* is unfree to do *x* if
(1)    she lacks the power to do it or refrain from it; or
(2)    she is prevented from doing it or refraining from it by some external obstacle;
and
(3)    there is some other practically possible situation in which neither (1) nor (2) would hold;
and
(4)    there is some agent or agency that can be identified as morally responsible for bringing about that situation.

## Section 3.3 -- W.A. Parent's View

Thomas Hobbes states:

> Liberty, or freedome, signifieth (properly), the absence of Opposition; (by Opposition, I mean externall Impediments of motion;) ...whatever is so tyed, or environed, as it cannot move, but within a certain space, which space is determined by the opposition of some externall body, we say it hath not Liberty to go further... [(a) But when the impediment of motion, is in the constitution of the thing it selfe, we use not to say, it wants the Liberty; but the Power to move; as when a stone lyeth still, or a man fastened to his bed with sicknesse]. And according to the proper, and generally received meaning of the word, [(b) a *'freeman', is he, that is in those things, which by his strength and wit he is able to do, is not hindred to doe what he has a will to do*]. (Hobbes' emphasis, my brackets) (Hobbes, 1968, pp.261-262)

This is a classic statement of the internal/external distinction, and yet this distinction is, as was seen in section 2.3, very difficult to draw in practice. Most impediments to motion will be a complex mixture of internal and external factors: what can impede an agent's actions (the external aspect) depends upon the agent's powers (the internal aspect). A brick wall may prevent the agent from getting from A to B, but it does not prevent a bird with the power of flight from getting from A to B; so is it external obstacle or internal power that thwarts the human agent here? A flight of steps does not prevent the able-bodied person from getting from A to B, but it does prevent the person confined to a wheelchair from getting from A to B; so is it external obstacle or internal power that thwarts the disabled person? Obviously it is a complex mixture of both aspects; actions take place where internal powers and external world meet. Therefore what counts as an external obstacle to action depends upon the internal powers and capacities of the agent. The frustration of an action can never be accounted for in purely internal or external terms: the best that can be done, if such a distinction must be made at all, is to ask which aspect, internal or external, plays the most significant role in that frustration under the circumstances.

According to the negative view, frustration of action is only an issue of freedom if external factors play the most significant role, and then only if those external factors are of a specific type (intentional interference by other agents). However, if the Alterability Thesis is taken seriously, then the significance of the internal/external distinction changes: now what has to be established is which aspect can be most effectively altered in order to enable the unabled. And now the question of freedom/unfreedom does not rest on whether what is altered or internal or external, but upon whether the *failure* to alter it is justifiable.

It may be objected that the external is still the essential dimension for issues of freedom, because even in terms of the impure theory, what is alterable must be an external factor. However, the crucial issue is not the *location* of what is to be altered, but the possibility of alteration. So a situation of inability can always, *prima facie*, be an issue of freedom: nothing is settled by fixing the location of what is to be altered as internal or external. The internal/external question is therefore irrelevant to settling whether this can be an issue of freedom: the relevant question is, instead, alterability. The only sense in which the external is still relevant is when it comes to identifying an agency that can be held morally responsible for the situation -- such an agency is, of course, going to be 'external' to the person who is unable to do *x*. And so both the agent's inability to do *x* and the factor that can be altered such that they are enabled to do *x* can be internal to the agent, and the situation be an issue of freedom.

W.A.Parent places great weight on the internal/external distinction and uses it to draw a clear and distinct boundary between the *power* or *ability* to do something and the *freedom* to do that thing. According to Parent, the two terms "ability to..." and "freedom to..." have distinct meanings, and therefore have nothing to do with each other in practice. If someone's ability to do *x* is taken away, their freedom to do *x* is not necessarily taken away: it depends upon how it is done. For example, if *X* deliberately shoots *Y* in the back, taking away their ability to walk, then "he does not thereby render *Y* unfree to walk; rather he deprives him of the physical capacity to do so" (Parent, 1974A, p.151). Parent's case is that "deliberate deprivation of ability" and "interference with liberty" have different designata.

Now, this looks like an appeal to the grammar of the concepts to settle the argument, but it is an appeal which settles very little. It must be conceded that "ability to..." and "freedom to..." have different meanings; but that can be accepted without also having to accept that deliberate deprivation of ability never interferes with freedom. The fact is that, independent of any considerations of grammar, depriving a person of the physical capacity to walk, however and whyever it is done, will have a wide effect over the whole range of her life, depriving her of a wide range of opportunities and life chances that depended upon that ability. So by depriving her of the ability to walk, she has been deprived of a whole range of life chances; and depriving her of these surely raises issues of freedom. "Ability to..." and "freedom too..." may not be logically or grammatically entangled, but they are surely practically entangled, such that to effect one must be to effect the other.

However, for Parent, effecting someone's opportunities is not to effect their freedom, because "freedom" and "opportunity" are not the same thing. "The terms 'liberty' and 'opportunity' have distinct meanings. Depriving someone of the liberty to act is not the same thing as refusing him the opportunity to do so..." (Ibid., p.153). But it can be accepted that "liberty" and "opportunity" have distinct meanings, without having to accept that they have nothing to do with each other in practice: two concepts can have distinct meanings and yet still be inseparably entangled when it comes to practice, such that to effect one is to effect the other.

Parent uses the same argument for the ideas of "social freedom" and "freedom of choice". For him, "The former is a political, the latter a metaphysical concept" (Ibid., p.156). But again, it can surely be allowed that they have distinct meanings, and at the same time recognized that they depend upon each other in practice, such that the reduction of an agent's freedom of choice must of practical necessity decrease their social freedom, and vice versa.

For Parent, social unfreedom only occurs when an agent's powers are blocked by an external obstacle, but they still possess those powers: where their powers are taken away from them, even deliberately, this is not an instance of unfreedom (see passage (a) of Hobbes' statement). Parent's case is that there are many ways to prevent someone from acting, and depriving them of their freedom to act is just one of these ways. Others are deprivation of means, ability, power, permission, authority, will (Parent, 1974B, p.434). Freedom is just one more element amongst these: they do not comprise freedom. So if *B* takes away *A*'s means or power or ability or will to act, they have not taken away their freedom to act, because freedom to act is not the same thing as the means or power or ability or will to act: it remains behind, intact.

The obvious reply is that while the means or power or ability or will to act are not the same thing as the freedom to act, they act as conditions for the freedom to act, such that if those conditions are taken away, freedom is taken away too. It can coherently be claimed that depriving someone of their means or power or ability or will to do

$x$ does deprive them of their freedom to do $x$, without the implication that the means or power or ability or will to act are therefore *the same thing* as the freedom to act.

Two conclusions seem to follow from what Parent says:

(1)    For someone to have their freedom to act taken away at all, they must already possess the means, power, ability or will to act.

(2)    For someone to possess the freedom to act, it is not necessary that they possess the means, power, ability or will to act.

Or, in other words:

(1)    For $A$ to be unfree to do $x$, it is a necessary condition that $A$ be able to do $x$ -- you cannot prevent someone from doing something they cannot do in the first place.

(2)    For $A$ to be free to do $x$, it is not a necessary condition that $A$ be able to do $x$ -- "...a man socially free to do $x$ may nevertheless be unable to do it for a variety of reasons" (Parent, 1974A, p.161).

But this would mean that the person unable to do anything cannot be made unfree in any way at all: their liberty is inviolable -- the less an agent can actually physically do, the more secure their liberty. A person without the means, power, ability or will to do $x$ is still at liberty to do it: "...a person's not being prevented from engaging in a certain activity constitutes *by itself* a sufficient condition of his liberty to do so" (Parent's emphasis) (Ibid., p.158). This is, of course, the classic statement of the pure negative theory, and it reveals an implication of that theory: that if a person cannot do $x$, their freedom to do it is perfectly inviolable -- the people with the most secure freedom to do $x$ are those people are lack the capacity to do it.

This implication is not merely bizarre, it is also dangerous, especially for the treatment of the physically disabled or the mentally handicapped. In order to ensure that these persons are not treated as mere objects, rather than as ends in themselves, their liberty must be respected. But according to the pure negative view, nothing counts as *not* respecting their liberty -- demanding that their liberty is respected places no practical limits upon what can be done to them. Anything can be done to them, without raising the accusation of the violation of their freedom. This is not because they have no freedom, but because that freedom is literally inviolable. If they lack the power or ability or will

70

to do anything, then they cannot be rendered unfree to do anything --
and they nevertheless remain perfectly free to do all those things they
cannot possibly do. Respect for freedom has been reduced to an empty
formality.

## Section 3.4 -- Patrick Day's View

This implication can be avoided if it is insisted that the *ability* to do $x$ is
a necessary condition for being free to do it. This is, of course, the
impure negative view, and this is also Patrick Day's position. It also
seems a better reading of Hobbes, especially if passage (b) of his
statement is noted: "a 'freeman' is he, that is in those things, which *by
his strength and wit he is able to do*, is not hindred to doe what he has
a will to do" (my emphasis). For Day, though, being able to do $x$ is a
necessary condition for being both free *and* unfree to do $x$: "...the truth
of '$A$ is able to $D$' is a necessary condition both of the truth and also of
the falsity of '$A$ is free to $D$'" (Day, 1977, p.260). Therefore the
person who is unable to do $x$ is neither free nor unfree to do it: they are
not freedom evaluable.

For Parent, the person unable to do anything could not have their
freedom violated because it was somehow logically inviolable; for
Day, their freedom cannot be violated because there is no freedom here
to violate. Both these positions agree that a person cannot be made
unfree to do something they could not do in the first place, but they
give very different perspectives upon the position of the disabled. For
Parent, the disabled person has equal liberty with the able-bodied
person to use public facilities, even though they have no access. For
Day, the disabled person does not have the freedom to use that facility,
but because no one has intentionally interfered to prevent them from
using it, they are not unfree to use it either -- the question of freedom
and unfreedom does not arise here. The inability of the disabled to use
such facilities therefore cannot be an issue of freedom. For Day, the
physically or mentally handicapped person unable to care for themself
has no liberty that can be respected or disrespected; for Parent, the
question of respect for liberty *does* arise, but then any answer will do.
Another important difference between Day and Parent is that the
former holds the strong intentionality thesis (IT1), offering a
Benthamite definition of freedom as, simply, the absence of coercion;
while the latter allows that even natural events like snowstorms can
restrict liberty (Parent, 1974A, p.159).

71

However, Day has another condition for unfreedom that acts as a restriction upon the cases of inability that can legitimately be described as constraints on freedom: that is the *retrievability* of the obstacle that prevents *A* from doing *x*. If *B* makes *A* unable to do *x* by chopping off both legs, then they have not made them unfree to act, merely unable. "We do not talk of *A* being unfree to *D* unless *B* has made *A* unable to *D* in such a way that it is possible for *A* to be again able to *D*" (Day, 1977, p.264). But this condition must be rejected as an element of the theory of freedom, because an irretrievable disability may not necessarily render *A* irretrievably unable to do *x*. Certainly, chopping off *A*'s legs is an irretrievable step, given the current state of medical surgery: but it does not necessarily render *A* irretrievably unable to travel from place to place, nor even irretrievably unable to walk. It is possible be that *A* could be enabled to travel from place to place by some simple alteration of social arrangements; or they may be enabled to walk by means other than their own legs. It is not the ability to walk that is at stake, but the ability to travel from one place to another -- and even if we cannot enable *A* to walk again, we can enable them to travel from place to place. So a more sophisticated Alterability Thesis is called for here than Day allows.

Finally, according to Day, *B* decreases *A*'s freedom by decreasing the number of alternative actions *A* can perform -- so can *B* *increase* *A*'s freedom by increasing the number of alternative actions available to *A*? Day says yes, but only if *A* was made unfree to do those things in the first place (Ibid., p.260). This means that the idea of being *made* free is limited by the ways in which someone can be made unfree -- and for Day the ways people can be made unfree are severely restricted by the strict intentionality thesis and his rather pessimistic notion of retrievability. Freedom can only be taken away, or restored after it has been taken away -- it cannot be created. Therefore the physically disabled can only be made free to use public facilities if that freedom was taken away from them in the first place -- and as that freedom was never taken away from them by anybody, as they were never free to use those facilities in the first place, their exclusion is not an issue of freedom.

## Section 3.5 -- The Strict Intentionality Thesis

As has been seen, Patrick Day opts for the strict intentionality thesis (IT1), and he discusses this aspect of the idea of freedom in a later paper, "Is the Concept of Freedom Essentially Contestable?" (Day,

1986). There he sets out to show that the concept of freedom in political philosophy is not essentially contestable: to do so he offers five definitions of freedom, and tries to show that, of these, four are clearly false and one is clearly true -- and if there is only one true definition of freedom then there is nothing to essentially contest. The true definition is that: "Liberty is the absence of coercion", where coercion implies intent -- there must be coercive intent by *B* for the act to be coercive.

To back his argument, Day tells two stories (Ibid., p.118):

(1)     *B* locks her premises for the night while her secretary, *A*, is still inside. She does so simply because she has forgotten or does not know that he is still inside the building. Clearly there is no coercive intent, and so *A*'s liberty has not been violated.

(2)     *B* locks *A* inside the building on purpose because she wants him to finish a backlog of work. Here there is clearly coercive intent, and so *A*'s liberty has been violated.

This seems straightforward: but if the stories are meant to show that liberty is simply the absence of coercion then far more work must be done. Clearly there is a difference between the two stories that makes one an act of coercion and the other not, but a number of elements differ: (i) in the second story *B knows* that *A* will be locked in as a result of her action; in the first she does not; (ii) in the second story *B intends* that *A* will be locked inside as a result of her action; in the first she does not; (iii) in the second story *B aims to achieve a specific goal* through locking *A* in the building; in the first she does not. So at least three factors differ: knowledge, intention and purpose. Two questions arise:

(1)     Are all three factors needed in order to say that *B*'s act was one of coercion?

(2)     Are all three factors needed in order to say that *A*'s freedom has been constrained?

The position taken here is that the answer to the first question is yes, but the answer to the second question is no; and therefore liberty cannot simply be the absence of coercion.

Day's position has some initial plausibility because he tells just two stories, one clearly an act of coercion and the other clearly not. But between these there may be other stories which are not so clear. Here are five possibilities:

(1)     *B* just forgets or does not know *A* is in the building and locks up for the night. This is the first of Day's stories.
(2)     *B* realises there is a possibility that *A* is in the building, and therefore a risk of locking him in for the night. She decides to take that risk.
(3)     *B* knows *A* is in the building and knows this is a good reason for not locking up for the night. But she decides that it is outweighed by other reasons she has, and so she locks up. If those other reasons had been absent, she would not have done so.
(4)     *B* knows *A* is in the building, but does not see this as any reason for not locking up; it does not enter into her reasoning.
(5)     *B* knows *A* is in the building and deliberately locks him in to force him to clear a backlog of work. This is the second of Day's stories.

It would seem that only story 5 is an unambiguous case of coercion, because only in story 5 is there clearly coercive intent; but it is not clear that only story 5 is a case of freedom violation -- some of the other stories can plausibly be seen as issues of freedom. Even in story 1, the possibility of negligence arises -- *should B* have known that *A* was in the building? Was it her responsibility to find out before she locked up? In story 2, *B* is clearly reckless about *A*'s welfare, and it could be argued that freedom can be violated by reckless, as well as coercive, actions. In story 3 it could be argued that *B* has made an error of judgment in concluding that she had good reasons that outweighed her responsibilities to *A*, and so her actions constitute a violation of his freedom. In story 4, it seems clear that *B* has violated *A*'s freedom, but through lack of respect and concern for his welfare, rather than through coercive intent.
What seems to follow is that:

(1)     the absence of coercion is a necessary but not sufficient condition for freedom -- just because an agent is not being coerced at the present moment, it does not follow that they are free to act; and
(2)     the presence of coercion is a sufficient but not necessary condition for unfreedom -- there may be ways other than coercion in which an agent can be made unfree to act.

A wide range of stories can be told about constraints on freedom: they can arise because, in the pursuit of their goals, people ignorantly

74

assume that the freedom of others is not at stake, under conditions in which they ought to have known; or knowing that it is at stake, they recklessly choose to take a risk with other people's liberty; or they selfishly decide that their goals outweigh the importance of that liberty; or they brutally decide that the freedom of certain others is irrelevant -- carries no weight at all. In none of these cases do they directly intend to constrain freedom -- it is a side-effect, either unknown or unfortunate or unimportant to them. A person's freedom can be constrained by being overlooked, ignored, put at risk, or given insufficient weight. There seems little reason to hold on to the strict intentionality assumption when it denies that any such cases can be issues of freedom.

Day explains why he opts for the strict intentionality thesis (Day, 1987). He says:

> *B* makes *A* unfree to do *X* if and only if *B* makes *A* unable to do *X* with *the intention* of making *A* unable to do *X*. For example, if *B* locks *A* in a room unintentionally, *B* makes *A* unable to leave the room, but not unfree to do so. The reasons for this are that all coercive acts are violations of the moral right to liberty; that all violations of a moral right are morally right or wrong acts; and that all morally right or wrong acts are intentional acts. (Ibid., p.102)

This is a helpfully clear statement of the strict intentionality thesis, but the final clause, "that all morally right or wrong acts are intentional acts", remains crucially ambiguous. If it amounts to the claim that all morally right or wrong acts are those actions which the agent *intends* to be morally right or wrong, then this would be an extremely odd moral theory. Someone can intend an action to be morally right but this obviously does not make it so. Day probably means that actions are judged to be right or wrong in terms of their *intended* consequences. This makes more sense as a moral theory, but it is not obviously right. In practice, people are not only morally blamed for the intended consequences of their actions, but, under certain circumstances, also blamed for unintended consequences. So Day is correct that all morally right or wrong actions are intentional actions, but mistaken in his claim that what must be right or wrong about them is their *intended* consequences. What follows for freedom talk is that Day is correct that all actions that violate freedom must be intentional, but incorrect that what they must intend is the violation of freedom. If the final clause of Day's argument is read in this way, then it simply no longer follows

75

that "*B* makes *A* unfree to do *X* if and only if *B* makes *A* unable to do *X* with *the intention* of making *A* unable to do *X*".

It was shown in section 2.3 that this controversial moral theory, that agents can only be held morally responsible for events they intend to bring about, was also at work behind Richard Flathman's appeal to the strict intentionality thesis. But the theory is simply implausible, and social reality, with the notions of negligence and recklessness, shows that it is not held in practice. Once that moral theory is rejected, then the strict intentionality thesis within the theory of freedom becomes groundless, and must also be rejected.

It was also shown in section 2.3 that moral responsibility for a situation does not necessarily imply moral blame for its existence -- people can hold moral responsibility for situations for which they are blameless. What is meant is that the responsibility for *altering* those situations falls upon particular agents or agencies, even though they have no causal connection with the situation. Refusal or failure to alter such situations *does* however, give rise to judgments of moral blame, and the possibility of freedom violation. And so the role of moral responsibility in freedom-talk does not justify the use of the strict intentionality thesis. The thesis can be discarded and still leave room for coherent judgments of moral responsibility within the theory of liberty. The impure theory of freedom, therefore, discards the strict intentionality assumption, and allows that *B* can constrain *A*'s freedom even though they do not intend to do so, and through omission as well as commission.

## Section 3.6 -- Liberty and the Physically Disabled

Neither position described so far -- the pure and impure negative theories of freedom as outlined by Parent and Day -- leave space for the claim that the freedom of the physically disabled is constrained by their exclusion from society's institutions and practices. Of course, both positions allow that some types of exclusion count as constraints of freedom, but the strict intentionality assumption, alongside other aspects of the theories, means that the exclusion of the disabled cannot be included as an issue of freedom. However, the pure and impure negative theories do not exhaust liberal views of freedom: there is a richer view available within modern liberal thought, one which sees liberty as absence of interference with the range of options open to the agent as an individual chooser, where that interference need not be intentional. Sir Isaiah Berlin develops such a position:

76

The extent of my freedom seems to depend on (a) how many possibilities are open to me...; (b) how easy or difficult each of these possibilities is to actualize; (c) how important in my plan of life, given my character and circumstances, these possibilities are when compared with each other; (d) how far they are closed and opened by deliberate human acts; (e) what value not merely the agent, but the general sentiment of the society in which he lives, puts on the various possibilities. (Berlin, 1969, p.130, footnote 1)

S.I. Benn and W.L. Weinstein state that "underlying and presupposed by the concept of freedom of action there is another but related concept, that of autonomy -- of the free man as chooser" (Benn and Weinstein, 1971, p.194). But while they want to see the idea of freedom based on a conception of persons as free choosers, they quite rightly point out that this does not mean that an agent can only be made unfree if they are prevented from doing what they want: "to eliminate an otherwise available alternative,...is just as much an interference with freedom, whether or not I should have chosen it had it been available" (Ibid., p.205).

Both Benn and Weinstein and Berlin use the Alterability Thesis. Benn and Weinstein state:

...if a restriction can give rise to discussions of freedom and unfreedom, it must make sense to ask 'What justifies it?' Now we do not seek justification for restrictions unless we suppose that things could have been otherwise than they are. (Ibid., p.199)

And Berlin says that the absence of freedom is due to the closing of options, or the failure to open them, "as a result, intended or unintended, of *alterable* human practices, of the operation of human agencies..." (my emphasis) (Berlin, 1969, p.xl). From this it can be seen that Berlin limits the Alterability Thesis by appeal to one of the weaker intentionality theses, IT2 or IT3, but it is not clear which -- however, it clearly cannot be the strict intentionality assumption, IT1. Benn and Weinstein, however, limit the Alterability Thesis through the natural/social distinction. Natural states are assumed to be given and inalterable, while social states, that is states which are such that "some rational being (or beings) can be held responsible for them, for bringing them about, or allowing them to continue" (Benn and Weinstein, 1971, p.199), are assumed to be alterable. This assumption

77

has unfortunate implications for the liberty of the disabled: a physical handicap is natural, not social, and therefore is assumed to be inalterable, and so cannot be the cause of unfreedom. This use of the natural/social distinction, with the added assumption that what is natural is necessarily inalterable, is a mistake. Given their view of responsibility for states of affairs, that some rational agent can be held responsible for "bringing them about, or for allowing them to continue", the natural/social distinction looks irrelevant; a rational agent can be seen as responsible for allowing a natural state affairs to continue, when they have the power to alter it.

What can be seen is that neither Benn and Weinstein nor Berlin insists upon a strict intentionality assumption, and both allow that omissions can constrain freedom as well as commissions. Berlin's position is complex: the 1969 introduction to *Four Essays on Liberty* constitutes a revision of the position he outlines in the original "Two Concepts of Liberty" essay. In the essay he sees freedom as the absence of impediments to the fulfilment of a person's desires. In the introduction he sees this as a mistake: it would allow the paradox that an agent's freedom is increased when their desires are decreased; the ultimate paradox would be that the person who wants nothing at all cannot be made unfree in any way whatsoever (this is similar to the paradox with the pure negative view of freedom, that the person who can do nothing at all cannot be made unfree in any way whatsoever -- see section 3.3). In the introduction, Berlin claims that freedom not only entails the absence of frustration with the agent's *actual* desires, it also entails absence of obstacles to *possible* choices and activities (Berlin, 1969, p.xxxix). And:

> ...absence of such freedom is due to the closing of such doors or the failure to open them, as a result, intended or unintended, of alterable human practices, of the operation of human agencies; although only if such acts are deliberately intended (or, perhaps, are accompanied by awareness that they may block paths) will they be liable to be called oppression. (Ibid., p.xl)

So the deliberate restriction of options, or at least acting with an awareness that other people's options may be limited by what I do is, strictly speaking, oppression; but unintended restriction of options, including restrictions caused by omissions as well as commissions, and restrictions the agent may not be aware they have caused, interfere with liberty too. Berlin clearly moves beyond the strict intentionality thesis, with his emphasis on the intended or unintended results of alterable human practices, and his description of oppression as a special case of the absence of freedom. But which the remaining versions of the intentionality thesis does he use to limit alterability -- IT2 or IT3? Two things are not made clear in Berlin's text: (1) whether the situations referred to in IT3 would count for Berlin as human *practices*; and (2) what Berlin regards as *alterable* human practices -- it cannot be assumed that all human practices will count as alterable. Until we know the answers to these questions it is pointless to try to pin Berlin down, and he does not supply the answers in his text.

However, there are still features of Benn and Weinstein's position which do not allow the articulation of the claim that the exclusion of groups like the disabled from society's institutions and practices is a moral violation of their freedom. There are at least three problems: (1) despite realizing that liberty requires positive conditions, they concentrate on the capacity to assess available options, at the expense of other capacities which might be needed, such as the basic causal power of movement -- they ignore the powers and capacities needed to *act out* choices; (2) they concentrate on interference with *available* options, not *possible* options; (3) they use the natural/social distinction. Even if they explicitly wished to claim that the physically disabled are unfree to use public facilities that do not take their disability into account, rather than merely unable to do so, these three features prevent them from doing so.

## 1. Powers of the Agent

John Gray endorses the conception of freedom suggested by Berlin and described by Benn and Weinstein, and states:

> Any view of freedom as the non-restriction of options is bound to remain radically incomplete...in the absence of an account of the nature and powers of the self whose options it is that are opened and closed by human action and omission. (Gray, 1984, p.338)

Yet despite this explicit reference to powers, Gray only speaks of one such power, that of rational choice, at the expense of any other powers and capacities; and in certain cases these other powers, or their lack, may be central to the account of freedom or its absence.

Suppose there is a library with the entrance at ground level, such that people in wheelchairs can use it. *B* redesigns the library with an elegant series of stairs leading to the entrance, thus enhancing its architectural beauty. *B* does not mean to interfere with anybody's options by redesigning the library, but now people confined to wheelchairs do not have the option to use it simply because they lack the basic causal powers needed to climb stairs. So the conditions of liberty include a range of positive powers and capacities of the agent, not only the power of rational choice: the able-bodied person and the disabled person may have equal powers of rational choice, but this does not mean they are equally free to use the library.

Of course, changing the design of the library may count as an external interference with liberty, but the point is that it only becomes an interference because certain groups lack certain basic causal powers; it does not count as an interference for those who possess those powers. What counts as an external interference depends upon the powers and capacities agents can be expected to have -- and so even a pure negative theory of freedom *must* have something to say about the powers and capacities of agents in order to make any sense at all.

## 2. Available versus Possible Options

In their 1971 paper, Benn and Weinstein talk of available options. One of their examples is of a person, *A*, who has no money and therefore cannot buy any eggs. They say it would be wrong to say that *A* is unfree to buy eggs because that option was not available to her in the first place -- if *A* has no money then she cannot buy eggs whatever the price; therefore charging a certain price for eggs does not close off any option that was once open to her. But this is odd: for it means that if there are no options open to *A*, then she cannot be made unfree -- her freedom is inviolable. And so Benn and Weinstein must embrace Parent's proposition 1 (section 3.3) that an agent cannot be made unfree to do something that they could not do in the first place; and this leads to the paradox that the person who can do nothing has perfect freedom.

This also leads to odd conclusions concerning the situation of the disabled. If people in wheelchairs could previously use the library, and it is redesigned so that they no longer can, then an option that was available has been removed, and their freedom has therefore been interfered with. But if a library is built where there was none before, and an entrance designed which people in wheelchairs cannot use, then no available option has been removed -- they did not have the option to use a library in the first place, and so the exclusion from *this* library does not interfere with their freedom. This would be the case even if the library was deliberately designed with the specific intention of excluding certain people -- no option they previously enjoyed has been removed, and so their freedom has not been interfered with. This would follow even if guards were placed in the doorways with instructions to prevent entry by people on grounds of race, colour, religion, whatever. This is clearly absurd, and so there must be something wrong with the theory.

In their 1974 paper, Benn and Weinstein see the limits of their approach -- their example only holds "...if we take the market and the laws of property for granted"; but if they are seen as alterable, then it makes sense to say that "his inability to buy eggs is a case of his being unfree to buy them" (Benn and Weinstein, 1974, p.437). This is to adopt the Alterability Thesis, but which version do Benn and Weinstein wish to work with? IT1 is too strict: it would mean that only if the library is designed with the specific intention of excluding people in wheelchairs has their liberty been constrained; and only if the market system was deliberately designed with the specific intention of preventing $A$ from have these particular eggs is she unfree to have them.

IT2, however, is more flexible. Now, even though the library is not designed with the intention of excluding the disabled, they have been deprived of the freedom to use it; and this is the case even where there was no library before because it was clearly possible to design a library that they could have used. Therefore the disabled are not merely unable to use the library -- a theory of freedom with combines the Alterability Thesis with IT2 allows the claim that they are unfree to use it, that their exclusion is a moral violation of their liberty.

But while IT2 can deal with the case of exclusion from the library, it would not allow Benn and Weinstein to claim that the person unable to buy eggs is unfree to do so, unless they wish to argue that the market system is a deliberately designed social institution and such a claim is not uncontroversial. For example, F.A.Hayek would describe the market as a "spontaneous order" (Hayek, 1973, pp.35-48) which arises from the intentional activities of social agents, but is not intended nor designed by them. In order to claim that $A$ is unfree to buy eggs, Benn and Weinstein must opt for IT3, the most radical of the intentionality theses: it would enable them to claim that the market system itself renders certain members of the community unfree. Where poverty interacts with other features to effectively exclude a great many people from participation in society's institutions and practices, IT3 looks to be the most effective thesis to work alongside the Alterability Thesis in the impure theory of freedom.

## 3. The Natural and the Social

The distinction between the natural and the social can still silence the claim that the physically disabled have been deprived of the freedom to use public facilities that exclude them. The Natural is seen as necessarily inalterable and so the Alterability Thesis cannot be applied to it; and it is seen as in some sense given -- it does not arise through social practice, and so no version of the Intentionality Thesis can be applied to it. Physical disability, whether caused by disease, accident or deliberate attack is natural in this sense, and so neither the Alterability Thesis nor the Intentionality Thesis are applicable. It therefore cannot feature as an issue of freedom.

The argument seems to depend on a simplistic appeal to a 'state of nature' -- the inability suffered by the physically disabled is natural, and so there is nothing that can be said about it, socially or politically. In a state of nature, certain obstacles would not be present; they must therefore be political or social constructs, and are suitable subjects for political or social theory. The obstacles faced by the disabled would still be present in a state of nature -- they are therefore natural and there is nothing that a political or social theory can say about them.

This kind of argument has already been dismissed. Simply, the natural is not inalterable. In the first place, any natural disability could be overcome and altered. In the second place, even where a disability cannot be overcome and altered at present, it need not act as an obstacle -- the natural inability may be inalterable, but the barriers it creates are not. Those barriers arise through the social practices which act as a context for the disability and make it truly unabling. The claim is not that the physical disability itself constrains the individual's freedom -- it is the way that the community responds or fails to respond to that disability.

It could be replied that the inability of the physically disabled is a natural fact about them. If wheelchairs were not provided, then the disabled person would not be able to use the library, ramps or no ramps. Therefore their inability to use the building *is* natural fact about them, not a *social* fact about the organization of the community. However, wheelchairs *are* provided (usually) to those who need them, and so the question why such people are excluded from certain areas of social life is a relevant political issue, an issue about social and political practices. The counter-claim seems to be that the unfreedom of the disabled has to be assessed in terms of the actions they can perform without artificial assistance: only if that range of actions is interfered with has their freedom been constrained. However, this is just as much an appeal to the state of nature as the previous argument: it claims that the disabled person is unfree only if that range of actions she could perform in a state of nature has been interfered with. The previous argument claimed that only obstructions that were *not* present in the state of nature could count as constraints upon freedom; this argument claims that only interference with the range of actions that would be possible in a state of nature can count as constraint of freedom. The point of the first argument is that only obstacles created through social practices can count as constraints upon freedom; the point of the second argument is that only interference with those actions that rest *directly* upon an agent's basic causal powers can give rise to issues of freedom.

Neither argument is particularly convincing, and so the natural/social distinction seems to have little relevance when it comes to assessing the freedom of the physically disabled in the community. It is true that in a state of nature there would be no wheelchairs and therefore no problem of access, but equally there would be no libraries either -- and if only interference with actions possible in the state of nature counts as constraining freedom, then stopping anybody from entering the library on whatever grounds cannot count as such a constraint, because this was not an available option in the state of nature. So the state of nature argument gives rise to some absurd implications, and appeal to 'natural facts' about the physically disabled amounts to such a state of nature argument.

The fact is that it is not only someone's physical handicap, the absence of the power to walk, that prevents them from gaining access to certain institutions, such as a library -- it is also the current social practices of the community, and those practices can always be altered to enable them to gain access to those institutions. The liberty of the disabled can therefore be both protected and increased. This can be done, not only by using medical, scientific and technological powers to see if their basic causal powers can be restored, but also be re-assessing social practices to see whether, by their alteration, a social context can be created within which the disabled can be full participants. This may require something as simple as providing ramps and lifts for people unable to walk, oral announcements and material for those unable to see, or visual displays for those unable to hear. None of this requires great foresight, imagination, or cost. If these alterations can be made, then there seems little excuse for not making them. The failure to make them, whether through ignorance, complacency or neglect, constitutes a moral violation of the freedom of the physically disabled.

# Section 3.7 -- Conclusion

The central dispute within the theory of liberty has concerned the relationship between freedom and ability and inability: any theory of freedom must identify which forms of inability constitute constraints of a person's freedom. Three possible views have been outlined:

*(A) Pure Negative Theory (Parent's position):*

(1)    For $A$ to be free to do $x$, it is *not* a necessary condition that $A$ be able to do $x$.

(2)    For $A$ to be unfree to do $x$, it *is* a necessary condition that $A$ be able to do it.

Therefore the unable person is *free* to do $x$, and cannot be made *unfree* to do it.

*(B) Impure Negative Theory (Day's position):*

(1)    For $A$ to be free to do $x$, it *is* a necessary condition that $A$ be able to do $x$.

(2)    For $A$ to be unfree to do $x$, it *is* a necessary condition that $A$ be able to do it.

Therefore the unable person is neither free *nor* unfree to do $x$.

*(C) Impure Theory:*

(1)    For $A$ to be free to do $x$, it *is* a necessary condition that $A$ be able to do $x$.

(2)    For $A$ to be unfree to do $x$, it is *not* a necessary condition that $A$ be able to do it.

Therefore the unable person is *unfree* to do $x$.

Set out like this, it seems clear that position (C) simply conflates inability and unfreedom, and so is unacceptable. However, it has been over-simplified to make clear the contrasting relationships between freedom and inability in all three theories. The Impure Theory is in fact supplemented by the Alterability Thesis and the Intentionality Thesis, and these clauses make it an improvement upon both (A) and (B). The unable person is unfree to do $x$, *if* there is some alternative, practically achievable situation in which she *would* be able to do it, and there is some agent or agency that can be identified as morally responsible for bringing about that alteration.

According to Impure Negative Theory, a person cannot be unfree to do *x* unless she was able to do it in the first place -- someone is now interfering to prevent her from using that ability. Impure Theory simply identifies some cases of inability (by no means all!) and asks whether the agent *would* be able to do *x* under a different set of circumstances, and suggests that this question is relevant to the freedom/unfreedom distinction. If there are alternative circumstances, if those circumstances are practically achievable at an acceptable cost, and if there is some agent or agency that can be identified as morally responsible for bringing about that alteration -- then the failure to bring about that alteration is a moral violation of freedom.

The project of this chapter was to show how the situation of the physically disabled within society can be described as an issue of freedom, in the context of a plausible theory of liberty. Admittedly the theory of freedom appealed to in order to reach that conclusion is more complex than its rivals: the concentration upon possible as opposed to available options; the realization that the conditions of freedom include a whole range of powers and capacities of the agent, rather than simply non-interference; these make assessing liberty or its absence a highly evaluative and disputable task. Judgments now have to be made about what is and is not possible to alter; what is an acceptable cost; what is and is not a power relevant to freedom; whether positive or negative conditions of freedom should receive priority under particular circumstances. The advantage of Benn and Weinstein's initial concentration upon available rather than possible options, and of Parent's and Day's approaches, is that they give very clear and precise answers to questions of freedom, by applying rigid theories of liberty to practical situations. But such clarity and precision are of no virtue whatever, if they allow these questions to be closed off *a priori* and eternally, despite society's growing capacity to both empower and disempower its members.

## Notes

[1]     Flathman (1987): "...the subject matter of the theory and practice of human freedom is not movement, it is action", p.31. And: "For the purposes of moral and political thought, our subject should be understood as freedom and unfreedom of action", p.1.

[2]     Epictetus: "There is but one way to freedom -- to despise what is not in our power." See Muller (1961), pp.229-230.

[3]     This is, of course, the same argument against the use of the internal/external distinction in section 2.3.

[4]     In fact more detail can be introduced into the conceptual map of freedom by introducing more refined differences into the Intentionality Thesis. For example, there is set ITA ITB and ITC, in which the phrase "or omission" is left out: in that case the failure to intervene to prevent or remove an obstacle does not violate freedom. And there is set ITX, ITY and ITZ, in which the phrase "or refraining from $x$" is left out: in that case the fact that an agent actually *does* $x$ demonstrates that they are free to do it, even if they are forced to do it. And of course there is another set in which both these phrases are omitted. Each set represents a different theory of liberty. The set chosen for the impure theory of freedom includes both phrases.

# 4 Freedom and Autonomy

## Section 4.1 -- Introduction

The previous chapters have developed a particular theory of freedom. That theory is described as impure, in that it holds that freedom has both negative and positive aspects and conditions, and that the absence of or interference with either kind of aspect or condition is a *prima facie* violation of the liberty of the agent. The aspects of freedom are the possession of both the space and the power to act, and the conditions of freedom are those that establish either the space or power to act. And it has been argued that negative and positive conditions can contribute to either the negative or positive aspect of freedom: the absence, for example, of a particular kind of negative condition can undermine both the negative and positive aspects of freedom.

Conditions of freedom seem to fall under three headings: first, the negative condition of being left alone to act; second, the positive condition of being able to make choices about which action to take; and third, the positive condition of being able to act out choices. Freedom can be violated by the absence of or interference with any of these types of condition. Benn and Weinstein provided the insight, highlighted in chapter 3, that the concept of freedom, if it is fundamentally connected with action, must also be fundamentally connected with choice; as it is not merely acting, but *choosing* to act, that signifies freedom: that one *does x* does not signify that one was free to do it; but that one *chooses* to do x does seem to signify that one was free to do it. As Benn and Weinstein observe: "The concept of man presupposed by the concept of freedom of action is that of the free (autonomous) chooser" (Benn and Weinstein, 1971, p.210). Amy Gutmann also emphasises the centrality of choice to liberty: "One cannot be a free person without continually engaging in a process of choice" (Gutmann, 1980, p.10). What follows is that freedom can be undermined not only by factors that undermine one's capacity to act, but also by factors that undermine one's capacity to choose. And therefore the second condition, the ability to make choices, is revealed to be a central concern for a theory of freedom.

The three types of condition can be named as:

(1)     The Non-interference Condition: being left alone to make choices about which life plan to pursue.

(2)     The Autonomy Condition: the possession of the ability to make rational choices concerning the best options open to one, given one's plan of life and social context.

(3)     The Power Condition: the possession of or access to powers and resources needed in order to pursue that life plan -- the power of enactment.

This chapter can be seen as a partial digression, in that the overall project of this book is to emphasise the importance of the Power Condition in a theory of freedom, and therefore the close connection between the impure theory of freedom and a particular theory of social justice. However, this chapter focusses upon the Autonomy Condition, and the digression is only partial, in that as Benn and Weinstein have shown, if the capacity to choose is a fundamental condition of being a free agent, then the Autonomy Condition must be a central concern of the impure theory of freedom.

This chapter is concerned with the quality of the will, and argues that factors which undermine the quality of the will are *prima facie* constraints of freedom, and that such constraints should be the concern of political philosophy. It is only when the Autonomy Condition is fulfilled that we can be sure that the agent is genuinely autonomous, and therefore free, rather than simply heteronomous.

Stanley Benn expresses his concern with the quality of the will in his paper "Freedom and Persuasion" (Benn, 1967). There he is concerned with the ways in which advertising and propaganda can manipulate opinions and shape preferences: this undermining of control over the agent's capacity to choose is surely a threat to freedom, and yet freedom in the negative sense cannot articulate this issue. The concept of freedom needed in order to form objections to these techniques is, says Benn, rational self-mastery: non-rational, subliminal techniques threaten freedom in this sense (Ibid., p.274). Lawrence Crocker agrees with this position, and makes a broader point about control over information:

> ...the management of information through control of the educational system and media by persons of a single political outlook may diminish the autonomy of those who base decisions upon that information. If the management of information leads people to fail to perceive alternatives to action or think them significantly less desirable than they otherwise would, then there would be a loss of liberty as well. (Crocker, 1980, p.34)

W.A. Parent's response is to appeal to a distinction between liberty and the worth of liberty: what is at stake here is not liberty itself, but its worth: "...all we need to say is that the widespread use of commercial advertising and political propaganda threatens man's ability to think for himself and consequently makes it very difficult to realise the full worth of his liberty" (Parent, 1974A, p.165). However, it can be replied that while liberty is obviously not the same thing as the ability to think for one's self, it may well depend in part upon that ability; such that if an agent loses that ability, they are likely to have lost a condition of their freedom, and therefore an important element of their freedom. The connection is practical, not logical nor grammatical: the distinction between liberty and its conditions, rather than between liberty and its worth, makes it clear that affecting the conditions of freedom -- amongst which may well be the ability to think for one's self -- must affect freedom too; and this is not to confuse liberty with its conditions.

Whatever the conditions of liberty, they cannot simply be an absence -- some of them must consist in the presence of certain powers or capacities of the agent. A theory of freedom must have something to say about the abilities of the agent, otherwise it falls into incoherence. John Gray comments: "...there are good reasons to doubt that any coherent conception of liberty can avoid incorporating requirements to do with the conditions of rational choice" (Gray, 1984, pp.336-337). And Amy Gutmann claims that: "...all plausible liberal theories of freedom are built upon some notion of what constitutes a rational will" (Gutmann, 1980, p.6). The impure theory of freedom clearly incorporates requirements to do with the conditions for the *enactment* of choices, a theme explored in Part 3 of this book; but it also clearly incorporates requirements to do with conditions for rational choice, and this chapter focusses upon that concern.

## Section 4.2 -- Berlin on Positive Liberty

A theory of freedom which has the capacity to make rational choice as a fundamental component may well be characterized as a theory of 'positive' liberty. However, the idea of positive liberty is complex. David Miller says that the concept embraces "a number of quite different doctrines", but isolates three:

(1) Freedom as the power or capacity to act in certain ways, as contrasted with the mere absence of interference.

(2) Freedom as rational self-direction, the condition in which a person's life is governed by rational desires as opposed to the desires that he just as a matter of fact has.

(3) Freedom as collective self-determination, the condition where each person plays his part in controlling his social environment through democratic institutions. (Miller, 1991, p.10)

The Autonomy Condition of the impure freedom is obviously close to the second of Miller's doctrines of positive liberty, which he further describes as "the idealist view of freedom as rational self-direction" (Ibid., p.12). It is this doctrine that Miller claims Sir Isaiah Berlin is concerned to attack in his essay "Two Concepts of Liberty" (Berlin, 1969). It could be argued that Berlin's attack on that doctrine must therefore also be an attack on the Autonomy Condition as it stands in the impure theory of freedom; and therefore that, to the extent that Berlin has disposed of that positive doctrine, he has also disposed of the Autonomy Condition, and therefore the impure theory of freedom has an incurable gap in its centre. This section will examine Berlin's arguments concerning positive liberty, and will show that those arguments strengthen, rather weaken, the role of the Autonomy Condition in the impure theory.

In the introduction to the 1969 edition of *Four Essays on Liberty*, Berlin is anxious to redress the distorted impression that seemed to arise from the "Two Concepts..." essay: that Berlin viewed negative liberty as the only true conception of freedom and dismissed the idea of positive liberty as a perverted dogma, appealed to only by totalitarian dictators and pernicious or misguided idealist philosophers. He says:

'Positive' liberty, conceived as the answer to the question, 'By whom am I to be governed?', is a valid universal goal. I do not know why I should have been held to doubt this... (Ibid., p.xlvii)

Indeed, the "Two Concepts..." essay contains one of the most eloquent statements of the ideals behind the idea of positive liberty:

I wish my life and decisions to depend on myself, not on external forces of whatever kind. I wish to be the instrument of my own, not of other men's acts of will. I wish to be a subject, not an object: to be moved by conscious purposes which are my own, not by causes which effect me, as it were, from outside. I wish to be somebody, not nobody, a doer -- deciding, not being decided for, self-directed, and not acted on by external nature or by other men as if I were a thing, or an animal or a slave incapable of playing a human role, that is, of conceiving goals and policies of my own and realizing them... I wish, above all, to be conscious of myself as a thinking, willing, active being, bearing responsibility for my choices and able to explain them by reference to my own ideas and purposes. (Ibid., p.131)

Berlin goes on to say that the conception of positive liberty is at "no great logical distance" from the idea of negative liberty -- they are "no more than negative and positive ways of saying much the same thing" (Ibid., pp.131-132). Debased forms of positive liberty have, indeed, been used to justify coercive paternalism, and so have led to injustice; but Berlin argues that negative liberty, too, has been debased and used to justify gross injustices:

Advocacy of non-interference...was...used to support politically and socially destructive policies which armed the strong, the brutal, and the unscrupulous against the humane and the weak, the able and ruthless against the less gifted and less fortunate. Freedom for the wolves has often meant death to the sheep. (Ibid., p.xlv)

And:

...the evils of unrestricted *laissez-faire*, and of the social and legal systems that permitted and encouraged it, led to brutal violations of 'negative liberty' -- of basic human rights. (Ibid., p.xlv)

And so Berlin rejects the "astonishing opinions which some of my critics have imputed to me" (Ibid., p.xlv), and underlines that "belief in negative liberty is compatible with, and (so far as ideas influence conduct) has played its part in, generating great and lasting social evils" (Ibid., p.xlv), pointing to the "bloodstained story of economic individualism and unrestrained capitalist competition" (Ibid., p.xlv). Emphasising the distinction between freedom and its conditions, Berlin notes that unrestricted free market systems fail to "provide the minimum conditions in which alone any degree of significant 'negative' liberty can be exercised by individuals or groups, and without which it is of little or no value to those who may theoretically possess it" (Ibid., p,xlvi). Indeed, Berlin's view is that:

The case for social legislation or planning, for the welfare state and socialism, can be constructed with as much validity from considerations of the claims of negative liberty as from those of its positive brother... (Ibid., p.xlvi)

However, there are valid reasons, argues Berlin, for the emphasis on the dangers of positive liberty expressed in the "Two Concepts..." essay. The first was that it struck Berlin that "whereas liberal ultra-individualism could scarcely be said to be a rising force at present, the rhetoric of 'positive' liberty, at least in its distorted form, is in far greater evidence..." (Ibid.9, pp.xlvi-xlvii).

It might be argued that this reason no longer has force; the "Two Concepts..." essay was first published in 1958, and the introduction to *Four Essays on Liberty* in 1969, both during the Cold War. Given the reason Berlin cites here, it is not unreasonable to describe "Two Concepts of Liberty" as a Cold War essay; given the collapse of the Communist block in Europe, and the dominance of free market ideology throughout the globe, the relevance of the essay in this respect has surely expired.

The second reason is that:

...the notion of 'negative' liberty..., however disastrous the consequences of its unbridled forms, has not historically been twisted by its theorists as often or as effectively into anything so darkly metaphysical or socially sinister or remote from its original meaning as its 'positive' counterpart. (Ibid., p.xlvii)

This reason still has great force. At its simplest, positive liberty appeals to the ideal of self-authorship, that the pattern of life I lead is genuinely chosen by me -- I am my own master. In itself, this appears to be harmless, and, as Berlin points out, is a valid universal goal. The problem is that it could be interpreted as the mastering of my desires and passions, which is to split my self in two -- the part that can be master, my reason, and the part that must be mastered, my passions and emotions. This becomes more problematic when it is supposed that my rational self is necessarily superior to my passionate self, or more real than my passions and desires -- my passions and desires are external to me, not part of my essential self. The notion of the self therefore suffers a "metaphysical fission into, on the one hand, a 'higher', or a 'real', or an 'ideal' self, set up to rule 'lower', 'empirical', 'psychological' self or nature, on the other..." (Ibid., p.xliv; and see pp.132-133). Geoffrey Parkinson comments:

Self-mastery is regarded as mastery of the passions by the reason; the passions are in a way external to one, they are not one's real self -- the real self being the reason. So the man who is free, in the positive sense of the term, is the man in whom reason rules -- rules over the passions. (Parkinson, 1984, p.41)

Therefore my use of reason should exclude any consideration of passions and desires; and as, in most moral theories, considerations of morality are thought to rest on passion rather than reason, it follows that my use of reason should exclude any considerations of morality.

For Berlin, the problem becomes even more vicious if it is assumed that there is, according to reason, only one true answer to any problem, and therefore that any alternative answers must be mistaken. If that is so, then if there is only one true answer to any social or political problem, the truly rational agent will be the one who perceives that answer correctly; truly rational activity will always be in complete harmony with all other rational activity. Where there is disagreement, one of the agents cannot be truly rational, and is therefore not in complete control over their passions and desires: the conflict can only be solved once that agent has been taught to be truly rational, or helped to establish control over their desires and passions. This, of course, leads to the possibility of 'forcing' someone to be free: if they do not act in accordance with the laws of reason, then they are made free if they are forced to act in harmony with those laws -- because freedom is to act according to reason, and not to be 'enslaved' by passions and desires. And as reason speaks with one voice to all rational people, whoever identifies themselves as rational can speak for all, and can force others to listen to reason by forcing them to act in the same way as they do.

Berlin says:

...some men are not as well attuned to the voice of their own reason as others: some seem singularly deaf. If I am a legislator or a ruler, I must assume that if the law I impose is rational (and I can only consult my own reason) it will automatically be approved by all the members of my society so far as they are rational beings. For if they disapprove, they must, *pro tanto*, be irrational; then they will need to be repressed by reason: whether their own or mine cannot matter, for the pronouncements of reason must be the same in all minds. (Berlin, 1969, pp.152-153)

Berlin cites Fichte:

To compel men to adopt the right form of government, to impose Right on them by force, is not only the right, but the sacred duty of every man who has both the insight and the power to do so. (Ibid., p.151, note 1)

And: "No one has...rights against reason" (Ibid., p.151).

This is a truly nightmarish vision for the pluralist liberal. Therefore, if the idea of positive liberty is to be appealed to in order to fully describe what it is to be free, then two dangers must be avoided: (1) the metaphysical division of the self into a rational and a passionate (and therefore irrational) part, and the distorted view of rationality that arises from that division; and (2) a value-monism, such that there will only be one and necessarily only one right and true answer to all moral and political questions. Certainly, for Berlin, as well as his commitment to value-pluralism, the value of freedom is itself internally complex -- being free will depend on many magnitudes:

> All these magnitudes must be 'integrated', and a conclusion, necessarily never precise, or indisputable, drawn from this process. It may well be that there are many incommensurable kinds and degrees of freedom, and that they cannot be drawn up on any single scale of magnitude... But the vagueness of the concepts, and the multiplicity of the criteria involved, is an attribute of the subject-matter itself, not of our imperfect methods of measurement, or incapacity for precise thought. (Ibid., p.151)

Berlin sums up his argument concerning the status of the idea of positive liberty like this:

> If it is maintained that the identification of the value of liberty with the value of a field of free choice amounts to a doctrine of self-realization, whether for good or evil ends, and that this is closer to positive than to negative liberty, I shall offer no great objection; only repeat that, as a matter of historical fact, distortions of this meaning of positive liberty (or self-determination) even by so well-meaning a liberal as T.H.Green, so original a thinker as Hegel, or so profound a social analyst as Marx, obscured this thesis and at times transformed it into its opposite. (Ibid., p.xli)

The position developed in this book is that the value of freedom can be identified with a field of free choice, but that such a conception of freedom unites both negative and positive aspects and conditions of freedom; for such a field can only exist where the agent has both the space *and* power to be free. The ideas of negative and positive liberty are not rivals here: they are seen as essential to each other. One without the other, as Berlin has so eloquently argued, must be debased and distorted; each needs the other if it is to contribute fully to what is valuable about freedom.

## Section 4.3 -- Rationality and Autonomy

Berlin, then, has shown that a theory of freedom must be concerned with both the positive and negative aspects of liberty, and with the conditions that underlie those aspects. I have described three kinds of condition: the Non-interference Condition, the Autonomy Condition, and the Power Condition. The focus of this chapter is the Autonomy Condition, the capacity for rational choice. The previous section defended that concern against the charge that the Autonomy Condition amounted to a concern with a tradition of 'positive liberty', and as that tradition has been discredited, primarily by Berlin, then one central element of the impure theory of freedom has collapsed. The defence had two elements: first, that this view is a distortion of Berlin's arguments, and is not one he would recognise as his position; and second, that the idea of positive liberty does express an important and legitimate aspect of the idea of freedom, and therefore some element of it should be included in any theory of freedom. However, the task remains of making sense of the Autonomy Condition and its place in the theory.

As was seen in section 4.1, John Gray believes that a concern with autonomous choice is legitimate, but he does recognise that this concern leads to a close flirtation with the traditional view of positive freedom as the 'authentic' or 'real' will. In the previous section it was argued that this flirtation need not be that dangerous, but Gray's way of dealing with danger is to claim that the appropriate conception of rationality must be kept minimalist and meagre. It stipulates "only that an agent *have a reason* for what he does" (Gray, 1984, p.337). And: "What such a requirement disqualifies as rational conduct is only the behaviour of the delirious agent, where no goal or end may be imputed to him which renders intelligible what he does" (Ibid., pp.337-338).

However, is this minimalist and meagre model of rationality sufficient to fulfil the requirements of the Autonomy Condition? It does not seem to answer the concerns which lie behind Benn and Weinstein's notion of the 'autonomous chooser'. What concerned

Benn in his "Freedom and Persuasion" paper (see section 4.1) was not that the agent be able to cite a reason for what they do, but that reason be, in some sense, genuinely their own; the central issue was not whether they could state a goal or end that counts as a reason for what they do, but the source or authorship of that goal or end or reason for their action. The Autonomy Condition seems to demand that the goal or end that counts as a reason must their own in some 'deep' sense: the reason for their action must be their's, not simply in the sense that they *have* it (it is the reason they give), but in the sense that they are its 'author'. So it is not enough simply to *have a reason*: it matters whether the agent is the genuine author of that reason, or whether it has been imposed upon them, overtly or through manipulation; or whether it has simply been uncritically accepted as the norm. This means that the concern with rational choice must go beyond Gray's commitment to the minimal and meagre model of rationality.

Stanley Benn gives a detailed account of the autonomous chooser in his paper, "Freedom, Autonomy and the Concept of a Person" (Benn, 1975/76). There he makes it clear that far more than Gray's minimal rationality is needed if the conception of the autonomous chooser is to provide a firm element of the theory of liberty. The standard chooser, says Benn, faces a standard choice situation:

> (a) he has a determinate set of resources at his disposal; (b) he is confronted with a set of opportunity costs: if he pursues *x* he must forgo *y*; (c) he has goals forming an ordered preference set, in the light of which he makes choices; (d) he has a set of beliefs about (a), (b), and (c), eg, about the relation of resources, as means, to his goals. (Ibid., p.111)

Benn calls conditions (a) and (b) objective choice conditions, and (c) and (d) subjective choice conditions. Classical liberal concern has been with the objective choice conditions, but Benn points out that the subjective choice conditions can be interfered with too. Importantly, unfreedom can be caused not only by interference with any or all four of the conditions, but also by the *failure* by some agent or agency to intervene when it is their responsibility to do so. By extension, unfreedom can be caused by "unreasonable social and economic conditions maintained by people with the power to change them..." (Ibid.).

Benn makes a distinction between *autarchy* and *autonomy*. Autarchy is the condition of being self-governed, being a self-chooser (Ibid., p.113), as opposed to being impelled or chosen for, which is the condition of *heterarchy*. The autarchic chooser has the rational capacity for decision: they have the capacity to recognise evidence and inferences which warrant changing beliefs; for making decisions when confronted by options; and for acting upon those decisions. They are capable of making appropriately different decisions and policies in the light of preferences, of formulating a project or policy so that a decision can be taken now for the sake of preferred future states (Ibid., p.116). Defects that disqualify an agent from autarchy are: (a) defects of practical rationality: e.g., compulsive behaviour, psychopathy; (b) defects of epistemic rationality: e.g., paranoia; (c) defects in psychic continuity: e.g., schizophrenia (Ibid.).

However, what the Autonomy Condition requires is the autonomous, not merely autarchic, chooser. More is required that simply choosing for one's self. Benn states:

> To be a chooser is not enough for autonomy, for a competent chooser may still be a slave to convention, choosing by standards he has accepted quite uncritically from his milieu. (Ibid., p.123)

So autarchy allows that the chooser, although they choose for themself, may be *heteronomous* rather than autonomous. The heteronomous chooser chooses for themself, but the standards by which they choose, the reasons they have for choosing, are given to them by others -- they are not truly theirs. Nobody forces them to choose this particular end, but the reason why they value this end has been accepted by them uncritically without examination. Another possibility is that the agent is *anomous*: they choose at random, for no reason at all. For Benn, what is at stake is the source of the *nomos*, the principles by which we choose. The autonomous person's life is based on beliefs, values and principles that are genuinely theirs; and "they are *his* because the outcomes of a still-continuing process of criticism and evaluation" (Ibid., p.124). And so the heteronomous, anomous and autonomous agents are all autarchic choosers, in that they all choose for themselves: but the heteronomous agent chooses according to rules laid down by others; the anomous agent chooses by no rules at all; and the autonomous agent chooses by rules they have legislated for themself. Benn says:

> The autonomous man is not merely *capable* of deciding for himself, he does so; he is not merely capable of considering reasons, he does consider them, and he acts on them. (Ibid.)

Ideally, the autonomous agent is the author of their own self-conception, their picture of who they are and what they can become. However, there is an obvious objection to this version of the Autonomy Condition: that it is surely too much to expect anybody to construct a new set of standards or rules or values for themselves -- to be a complete author of one's self is a worthy ideal but an unachievable one in practice. If this is what the Autonomy Condition requires, then it is difficult to imagine that *any* agent is truly free in the sense the impure theory demands. There are two possible responses to this objection. Firstly, the impure theory recognises the possibility of degrees of freedom -- it precisely denies that freedom is an either/or condition; therefore, while the strict Autonomy Condition probably rules out that any agent is *absolutely* free, it still allows that some are more free than others in terms of this condition. Secondly, the strict Autonomy Condition need not be insisted upon and Benn does not insist upon it:

> To be autonomous one must have reasons for acting, and be capable of second thoughts in the light of new reasons; it is not to have a capacity for conjuring criteria out of nowhere. (Ibid., p.126)

Therefore, the description of the autonomous chooser does not have to be one of the existentialist gone mad, or a Nietzschean superman, or a complete neurotic. Rather, they are "someone committed to a critical and creative conscious search for coherence" (Ibid.). For Benn:

> ...the autonomous man is not necessarily one who can give reasons for *all* his principles and values -- it is necessary only that he is alive to, and disposed to resolve by rational reflection and decision, incoherences in the complex tradition he has internalised. (Ibid., p.128)

The autonomous person is someone, then, who is prepared to subject their beliefs and values to a critique, and who is prepared to alter those beliefs and values in the light of that critique. It is not enough, as Gray suggests, that the agent simply be able to give a reason for their action: the authorship of that reason matters. Charles Taylor reinforces such a view: "...we cannot defend a view of freedom which does not involve at least some qualitative discriminations as to motive..." (Taylor, 1985, p.217). He says:

...our attributions of freedom make sense against a background sense of more or less significant purposes, for the question of freedom/unfreedom is bound up with the frustration/fulfilment of our purposes. Further, our significant purposes can be frustrated by our own desires, and where these are sufficiently based on misappreciation, we consider them as not really ours, and experience them as fetters. A man's freedom can therefore be hemmed in by internal motivational obstacles, as well as external ones. (Ibid., p.227)

And:

...freedom now involves my being able to recognise adequately my more important purposes, and my being able to overcome or at least neutralise my motivational fetters, as well as by way of being free of external obstacles. But clearly the first condition (and, I would argue, also the second) require me to have something, to have achieved a certain level of self-clairvoyance and self-understanding. I must be actually exercising self-understanding in order to be free. (Ibid.)

William Connolly is another writer who sees autonomy as an essential element of a theory of freedom, proposing a paradigm of 'freedom' that "appeals to the idea of autonomy for nourishment" (Connolly, 1983, p.153). He gives his own version of the autonomous chooser:

Creatures of habit and convention, we are also able to submit particular habits and conventions to critical scrutiny. Capable of understanding our established practices, we are also capable of deliberately creating new paths and of following old ways more reflectively. Capable of some degree of self-understanding, we are therefore capable of changing ourselves to some degree through action based upon that understanding. (Ibid.)

And he clearly spells out the implication of the Autonomy Condition:

Suppose...a well socialized consumer unreflectively accepts the consumptive role expected of him and is able to buy the goods he wants, while another citizen, similarly situated, reflectively considers the pressures pushing him into that role, explores alternative styles of life available, and chooses to continue or not

99

continue his previous consumptive habits in light of these reflections. The latter agent...acts more freely with respect to that consumptive role than the former; and that judgment might indeed be worth making. (Ibid., pp.159-160)

He concludes: "A person is autonomous to the extent that his conduct is informed by his own reflective assessment of his situation" (Ibid., p.154).

The full implication of the Autonomy Condition is now clear. It introduces another level of possible constraints upon freedom: for now there can be constraints not only upon the agent's power to act out choices, but also upon their power to *make* choices. Connolly offers the following description of freedom:

> $X$ is free with respect to $z$ if (or to the extent that) he is unconstrained from conceiving or choosing $z$ and if (to the extent that), were he to *choose $z$*, he would not be constrained from doing or becoming $z$.
>
> $X$ acts freely in doing $z$ when (or to the extent that) he acts without constraint upon his unconstrained and reflective *choice* with respect to $z$. (Ibid., p.157)

Connolly's specification of constraint upon *conceiving* and *choosing* as well as acting, corresponds with Benn's distinction between the objective and subjective conditions of choice.

Connolly has also supplied a convincing objection to the view that freedom is absence of interference with what the agent wants to do. One objection to that view is that, while the agent may not, for example, want to join the military forces, any law or policy that excludes them from doing so still infringes their freedom: it removes an option that ought to remain open to them. In response to this difficulty, freedom could be re-described as absence of interference with what the agent wants or *might* want. But Connolly's point is that constraint can act upon the formation of choices, as well as upon the acting out of those choices. Therefore another possibility arises: that there might be no law or policy excluding the agent from joining the military, but their wants may have been shaped such that they never formulate the desire to join the military. This means that even though $X$ does not want to do or become $z$, and even though $z$ remains available to them, they may still be unfree to do or become $z$. The question that must be addressed is whether their choice never to do or become $z$ is autonomous, or whether it is a decision based upon uncritical acceptance of pre-established values or propaganda or ignorance.

And this surely matters both philosophically *and* politically. Suppose there are three agents, $A$, $B$, and $C$, each faced with the possibilities $x$, $y$ and $z$. Agent $A$ chooses $x$ purely at random, without even considering whether there are other possibilities; agent $B$ chooses $x$ because they have been told to choose it; and agent $C$ chooses $x$ after careful, reflective, critical consideration of all the possibilities. Certain political philosophies may claim that there is no politically important difference between these choices -- the difference between them is metaphysical. However, there may be enormous and possibly horrific implications in agents performing actions purely at random without consideration of other options, or simply because they have been told to do this by others without considering whether this is what they ought to do. The impure theory of freedom, with the prominence of the Autonomy Condition, clearly states the differences between the choices taken by $A$, $B$ and $C$.

However, it could be objected that there is still a serious problem with the Autonomy Condition. While Berlin's concern over the notion of positive liberty was acknowledged in section 4.2, it was not dealt with adequately. There may be good political reasons for dropping the Autonomy Condition and returning to the minimal and meagre model of rationality that Gray advocated. The minimal and meagre model could be defined as: "Given the set of available actions, the agent chooses rationally if there is no other action available to him the consequence of which he prefers to that of the chosen action" (Hahn and Hollis eds., 1979, p.4). It is important, however, to note that the model has a specific function in political theory: it is doubtful that anybody has claimed that it is a true picture of human powers of reasoning -- rather, it is meant as a useful theoretical model rather than an accurate representation of the way people actually think. The use of the model is to guard against the dangers Berlin identified. If 'irrational' actions are unfree, then the richer the notion of reason, the wider the range of 'unfree' action. There is a danger that, in proclaiming wide areas of human activity to be unfree on such grounds, this allows that these people can be legitimately forced to be free, by compelling them to act according to reason. The richer the model of reason, the more scope there is for forcing people to be free; the minimal and meagre model allows that most human activity is rational, and therefore provides very little scope for interfering with that action in the name of freedom. Therefore there are good political reasons for holding the minimal and meagre model.

This is a very powerful objection to the impure theory of freedom. However, it should be noted that, if freedom has many conditions, both positive and negative, then those conditions can be more or less present or absent, and so the agent can be more or less free: there is no simply dichotomy between the free agent and the unfree agent. That means that we have to consider how to respond to the absence of any condition in the light of the consequences of that response for other conditions: the response would be one that restored the missing condition without damaging other conditions. For example, if the positive condition of the power of reason was absent, then forcing people to act as though they *were* rational will not make them more free: firstly, forcing people to act as though they enjoyed the power of reason does not supply them with that power; secondly, it would additionally destroy the negative conditions of their freedom. So forcing people to act as though they were rational not only fails to provide the missing positive conditions for freedom, it at the same time destroys the negative conditions for freedom. The strategies for providing or protecting the positive conditions for liberty will be ones which, as much as is possible, respect the negative conditions for liberty, and *vice versa* [1].

This picture is, of course, over-simplistic. The negative and positive conditions for liberty may clash in some circumstances. The important point, though, is that they do not *necessarily* clash: most often they will need each other if each is not going to be rendered hollow. However, there will be cases where positive and negative conditions clash, where one condition cannot be supplied or preserved without coming into conflict with the other -- the question of which should take priority in such a case cannot be decided at the level of theory: any view that claims that one type of condition must always take priority over the other in all circumstances is mistaken. Judgment will have to be used to decide which should take priority in particular cases; such judgments will never be clear, never precise, will be fraught with difficulties and dangers -- but they are judgments which will have to be made despite those difficulties and dangers.

The freedom of any particular agent will therefore depend upon a balance between the three types of condition of freedom. To the question: which balance? there is no fixed answer. Just as the value of liberty must be balanced against other values held by the political community, liberty is itself a question of balance between conditions, and that balance is, in practice, a constant political issue. It is unlikely that it can be answered in isolation from other values, such as equality, social justice, democracy and public order. Therefore the impure theory of freedom, with the Autonomy Condition playing a central role, does not justify forcing people to be 'free': any such approach is a direct contradiction of the theory.

## Section 4.4 -- The Problem of Evil

The aim of this chapter has been to establish the important of the Autonomy Condition within the theory of freedom. However, it set out to do more than that -- the goal was to show that the Autonomy Condition was not merely theoretically important, but also politically important; that is, a proper concern for a *political* philosophy. This was to oppose the position taken by Joel Feinberg who states: "...political and social philosophy are concerned with freedom only when conceived as absence of coercion by others. Ethics and metaphysics may quite properly concern themselves with more varied sorts of constraints..." (Feinberg, 1973, p.9). In the previous section it was claimed that the difference between choosing anomously, heteronomously or autonomously was of political significance. Taking Charles Taylor's characterization that to act autonomously is, in part, to act with self-understanding, why should it be a matter of concern to a community that its members act with such self-understanding, rather than, in John Gray's terms, merely be able to give reasons for what they do?

Suppose someone is faced with a practical task of shifting a set of objects from point $A$ to point $B$ by train. They must choose from a set of options, and will rank those options in terms of their efficiency in getting the objects from $A$ to $B$ as quickly as possibly at the minimum cost, while at the same time ensuring that they arrive in the optimum condition. If this is their objective, then they choose rationally if there is no other option available that will achieve these objectives equally well or better. However, what if more detail of the task to be performed is supplied. Suppose the objects in question are the Hungarian Jews, and point $A$ is Budapest, and point $B$ is Auschwitz, and the name of the person making the choice is Adolf Eichmann. Now, is it possible to say that the choice Eichmann made concerning the transportation of the Hungarian Jews to the death camps was the most rational choice available to him? One reply is that Eichmann excluded other concerns from his decision-procedure: he considered it purely in terms of achieving the given objectives -- in Gray's terms, he could give reasons for what he did. What was excluded was any moral consideration of the problem. It could be argued that if the question is concerned with the *rationality* of Eichmann's actions, then the *morality* of those actions must be excluded, as rationality and morality are separate issues. While it is true that Eichmann should have considered the morality of what he was doing, that questioning fell outside the scope of the rationality of what he was doing; he made the morally wrong choice, but that does not mean that he made the wrong choice from the point of view of rationality. Therefore Eichmann may well have made the most rational choice available to him.

However, this is to restrict rationality purely to means-ends considerations, working out the means to achieve a given end without any critical examination of the end in question, and this is precisely the minimal and meagre model of rationality at work. This separation of rationality and morality can be questioned: it could be argued that rationality should *include* moral questions, such that the most rational choice may well be the most moral choice; full rational consideration would include such an element of moral examination. If this view is taken, then Eichmann did not make the most rational choice available to him, because the most rational choice in this case was to reject the objectives altogether. If there was a conflict here it was not between rationality and morality, but between different kinds of values that had to be rationally weighed against each other -- for example the values of efficiency and certain moral values. Eichmann seems to have attached no weight at all to the moral value of what he was doing.

This is not to identify rationality and morality: it is simply to suggest that if there is such a thing as moral reasoning, then it must be an element of rationality as such; and therefore that any rational consideration of what action to take in particular circumstances must include that element of moral reasoning. This is not to say that the most rational choice will always be the most moral choice: it is simply to say that moral consideration will always have some role to play in arriving at the most rational choice. It may be that in some situations the moral considerations are not so weighty as to determine the choice; it may be that in such a situation the moral features are relatively light and so are easily outweighed; or that, while the moral features carry considerable weight, there are still other features that outweigh them. The point is that if a person arrived at a choice without taking relevant moral features into consideration they would be incompletely rational -- there would be something essential missing from their reasoning. In any situation, then, the relevant moral features must be recognized and weighed, and judgment used to decide to what extent those moral features should determine the choice. The person who *never* considered the moral aspects in arriving at their choice would be

104

making incomplete and inadequate judgments; at the same time the person who *always* attached absolute weight to those moral aspects might be seen also making inadequate judgments. There is, therefore, an art to judgment which the minimal and meagre model of rationality fails to capture. If that model of reasoning is applied then there is no difference between Eichmann's task and transporting potatoes. Barry Clarke complains of Eichmann that during a time of great moral crisis he continued to act as though times were normal; he "failed to discriminate between the normal routine aspect of his task and the reality of that task" (Clarke, 1980, p.438). The minimal model does not enable people to distinguish between normal times and times of horror.

Eichmann's actions, then, have to be considered in the context of the Holocaust. How did an evil such as the Holocaust ever happen? It depended on different sorts of people. First, there were the proposers of the evil, in this case the 'arch-Nazis' who devised the idea of exterminating certain racial groups and those members of their own 'race' they considered to be 'unhealthy'. Second, there were the administrators, the people like Eichmann who organized the programme and made the extermination possible. Third, there were the executors, those who actually carried out the extermination. And fourth, there were the tolerators, those who were aware of the evil, and had the capacity to intervene and prevent it, but who stood by and allowed it to take place for whatever reason. There is, therefore, a fourfold distinction between those who propose, those who administrate, those who execute, and those who tolerate.

The traditional view of evil restricts the notion to the first category, those who propose; evil lies in the individual and their consciousness, rather than in their actions and their consequences. David Hume stresses that mere indifference to virtue is not enough:

A creature, absolutely malicious and spiteful, were there any such in nature, must be worse than indifferent to the images of vice and virtue. All his sentiments must be inverted, and directly opposite to those, which prevail in the human species. (Hume, 1975, p.226)

However, this is to make the truly evil person someone inhuman, beyond humanity. "Absolute, unprovoked, disinterested malice has never perhaps place in any human breast...." (Ibid, p.227). Kant, too, describes the evil person as someone who wills evil for its own sake, and again this is something essentially inhuman, beyond the capacity of the human will (Kant, 1960, see p.32 and p.60) -- the Holy Will and the Evil Will are at opposite ends of the moral spectrum, but each is beyond the limits of the human. David Pocock, in an anthropological study of the idea of evil, points out that this is precisely how evil persons are understood in 'primitive' societies: a "belief in creatures who are and are not human beings, at once within and beyond the limits of humanity" (Pocock,1985, p.48). The motives of the truly evil person are beyond understanding, incomprehensible to normal human beings. It is precisely this inability to explain which leads to the use of the concept 'evil' (Ibid., p.49); if the person's actions could be explained in terms of motives that were understandable, then they would no longer be described as evil -- rather as selfish or misguided. However, if the motives and actions cannot be understood, then they cannot be judged. Pocock says: "...the evil act itself is beyond the comprehension of human justice..." (Ibid., p.52).

This is exactly how the arch-Nazis are seen by commentators. Barry Clarke says they cannot be accounted for in normal moral discourse (Clarke, 1980, p.432); they "defy explanation in readily understood moral terms. Moral discourse applies to those acts which are recognizably human and is of limited application to those acts which exceed human understanding" (Ibid.). Hannah Arendt says of 'radical' evil: "All we know is that we can neither punish nor forgive such offences and that they therefore transcend the realm of human affairs" (Arendt, 1958, p.241). The arch-Nazis are therefore beyond the powers of normal moral judgment.

Arendt was almost equally speechless when she was confronted by Adolf Eichmann at his trial in Jerusalem, but for opposite reasons. Instead of being confronted by radical evil, she found herself confronted by banality. She comments on:

> ...a manifold shallowness in the doer that made it impossible to trace the uncontestable evil of his deeds to any deeper level of roots or motives. The deeds were monstrous, but the doer -- at least the very effective one now on trial -- was quite ordinary, commonplace and neither demonic nor monstrous. (Arendt, 1978, p.4)

And: "It was as though in those last minutes he was summing up the lesson that this long course in human wickedness had taught us -- the lesson of the fearsome, word- and thought-defying *banality* of evil" (Arendt, 1976, p.252). Eichmann was neither "perverted nor sadistic", he was "terribly and terrifyingly normal" (Ibid., p.256); and "this normality was much more terrifying than all the atrocities put together..." (Ibid.). For her, Eichmann was a new type of criminal, who "commits his crimes under circumstances that make it well-nigh impossible for him to know or feel that he is doing wrong" (Ibid.).

There seems to be a paradox. There is a distinction between the proposers of evil and those who execute it, a distinction which renders each impossible to judge. The former cannot be judged to be guilty because they are beyond the powers of normal human judgment. The latter can be judged to be guilty of some lesser offence, but they cannot be held responsible for evil as they had no evil intent, only the intent to carry out instructions issued by those in authority. However, the gap between the inhuman will of the evil genius and the all-too-human will of the dull administrator is not that clear. Arendt writes as though she expected to see a demon or a monster on trial, and seems taken aback that Eichmann was neither: he was a very ordinary human being. But the accounts of the Nuremberg trials contain much the same observations about the defendants; and the defendants said much the same thing as Eichmann. Peter Padfield writes:

> When William Shirer, anticipating the moment he had been awaiting 'all these black, despairing years' entered the courtroom the prisoners were in their places. He found his first sight of them in there changed condition indescribable. Shorn of their former glittering symbols of power, 'how little, mean and mediocre' they looked. At the left of the lower row Goering was scarcely recognizable in a faded *Luftwaffe* uniform shorn of insignia; he had lost weight and reminded Shirer of 'a genial radio operator on a ship.' Above him at the left of the second row Donitz sat wearing a civilian suit and looking ' for all the world like a grocers clerk. Hard to imagine him as the successor of Hitler'; next to him Raeder looked 'a bewildered old man'. (Padfield, 1984, p.411)

Werner Maser says: "All were downcast and cut sorry figures, with their lined faces, some without ties, and the officers in faded uniforms without badges of rank or decorations" (Maser, 1979, p.74; and see p.234). It could always be argued that the evil genius was not present at those trials, but then how would Hitler have appeared in such a situation -- as a demon or a monster? Or as human-all-too-human? The claim that the evil genius was not present at the trials pushes the responsibility for evil further and further up the ladder of command until it rests upon the shoulders of one person alone, and that person becomes an incomprehensible monster.

This characterization of 'true' evil makes it disappear altogether from understanding. By making ultimate responsibility for evil rest upon inhuman monsters, we, in the end, absolve any *human* of responsibility for evil, because evil is not an activity that any human can possibly carry out. But evil *is* something that humans do -- this is undeniable! And so the evil that people do must be made comprehensible in terms of *being human*: the possibility of evil must lie within the limits of humanity, not beyond them. Eichmann and his 'banality' display one form of this possibility. Christopher Browning writes:

> ...many of the perpetrators of the Holocaust were so-called desk murders whose role in the mass extermination was greatly facilitated by the bureaucratic nature of their participation. Their jobs frequently consisted of tiny steps in the overall killing process, and they performed them in a routine manner, never seeing the victims their actions affected. (Browning, 1993, p.162)

While Browning does not consider Eichmann to be the best example of a 'banal bureaucrat', the concept "is still valid for understanding many Holocaust perpetrators" (Ibid., p.216, note 5). We should not underestimate "the extent to which ordinary bureaucrats, performing functions vital to the mass murder program in exactly the same routine way they performed the rest of their professional duties, made the Holocaust possible. The evil was not banal; the perpetrators most certainly were" (Ibid., p.216, note 5).

How does this relate to the importance of self-understanding, and the art of judgment that comes with it? One step is to recognise that evil is something that all humans are capable of committing. Browning quotes Ervin Staub who argues that:

> ...'ordinary psychological processes and normal, common human motivations and certain basic but not inevitable tendencies in human thought and feeling' are the 'primary sources' of the human capacity for mass destruction of human life. 'Evil that arises out of ordinary thinking and is committed by ordinary people is the norm, not the exception'. (Ibid., p.167) [2]

It would also seem that much evil is to do with lack of self-understanding, a lack of understanding of what is being done, and a failure to use judgment properly. It cannot be assumed that all humans possess a Cartesian consciousness, within which evil intent will be transparent. Indeed, it is questionable whether there need be any evil intent at all. Arendt puts the question:

> Is evil-doing (the sins of omission as well as the sins of commission) possible in default of not just 'base motives'...but of any motives whatever, of any particular prompting of interest and volition? Is wickedness...*not* a necessary condition for evil doing? (Arendt, 1978, pp.4-5) [3]

The *meaning* of what an agent does is not obviously available to that agent, such that they would be fully aware of the evil of their actions. Arendt comments:

> Action reveals itself fully only to the storyteller, that is, to the backward glance of the historian, who indeed always knows better what it was all about than the participants... What the storyteller narrates must necessarily be hidden from the actor himself, at least as long as he is in the act or caught in its consequences, because to him the meaningfulness of is act is not in the story that follows. Even though stories are the inevitable results of action, it is not the actor but the storyteller who perceives and makes the story. (Arendt, 1958, p.192)

And Maurizio Passerin D'Entreves, in his discussion of Arendt, comments:

> Being absorbed by their immediate aims and concerns, not aware of the full implications of their actions, actors are not often in a position to assess the true significance of their doings, or to be fully aware of their own motives and intentions. (D'Entreves, 1994, p.74)

Therefore there is no transparent Cartesian consciousness for evil to lie within: evil is part of actions such that it may only be recognized in the doing of them or even after they have been done. It may be that the only adequate protection against evil is the agent's own critical self-understanding of what they are doing. That understanding will not be found by searching one's consciousness for a clear intent, but only by closely examining one's action and the context within which one is acting.

Is it too simple to say of Eichmann that he lacked such a self-understanding? Arendt thinks not -- for her, Eichmann was "thoughtless" (Arendt, 1978, p.4); and she says: "The manifestation of the wind of thought is not knowledge; it is the ability to tell right from wrong, beautiful from ugly" (Ibid., p.193). Elsewhere she states that one of the "outstanding characteristics of our time" is thoughtlessness, "the heedless recklessness or hopeless confusion or complacent repetition of 'truths' which have become trivial and empty..." And she says: "What I propose, therefore, is very simple: it is nothing more than to think what we are doing" (Arendt, 1958, p.5).

For Arendt, thinking liberates judgment, because it enables people to judge the *particular* without resorting to old general or universal rules. Thinking is a capacity all possess, but not thinking, thoughtlessness, is "an ever-present possibility for everybody" (Arendt, 1979, p,191). This capacity for thinking is especially important when facing up to atrocities such as the Holocaust or the Gulag, because it is crucial that these are faced up to and understood, rather than explained away. The problem faced is that inherited moral categories may not be adequate for making sense of these modern horrors -- there is therefore a crisis in understanding, a crisis in judgment. People can, however, still judge and understand, in that they can use their imagination. Imagination "allows us to view things in their proper perspective and to judge them without the benefits of a pre-given rule or universal" (D'Entreves, 1994, p.106). Arendt says:

> Imagination alone enables us to see things in their proper perspective, to put that which is too close at a certain distance so that we can see and understand it without bias and prejudice, to bridge abysses of remoteness until we can see and understand everything that is too far away from us as though it were our own affair. (Arendt, 1953, p.392)

And:

> Without this kind of imagination, which actually is understanding, we would never be able to take our bearings in the world. It is the only inner compass we have... If we want to be at home on this earth, even at the price of being at home in this century, we must try to take part in the interminable dialogue with its essence. (Ibid., p.392)

110

It is through the use of imagination that we can come to terms with a reality that may initially defy human comprehension. This was Arendt's task when confronted by Eichmann in Jerusalem. D'Entreves comments:

> In her encounter with the person of Eichmann Arendt had first to show the intelligibility of his actions, the fact that they stemmed from a lack of thought and an absence of judgment, so that ultimately we could come to terms with their enormity, with their absolutely unprecedented nature. Once Eichmann's deeds were rendered intelligible they could be judged, and judged to be not only monstrous but 'banal'. In other words, in order to be in a position to pass judgment, Arendt had first to come to terms with what 'irrevocably happened' and find some meaning for actions that would otherwise escaped human understanding. (D'Entreves, 1994, p.108)

And:

> Eichmann's guilt resided in his banal thoughtlessness, in his failure to engage in responsible judgment when confronted with Hitler's orders to exterminate the Jews. Those few individuals who refused to carry out the orders of their superiors were thus left entirely to their own resources... (Ibid.)

They had to be able to tell right from wrong even though all that was left to guide them was their own judgment (Arendt, 1976, p.294). Arendt says:

> Those few who were still able to tell right from wrong went really only by their own judgments, and they did so freely; there were no rules to be abided by under which the particular cases with which they were confronted could be subsumed. They had to decide each instance as it arose, because no rules existed for the unprecedented. (Ibid., p.295)

Thinking and judgment are therefore required where traditional standards collapse, and people must judge autonomously, "judge according to their own autonomous values" (D'Entreves, 1994, p.111).

In the end, at the extreme, people cannot rely on the application of rules and principles to find out what is the right or wrong thing to do -- the state of heteronomy; they must be autonomous, that is rely on their own power of judgment. That power of judgment can be overwhelmed, by desire, propaganda, illusion, by force of circumstances. For Arendt the capacity to judge is a particularly *political* ability, and its possession and practice is therefore a particularly political issue. The question posed at the start of this section was whether the community should be concerned that its members have a critical self-understanding, rather than merely be able to give reasons for what they do. It has been shown that the consequences of people failing to have a critical self-understanding of what they are doing and the context in which they are acting, or of what their community is doing in their name, can be horrific. The only protection there can be against evil is people's own self-awareness, and the openness of their community to that same critical scrutiny.

## Section 4.5 -- Life Chances

It has been argued that the concept of freedom, if it is fundamentally connected with action, must also be fundamentally connected with choice, and therefore that one condition for freedom is autonomous choice -- the free agent is, amongst other things, an autonomous chooser. It has also been argued that the autonomous chooser should not be characterized as someone who creates new reasons and values for all that they do, and therefore become an impossible ideal. Rather, they have a context of choice, some sort of social framework, and that context must, to a greater or lesser extent, influence and shape their choices. Equally, it is a mistake to see that context of choice as essentially opposed to autonomy, the view that the greater the social context, the lesser the opportunity for autonomy. Instead, it is the kind of context that matters: some kinds of social framework increase autonomy, others erode it: the idea of a contextless autonomy is incoherent. Therefore something must be said here, however sketchy, about the context of choice.

One obvious answer is that a context of choice that increased or enriched autonomy would be one that included a wide range of options: quite simply, the wider the range of options, the greater autonomy, the narrower the range of options, the lesser autonomy. However, this equation, like the last one, is too simplistic -- the situation is far more complex, as Berlin points out:

The extent of my freedom seems to depend on (a) how many possibilities are open to me (though the method of counting these can never be more than impressionistic. Possibilities of action are not discrete entities like apples); (b) how easy or difficult each of these possibilities is to actualise; (c) how important in my plan of life, given my character and circumstances, these possibilities are when compared with each other; (d) how far they are closed or opened by deliberate human acts; (e) what value not merely the agent, but the general sentiment of the society in which he lives, puts on these various possibilities. (Berlin, 1969, p.130)

However, it does seem obvious that at a certain level, the freedom of the agent will depend not only upon the powers necessary to make and enact choices, but also upon the presence of a particular kind of range of options from which they can choose. Amy Gutmann comments: "...freedom must entail the possibility of *choosing* among a *broad range* of attractive alternatives" (Gutmann, 1980, p.6). It also seems obvious that a person can be free in the first sense of possessing the powers necessary to make and enact choices without being free in the second sense of having access to the range of options necessary for freedom, and *vice versa*. The dispute between the negative and positive theories of freedom can be displayed through this contrast. Positive theories allow for the possibility of the person who possesses all the capacities and powers needed to make and act upon choices, but who has a very narrow range of options from which to choose, if any -- for example, the well-fed, well-equipped, highly trained conscript soldier. Negative theories allow for the possibility of the person who has a wide range of possibilities to choose from, but who possesses none of the resources needed to enact those choices -- for example, the free beggar.

There are obvious problems in describing either the soldier or the beggar as free, as neither soldiers nor beggars can be autonomous choosers. And so the autonomous chooser must be free in both senses -- they have both the space and power to make choices and act them out, and a particular range of options to choose from. Of these two elements -- the space and power to make and act out choices, and the range of options from which to choose -- it may be felt that the former is highly complex, while the latter is relatively simple and need not take much theoretical space. However, as has been argued, autonomy cannot simply be equated with a wider range of options, and therefore this aspect of the theory of freedom has to be developed with some care. In this section, the notion of "life chances" as developed by Ralf

Dahrendorf (Dahrendorf, 1979) is used to develop this aspect of the theory.

Life chances, says Dahrendorf, emerge through the process of history. They are: "...the moulds of human life in society; their shape determines how and how far people can unfold" (Ibid., p.11). They are situated in societies and communities, they are *not* attributes of individuals:

> Life chances are a mould. They may be too big for individuals and challenge them to grow; or they may be too restricted and challenge them to resist. Life chances are opportunities for individual growth, for the realization of talents, wishes and hopes, and these opportunities are provided by social conditions. (Ibid., pp.29-30)

John A. Hall endorses this concern when he declares that increasing the life chances of individuals allows "for identities to become achieved rather than socially ascribed" (Hall, 1988, p.173).

But life chances are not simply options, argues Dahrendorf. Options *are* important -- options are possibilities of choice or alternatives of action presented in a social framework; directions in which the individual can move in their development. However, the other aspect of life chances is equally important, and this is the existence of "ligatures". Ligatures are allegiances, bonds or linkages. "By virtue of his social positions and roles, the individual is placed into bonds or ligatures" (Dahrendorf, 1979, p.30). These bonds or linkages give meaning to the place the individual occupies in society; it is the anchoring of persons and their actions. They act as "the foundations of action" (Ibid., p.31). It is ligatures which situate actors within a specific community -- without ligatures, the agent remains unsituated, marginalized, excluded, without a place in the community.

Life chances are a function of both options and ligatures; these two elements can vary independently of each other, and their specific combination at any one time constitutes the individual's life chances. This means that a wide range of options does not necessarily mean a wide range of life chances. "Ligatures without options are oppressive, whereas options without bonds are meaningless" (Ibid., 1979, p.30). Richard Flathman expresses this in terms of the "situatedness" of action (Flathman, 1987, pp.1-3) -- action is always situated within a particular community, and that community will act as the foundation of that action: it acts as "a 'structure' which is a necessary condition of meaningful action" (Flathman, 1987, p.180), a structure consisting of "substantive conventions, rules, shared understandings, beliefs, values and the like" (Ibid., p.181).

Obviously there must be some optimal balance of options and ligatures which would constitute being free to the most extensive degree possible within a particular community -- but, says Dahrendorf, it would be difficult to spell out such a balance. Measuring options may sound plausible, but measuring ligatures is much more problematic:

> They are the (often bizarre) patterns by which social positions are tied to others in order to provide their incumbents with bonds. Such patterns are railings to which people can cling as they walk into the mist of their social lives, just as they can be barriers too which they encounter in this mist. (Dahrendorf, 1979, p.32)

Their intensity is perhaps more important than their number. Dahrendorf says:

> At any time, there is an optimal relationship between options and ligatures -- choices and linkages, or bonds, from the individual's point of view -- and thus there is a function of options and ligatures which defines a maximum of life chances. Both options and ligatures, however, can grow as well as shrink, thus life chances are capable of increase and extension. (Ibid., p.34)

Dahrendorf concludes: "Exploring the conditions of an increase in life chances is the first problem of the social theory of change and the first objective of the political theory of liberty" (Ibid., p.34).

The theory of freedom outlined here does allow for something similar to the notion of Dahrendorf's ligatures in its emphasis upon the powers and capacities the agent needs in order to formulate plans of action and enact them. This emphasis does situate liberty within a social framework, as the powers and resources needed by the agent go far beyond powers of reason -- such basic powers as the power of movement are also needed, and these depend upon the way the community is organized. This is freedom *in* a society, not freedom *from* it (Ibid., p.62). The unsituated, contextless person enjoys few of the powers and resources that attach themselves to positions within the community -- the basic powers and capacities that attach themselves to recognized *membership* of that community. The unsituated person is not a member -- or if they are formally a member of the community, that membership has been rendered empty precisely by their lack of context.

However, Dahrendorf's notion of ligatures means more than this, for they carry an intrinsically moral element: they may be restrictions or fetters or foundations of action, but they may be values too -- they may give meaning to action: "The mere opportunity of choice without a defined position from which to choose (in a sense without co-ordinates) is bound to remain random" (Ibid., p.42). And: "Mere opportunities for choice are the absence of morality; a world of mere options is beyond good and evil. This means, however, that the opportunities for choice lose their meaning; a feeling of pointlessness is spreading" (Ibid., p.42). Ligatures situate actions morally; they make freedom significant and meaningful. For Dahrendorf, this means that "...a liberal position which aims at the extension of human life chances must have the formation of ligatures as much (and at times perhaps more) in mind as the opening-up of options" (Ibid., p.43).

The idea of life chances gives the theory of freedom a dynamic quality which is missing from the purely negative position. Dahrendorf states:

> Liberty is the absence of constraint, certainly. But this is merely the passive, negative side of the picture. All too often this negative side has dominated men's concerns, and has had to do so. Even so, the absence of constraint is not enough. The road into the unknown, the uncertain and insecure is also one towards the extension of human life chances. (Ibid., p.38)

And, dramatically:

> I despise that negative attitude which calls itself liberal, and is in fact little more than the defence of the vested interests of the haves... The active concept of liberty advocated here does not allow us to rest before all avenues of extending human life chances have been explored, and that means we must never rest. (Ibid., p.38)

Dahrendorf protests against those negative views that claim that people are free to make the best use of the existing options open to them -- these theories suggest that freedom lies in deciding "what use we shall make of the circumstances in which we find ourselfs" (Hayek, 1960, p.19). Dahrendorf protests that this attitude is deeply conservative:

116

The 'circumstances in which we find ourselves' define as a constant the very things which are variable. Liberty in this case is no more than the implementation of the life chances which are available here and now. But there are other fetters on human development. That which we do not (yet) know or are not (yet) able to do is a limitation of what we know and do which can be removed... The classical liberal concept of liberty is negative because it seems to be resigned to, indeed pleased with existing conditions. (Dahrendorf, 1979, pp.91-92)

Seeking to expand life chances is a difficult challenge:

...extending options is a complicated process which...does not end with the promise of rights, but merely begins with it. People's standard of living, and their social status generally, are important as a real condition of options. (Ibid., p.93)

Dahrendorf seems to be appealing to a radical alterability thesis here, which demands intervention, as opposed to a conservative reluctance to intervene. Elsewhere he appeals to it explicitly when he says: "It is not the human condition which is at fault; rather, it is real conditions created by human beings, and they can therefore be changed" (Dahrendorf, 1975, p.22). Therefore providing formal rights is insufficient, as people's standards of living can undermine their opportunity to make full use of those rights.

Two important points seem to emerge from Dahrendorf's discussion. Firstly, it is clear that the degree of autonomy cannot simply be equated with the width of a range of options, such that the narrower the range the lesser the autonomy, or the wider the range the greater the autonomy. The significance of the options matters: autonomy does not exist over and above or separate from the social context -- it is embedded within the community, such that the shape and form of that community contributes to the shape and form of the autonomy of the agent. Secondly, for choices to be meaningful, the agent must be situated within a community, that is, be recognized as a member of the community. Dahrendorf has argued that life chances are made meaningful by ligatures, that is, social position. Positionless people lack genuinely meaningful options. The significance of this is that a person could be supplied with a wide range of options, but deprived of any position that makes those options meaningful. Therefore people must have access not only to the material benefits of social cooperation, but also to the burdens of social position. To exclude people from such position is to deprive them of membership, and to deprive them of membership is to deprive them of the opportunity to make meaningful choices. The lack of ability to make meaningful choices is the absence of the Autonomy Condition of freedom, and therefore is highly damaging to a person's liberty. Therefore, if the community is to ensure that its members enjoy liberty, it must ensure that they are not deprived of the opportunity to be active participants in that community -- to be genuine members. No amount of compensation for the lack of that active membership -- in terms of 'welfare' payments, etc. -- can make up for the cost of its loss.

## Section 4.6 -- Conclusion

This chapter distinguished between three conditions of liberty: the Non-interference Condition; the Autonomy Condition; and the Power Condition. It has examined the Autonomy Condition -- the possession of the ability to make rational choices concerning the best options open to one, given one's plan of life and social context. It defended the place of the Autonomy Condition within the theory of freedom against an attack based upon Berlin's critique of positive liberty, by arguing firstly that Berlin's critique has been misrepresented, and secondly that to the extent that Berlin *does* criticise the idea of positive liberty, the Autonomy Condition can be characterized in a way that meets that criticism.

The concept of rationality was examined, to see whether a 'minimal and meagre' model of rationality would be sufficient to fulfil the Autonomy Condition, or whether a richer notion of rationality was required. It was concluded that while the minimal model had political attractions, there were also good reasons to prefer a richer model of rationality. Finally, Dahrendorf's notion of 'life chances' was examined to give substance to the notion of a range of options from which the autonomous agent can choose. It was concluded that options needed to be embedded within a community, and that the autonomous agent must be a member of a community -- positionless people lack genuinely meaningful options. The exclusion of people from membership of the community deprives them of the opportunity to make genuinely meaningful choices, and so deprives them of their autonomy. Therefore the autonomy of the agent does not only rest on their power of rational decision-making, their self-understanding -- it also rests upon the nature of the community, and the opportunity to be an active participant in that community. The freedom of the agent

118

therefore rests upon the opportunity to be an active member of the community. Freedom is not the *absence* of social context -- it is the presence of a certain form of social context, a context that ensures the three kinds of conditions of freedom. Therefore the theory of freedom must be concerned with the social context of action, and to that extent touches upon the question of social justice. One aspect of a theory of social justice must be a concern with the freedom of the members of the community. How this theory of freedom shapes a theory of social justice is explored in Part 3 of this book.

## Notes

[1]    A challenge put to me in a research seminar was what the impure theory of freedom has to say about members of a 'cult', who were 'brainwashed' into wanting to lead a certain kind of life. My response is that the theory does not supply a solution to such a problem, but it does reveal what is at stake. The best solution would be one that restored the positive aspect of their freedom without destroying the negative aspect. If there was no such solution available to those who had to decide what to do, then they would have to decide whether it was worth destroying the negative aspect of liberty for those cult members, for example by abducting and 'deprogramming' them , for the sake of the positive aspect of their liberty: and there is no simple answer to such a problem -- a theory of freedom cannot be expected to supply a specific answer, rather it brings to the fore those aspects of the situation which must be taken into account when making a judgment.

[2]    See Staub (1989). See especially Browning (1993), chapter 18.

[3]    Much of this discussion is based upon D'Entreves (1994).

# Part 3
# Issues of Justice

# 5 Freedom and Neutrality

## Section 5.1 -- Introduction

The project of Part 3 is to examine the relationship between the impure theory of freedom and the practice of social justice, and to establish whether the theory of freedom places any positive demands upon programmes of social justice. If the practice of social justice is taken to be intervention to secure the well-being or welfare of members of the political community, then this book rejects a view of freedom that simply places negative side-constraints around such a practice, that constrains intervention rather than demands it. Rather, freedom is seen as a component of human well-being, as a goal rather than merely a boundary; and therefore freedom will on occasions demand intervention.

So far two ways in which the impure theory can demand intervention have been identified: of the three conditions of liberty -- the Non-interference, Autonomy, and Power conditions -- the final two clearly can demand intervention. The Power Condition requires the possession of or access to powers and resources needed in order to pursue chosen plans of life, the power of enactment; if this power of enactment is indispensable to freedom, then intervention may be required to ensure that all possess it. The Autonomy Condition can also demand intervention: chapter 4 established that the free agent must be a genuine member of the community. If the free agent is an autonomous chooser, they must have a social context within which they can make meaningful choices, and meaningful choices can only be made from a recognized position within the community. Therefore the autonomy of the agent does not only rest upon their powers of rational decision-making, but also upon the nature of the community and their membership of it. To exclude any person from full membership of the community is to deprive them of the opportunity to make meaningful choices: this is to deprive them of their autonomy, which, finally, is to deprive them of their freedom. The free agent is therefore an active chooser, doer and participator in the community, and the connection between the theory of freedom and the practice of social justice is clear. Part of the programme of social justice will be to ensure that all members of the community are in a position to be equally active choosers, doers and participators. This by no means supplies a total theory of social justice, but it does supply a significant component of

123

such a theory -- that component that connects with the theory of freedom.

Therefore, with the move from the negative to the impure theory of freedom, the boundaries of intervention have been transformed. However, before we can move to a radically interventionary theory of social justice, other arguments that could still constrain the scope of the theory have to be considered. The whole argument of this book rests on the assumption that the question of which theory of freedom to adopt cannot be settled only by comparing the internal coherence of rival theories: the value of freedom, and the theory that best articulates that value, has to be settled in the context of other political values, such as justice, equality, welfare, public order, etc. The preferred shape of those other values may provide a context for the value of freedom that rules out that suggested by the impure theory. It has never been part of the argument that the value of freedom is prior, theoretically or practically, to other political values. For example, while it has been argued that the value of freedom will shape, at least in part, the theory and practice of social justice, the concept of social justice has also shaped the theory of freedom. The argument rests on a theory of social justice that is egalitarian, that assumes that all members of the community are entitled to the equal value of membership, and that the task of a programme of social justice is to ensure that all members of the community have equal access to the conditions necessary for the equal value of membership. Membership comprises being an equally active chooser, doer and participator in the community. This view of social justice has shaped the impure theory of freedom, with its emphasis on the *activity* of freedom, and the conditions needed to act as a foundation for that activity.

However, there are other values that may have a role in shaping the theory of freedom or the choice of that theory, or in constraining the theory of social justice. So while the boundary of intervention may change with the shift from the negative to the impure theory of freedom, other political values may dictate that it remains the same. One of the central values of political theory is neutrality. Indeed, the principle of moral equality would seem to have a close connection with the value of neutrality -- it could even be interpreted *as* a principle of neutrality. And it may be that the value of neutrality either dictates against the choice of the impure theory of freedom and/or constrains the intervention that the theory of freedom calls for. The impure theory of freedom states that when the positive and negative conditions of freedom clash, the question of which should take priority cannot be settled at the level of theory: they are *prima facie* equally important.

However, if the community is going to respect the value of neutrality, it may be that the negative conditions of freedom should always be given priority -- to prioritize the positive conditions may violate the principle of neutrality, and therefore violate the principle of moral equality. The possibility that the value of neutrality could perform this constraining role is examined in this chapter, and is, in the end, rejected. Rather, it is argued, the value of neutrality may demand the priority of the positive conditions of freedom, and therefore also demand radical intervention.

## Section 5.2 -- Two Senses of Neutrality

Two senses of 'neutrality' can be distinguished. It is important to keep in mind that these are senses in which the community or state can be neutral; whether it makes sense for individual agents to be neutral in these ways is a different question.

(1)     The community can be neutral on the question of the valuable or worthwhile life: the community is neutral between rival conceptions of the good.

(2)     The community can be neutral between persons: it does not pick out anybody for special or different treatment, unless there are justifiable grounds for doing so.

The position argued for in this chapter is that the second sense of neutrality is fundamental, and that the first is of value only to the extent that it is necessary to achieve the second: where some conception of the valuable life must be presupposed in order to achieve neutrality between persons, then the community must fix upon such a conception. The claim is that any recognizably liberal political theory holds the same position: the fundamental commitment is to neutrality between persons (this is the sense in which the moral equality principle can be understood as a neutrality principle); where a conception of the good is required to achieve such neutrality, then the theory should be committed to such a conception -- neutrality on the valuable life is secondary and derivative. This may initially sound incoherent: how can the community ensure neutrality between persons by *not* being neutral on the question of the valuable life? The answer is that there are two forms of neutrality between persons: negative and positive neutrality. Negative neutrality between persons amounts to leaving them equally alone to pursue their own life plans -- this demands that the community be neutral on the question of the valuable life. Positive neutrality between persons amounts to ensuring that the welfare of each person is equally realized -- this demands that the community take a position on the question of the valuable life. Therefore, to the extent that liberal theories are committed to positive neutrality between persons, they are committed to a particular conception of the valuable life; the question is, of course, how far they are committed to positive neutrality. The position argued for here will be that positive neutrality between persons is a legitimate and important goal for a political theory, and that it makes room for the impure theory of freedom, and for a radically interventionary theory of social justice.

*Section 5.2.1 -- Neutrality on the Valuable Life*

Neutrality on the question of the valuable life has been seen as central to the liberal tradition. One argument for it goes like this:

It can be assumed that there is a variety of conceptions of the good in the community. Two normative assumptions can also be made: (1) that no single agency should impose any conception of the good upon members of the community which would limit the range of conceptions of the good available; and (2) that this kind of plurality is itself valuable to the community. John Rawls makes these assumptions: "A crucial assumption of liberalism is that equal citizens have different and indeed incommensurable and irreconcilable conceptions of the good" (Rawls, 1982, p.17); and: "...liberalism accepts the plurality of conceptions of the good as a fact of modern life... It tries to show both that a plurality of conceptions of the good is desirable and how a regime of liberty can accommodate this plurality so as to achieve the many benefits of human diversity" (Ibid., p.18).

If such a view is taken, then what is required is a framework within which the individual is left free to pursue their own conception of the good, a 'regime of liberty'. Neutrality is therefore a liberty-preserving device, because it prevents the demand that members of the community should pursue a designated vision of the good that they have not chosen for themselves. Therefore a framework of rules that is genuinely neutral between conceptions of the good has to be put in place. Such a framework aims to achieve a kind of equality: the equal freedom of individuals to pursue their self-chosen goals.

John Rawls expresses this idea through two distinctions: between the Right and the Good, and the Reasonable and the Rational [1]. The idea of the Right defines the framework through which people must pursue their chosen ends -- any goal can be pursued as long as it does not interfere with the ability of others to pursue their goals. Therefore the only constraint upon which goals can be pursued is that they must respect the similar right of others. The idea of the Good represents whatever the individuals or the community as a whole identifies as a goal worth pursuing. Under Rawls' scheme, the Right is prior to the Good: all goods must be pursued within the context of a framework of rights, and the framework of rights is neutral between goods. The only constraining force is mutuality.

The distinction between the Reasonable and the Rational expresses the same basic idea. The Rational expresses whatever the individual or the community considers most rational to pursue, and the Reasonable expresses those limits upon the ways such goals can be pursued that people would accept as reasonable for them. Therefore the framework of neutrality expresses the limits the conception of the Right or the Reasonable places upon the ways in which people can pursue what they consider to be Good or Rational. No judgment is necessary here about what actually *is* good or rational.

Rawls' two principles of justice can be seen as fitting this distinction:

(1)     Each person has an equal right to a fully adequate scheme of equal basic liberties which is compatible with a similar scheme of liberties for all.

(2)     Social and economic inequalities are to satisfy two conditions:
(a) they must be attached to offices and positions open to all under conditions of fair equality of opportunity; and
(b) they must be to the greatest benefit of the least advantaged members of society. (Ibid., p.5)

The first principle can be interpreted as the framework of neutrality, the second as a framework of social justice; or the first principle is a non-interference principle while the second is an intervention principle. Or in Rawls' terms, the first principle expresses the Right while the second expresses the Good -- and as the Right is prior to the Good, the first principle has priority over the second.

There are two questions that can be raised about this division of the principles. First, does the first principle genuinely represent neutrality on the question of the good life or does it presuppose a particular conception of the good? There are grounds for supposing the latter, especially when one takes into account that Rawls emphasises a list of 'basic liberties' rather than the notion of liberty as such: he could be interpreted, therefore, as identifying a set of activities that people *ought* to be free to do; and the only way of doing that is to fix upon these activities as being of particular value -- and this is, of course, to fix upon a conception of the valuable life. Rawls lists the basic liberties as:

> ...freedom of thought and liberty of conscience; the political liberties and freedom of association, as well as the freedoms specified by the liberty and integrity of the person; and finally, the rights and liberties covered by the rule of law. No priority is assigned to liberty as such, as if the exercise of something called 'liberty' has a pre-eminent value and is the main if not the sole end of political and social justice. (Ibid., p.5)

There are two ways a list of basic liberties can be arrived at, according to Rawls. The first is historical:

> ...we survey the constitutions of democratic states and put together a list of liberties normally protected, and we examine the role of these liberties in those constitutions which have worked well. (Ibid., p.6)

The second way is:

> ...to consider which liberties are essential social conditions for the adequate development and full exercise of the two powers of moral personality over a complete life. (Ibid., p.7)

This is the method Rawls uses. The basic liberties are "founded on the conception of citizens as free and equal persons" (Ibid., p.4); and their function is "the adequate development and full exercise of the two moral powers of citizens as free and equal persons" (Ibid., p.11). The two moral powers are:

> ...the capacity for a sense of right and justice (the capacity to honor fair terms of cooperation and thus to be reasonable), and the capacity for a conception of the good (and thus to be rational). In greater detail, the capacity for a sense of justice is the capacity to understand, to apply and normally to be moved by an effective desire to act from (and not merely in accordance with) the principles of justice as the fair terms of social cooperation. The capacity for a conception of the good is the capacity to form, to

128

revise, and rationally to pursue such a conception, that is, a conception of what we regard for us as a worthwhile life. (Ibid., p.16)

Rawls claims that the clarification of his theory offered in "The Basic Liberties and Their Priority" will prevent misinterpretations:

...for example, that it is intended to be morally neutral, or that it models only the notion of rationality, and therefore that justice as fairness attempts to select principles of justice purely on the basis of a conception of rational choice as understood in economics or decision theory. (Ibid., pp.20-21, note 20)

Rawls makes it clear that his theory is based on a conception of the person that can be understood as 'liberal':

...it takes the capacity for social cooperation as fundamental and attributes to persons the two moral powers which make such cooperation possible... Thus citizens are regarded as having a certain natural political virtue without which the hopes for a regime of liberty may be unrealistic. (Ibid., pp.86-87)

It could therefore be argued that underlying all liberal political theory is a conception of the person as a free and equal citizen, a conception that requires some position on the basic activities that are of value to free and equal citizens: basic liberties will protect these activities. There is, therefore, some commitment here to a conception of the valuable life for such citizens.

The second question concerning the division of the principles is why *should* the ideal expressed in the first principle have priority over the ideals expressed in the second? Why should the Right be prior to the Good? The answer is that it is debatable whether Rawls thinks that it should. It is important to remember that his is a two-stage theory, and in the first stage the first principle has no priority. It gains its priority in the second stage, but only because specific conditions are in place. Rawls distinguishes between the general and the special conceptions of justice. The special conception is expressed by the principles as stated above, characterized by the priority of the first principle. But in the general conception there is no such priority:

All social primary goods -- liberty and opportunity, income and wealth, and the bases of self-respect -- are to be distributed

129

equally unless an unequal distribution of any or all of these goods is to the advantage of the least favored. (Rawls, 1972, p.303)

Under the special conception, equal liberties and equality of opportunity are exempt from the difference principle (principle 2b); under the general conception, they fall under the difference principle. Rawls says:

...this general conception imposes no constraints on what sorts of inequalities are allowed, whereas the special conception, by putting the two principles in serial order...forbids exchanges between basic liberties and economic and social benefits. (Ibid., p.151)

The logic of this move is expressed by the parties in Rawls' original position:

...if the parties assume that their basic liberties can be effectively exercised, they will not exchange a lesser liberty for an improvement in economic well-being. It is only when social conditions do not allow the effective establishment of these rights that one can concede their limitation; and these restrictions can be granted only to the extent that they are necessary to prepare the way for a free society. The denial of equal liberty can be defended only if it is necessary to raise the level of civilisation so that in due course these freedoms can be enjoyed. (Ibid., pp.151-152; and see pp.542-543)

The reasoning, therefore, is that if the economic and social conditions are such that the basic liberties cannot be exercised, it is reasonable to accept these limitations on freedom -- but only if the objective of these limitations is to enable society to move to a situation of greater economic and social prosperity such that all can exercise their basic liberties.

Two problems occur here. The first is that Rawls argues priority can only be given to the first principle once specific conditions are in place. If those conditions are not in place, it would be positively damaging to give the negative requirements of the non-interference principle priority over the positive requirements of the intervention principle; in fact it may be justified under those conditions to give the positive requirements priority over the negative [2]. However, Rawls does not indicate what the relevant conditions are, and writes throughout on the assumption that this question has been answered theoretically and practically, and that he is dealing with a society in which the relevant conditions have been met: "For the most part I shall assume that the requisite circumstances for the serial order obtain" (Ibid., p.152).

One extremely important question concerning the transition point will be the conception of freedom used to judge when it has been reached. For Rawls, whether the basic liberties can be effectively exercised is the crucial question; but if the richer conception of freedom being developed here is used as the measure, than the transition point will come far later than if 'thinner', more negative, conceptions of freedom are used. The question becomes whether all members of the community are in a position to be equally active choosers, doers and participators. On that measure, it is doubtful whether many western capitalist societies, if any, have met Rawls' condition; and attempts to enforce the priority of the non-interference principle over the intervention principle must cause immense damage to the freedom of members of those societies, and lead to widespread damage and destruction of their life chances. It could be argued that, in a period of history where there has been a significant shift towards the priority of the non-interference principle over the intervention principle, this destruction has taken place in a dramatic form, and continues to do so. Rawls' assumption that the transition point has been unproblematically reached is highly questionable.

A second problem is that a society cannot move to the priority of the Right over the Good, unless it can identify a set of conditions under which the move is appropriate -- it must fix the transition point. However, in order to identify such a set of conditions, some conception of the good has to be appealed to; how else can it be judged that the move from the general to the special conception of justice is appropriate? If this is right, then the Good is ultimately prior to the Right. In other words, some conception of the valuable life must lie behind Rawls' theory of justice in order to give it any coherence. And this must be true of any liberal political theory.


*Section 5.2.2 -- Neutrality between Persons*

Another argument for neutrality on the question of the valuable life concedes that it is not fundamental as an end in itself, but argues that it is necessary as a means for achieving neutrality between persons -- neutrality between persons *is* fundamental, but requires neutrality on

131

the valuable life. Ronald Dworkin spells out the importance of this neutrality ideal to liberal thought in a discussion of equality (Dworkin, 1978). For Dworkin, the core of liberalism is its conception of equality -- it regards people as equals; and to treat people as equals is to treat them with equal respect and concern. However, there are two incompatible ways in which a state can treat its citizens as equals (Ibid., p.127):

(1)  ...government must be neutral on what might be called the question of the good life.
    ...political decisions must be, so far as is possible, independent of any particular conception of the good life, or of what gives value to life.
(2)  ...government cannot be neutral on that question, because it cannot treat its citizens as equal human beings without a theory of what human beings ought to be.
    ...the content of equal treatment cannot be independent of some theory about the good for man or the good life, because treating a person as an equal means treating him the way the good or truly wise person would wish to be treated.

To treat someone as an equal is to treat them as though they desired the good life.

For Dworkin, the first version of equality, with neutrality over what constitutes the worthwhile life, is the constitutive political morality of liberalism. The ideal of neutrality within liberal theory is, however, not based on a scepticism about what is good for people:

Liberalism cannot be based on scepticism. Its constitutive morality provides that human beings must be treated as equals by their government, not because there is no right and wrong in political morality, but because that is what is right. (Ibid., p.142)

And this does not involve a contradiction:

Liberalism is not self-contradictory: the liberal conception of equality is a principle of political organization that is required by justice, not a way of life for individuals, and liberals, as such, are indifferent as to whether people choose to speak out on political matters, or to lead eccentric lives, or otherwise to behave as liberals are supposed to prefer. (Ibid., pp.142-143)

However, the movement from the importance of neutrality between persons -- Dworkin's equality -- to neutrality on the question of the valuable life, is not obvious. There are two ways to be neutral between persons, negatively and positively; and neutrality on the question of the valuable life only follows from the negative interpretation. Such neutrality is impossible on the positive interpretation. Therefore before neutrality on the valuable life is confirmed, the priority of negative neutrality between persons over more positive neutrality has to be established. First, the difference between these two forms of neutrality between persons should be made clear.

Frameworks of rules can be neutral between persons in two ways: negatively or positively. A negatively neutral framework would be completely general and apply to all persons equally, and would specify no goals those persons must pursue. The important aspect of such a framework is that it takes persons and their circumstances as it finds them, and leaves them to make the best of those circumstances -- it does not intervene to assist any particular individuals to achieve their individual goals, as that would be to pick out those individuals, and by implication the goals they have chosen, for special treatment. Such a framework is therefore radically non-interventionary. Note that to be completely neutral in this negative sense, the framework must not only specify no end-point at which people must aim, but also no start-point at which they must begin: to specify that people must *start* as equals is to violate negative neutrality and requires some measure of intervention to ensure that they do. A genuinely negatively neutral system would, therefore, be completely indifferent to where people have started, where they are at any given time, and where they are going to finish. All such a framework would specify is that the rule of non-interference be applied equally to all.

A positively neutral framework would aim to neutralise the effects of contingent differences between people upon their life chances, to ensure that all life chances are of roughly equal value -- as all people are morally equal, all are entitled to equally valuable lives. Such a framework would intervene to pick out particular groups or individuals for particular treatment, if the value of their life chances is threatened by some factor that does not threaten others. The positive framework could have two roles: either specifying a start-point where all should begin or specifying an end-point which all should reach -- and it could, of course, do both.

The negative framework is therefore a framework of equal non-interference which rules out intervention to assist particular individuals to achieve their goals. The positive framework is a framework of powers and resources which aims to establish the equal value of life chances through intervention. Neither framework is concerned with what people choose, but each aims to provide a context within which people are free to make a choice and enact it. However, the negative framework is neutral in a purely formal sense: it achieves neutrality by leaving people to make the best of the circumstances within which they find themselves, whatever they might be -- and this form of neutrality could lead to radical inequality of the value of life chances. The positive framework is practical: it achieves neutrality by ensuring that all have access to the powers and resources they need in order to choose and enact a life goal -- this form of neutrality is committed to some degree of practical equality.

There are other ways of drawing the contrast. Within the negative framework, neutrality is a quality of the *rules* of the framework, and the rules aim at no particular outcome. Within the positive framework, neutrality is a quality of the *outcomes*, and that quality of outcomes is the goal of the framework. The negative framework is a deontological, rights-based position; the positive framework is a teleological, goal-based position. Within the negative framework, freedom is interpreted as a side-constraint upon the goals that individuals and the community can pursue and the way they can pursue them; within the positive framework, freedom is one of the practical goals that the framework can aim to achieve. [This gives us another way of understanding the contrast between negative and positive freedom. Negative freedom sees freedom as a side-constraint, as a formal feature of the process; positive freedom sees freedom as an outcome, as a goal of the process. The impure theory of freedom sees both understandings as valid, but each as incomplete without the other.]

If this contrast is correct, then being neutral between persons can mean either:

(1)     guaranteeing equal non-interference such that all are left alone to do what they wish within the circumstances in which they find themselves; or
(2)     guaranteeing equal access to the resources needed in order to be an equally participating member of the community.

Neither kind of neutrality is concerned with what people do, but the second is concerned with what they *can* do. Neutrality on the question of the valuable life follows from the first kind of neutrality, but is ruled out by the second in that it identifies being an equally participating member of the community as a valuable component of life chances. Given these two forms of neutrality between persons, is there any reason at the level of theory for preferring the negative version over the positive, and therefore ruling out the sort of interventionary strategies called for by the impure theory of freedom?

One way of defending negative neutrality would be to argue that it aims to preserve liberty, while positive neutrality aims to achieve equality; and therefore the latter would appeal only to egalitarians. Liberal theorists should therefore prefer the negative interpretation, which rules out the impure theory of freedom. However, such a move is too simplistic. Freedom has both negative and positive conditions, and the positive conditions require the kind of intervention ruled out by the negative version of neutrality: to the extent that freedom is recognized as having conditions, freedom can be interpreted as a goal, not merely a side-constraint. The claim that the negative framework is best for protecting liberty is therefore mistaken -- a purely negative framework would allow the destruction of the conditions of freedom.

It might still be argued that negative neutrality would secure freedom as a side-constraint, while positive neutrality would achieve freedom as a goal; and that there are good grounds for preferring freedom as a side-constraint over freedom as a goal, and therefore for giving negative neutrality priority over positive neutrality. But such an argument is mistaken. First, there must be some over-riding reason to prefer freedom as a side-constraint over freedom as a goal, and it is not obvious what that reason could be. Second, freedom must not be confused with its conditions: providing the negative conditions of freedom does not necessarily secure its negative aspect, just as securing the positive conditions does not necessarily secure its positive aspect. The absence of positive conditions undermines both the negative and positive aspects of being free. And therefore negative neutrality on its own, while it may put in place the negative conditions of freedom, does not guarantee the negative aspects of freedom.

The dispute here is not over the relative weights that should be attached to freedom and equality, but over how to create, maintain and protect the conditions of freedom. The position being developed here does not advocate the priority of either the negative or positive framework when it comes to that task: both are indispensable -- a mixture of rights-based and goal-based strategies is essential for ensuring the equal freedom for all. One strategy without the other, or one given priority over the other in the wrong political, social or economic conditions, will destroy the value of freedom for many members of the community. What is being questioned here is a picture that presents freedom and social justice as necessarily at odds, with freedom as negative and anti-interventionary, and social justice as positive and interventionary. In its place is a picture that presents freedom and social justice as having a positive relationship, and therefore the idea of freedom does not necessarily block any interventionary programme of social justice because freedom can be a goal of that intervention. Equally the appeal to neutrality does not necessarily block such moves, because the goal of intervention could be positive neutrality between persons.

## Section 5.3 -- Nozick's Critique of Positive Neutrality

The argument so far has distinguished between negative and positive neutrality between persons, and claimed that while negative neutrality rules out a commitment to a conception of the good, positive neutrality requires one; and has established that positive neutrality is an ideal which plays an important role in liberal political theory. The question has been posed whether there are any grounds to prefer one conception of neutrality between persons over the other, and so far the answer has been that at the level of theory there are no such grounds: both forms of neutrality are *prima facie* equally important. However, Robert Nozick (Nozick, 1974) can be seen as articulating a fundamental theoretical objection to positive neutrality. The objection is that the positive framework involves neutralising the effects of what are identified as 'morally arbitrary' factors upon outcomes, but what if these 'arbitrary' factors are simply the natural differences between people? How can people be prevented from using their natural features to their advantage without limiting freedom in a highly problematic way? People ought to be left free to use their natural features as they see fit, and any attempt to prevent them from doing so is an unacceptable limitation of liberty. Positive neutrality, to the extent that it involves intervention to determine outcomes, is therefore ruled out; the only legitimate form of liberal neutrality is negative.

Nozick uses this argument as an objection to any interventionary programme, but his argument is specifically aimed at Rawls' difference principle. According to the difference principle, people are allowed to use their natural advantages to benefit themselves only if they also benefit the worst off (Rawls, 1972, pp.75-83). The logic behind the principle is that the most rational choice of distribution is equality, unless an unequal distribution can improve the position of the worst off -- in which case, the most rational choice is to move to that situation of inequality. Rawls says:

> We see then that the difference principle represents, in effect, an agreement to regard the distribution of natural talents as a common asset and to share in the benefits of this distribution whatever it turns out to be. Those who have been favored by nature, whoever they are, may gain from their good fortune only on terms that improve the situation of those who have lost out... No one deserves his greater natural capacity nor merits a more favourable starting position in society. But it does not follow that one should eliminate these distinctions. There is another way to deal with them. The basic structure can be arranged so that these contingencies work for the good of the least fortunate. (Ibid., pp.101-102)

So rather than these natural differences being neutralised in some sinister sense, people can exploit them but only if this exploitation benefits others too -- and this is a far more benign and acceptable form of neutralization.

However, Nozick does not see it as benign at all -- rather, the claim that natural talents should be seen as a collective asset clashes with the strong intuition that such talents are the property of their possessors, and they therefore should have the right to use them as they see fit. According to this view, the accidental differences between persons should be allowed to play a free role in determining life chances because people must be left free to exploit their private property in whatever way they wish within the limits of mutual liberty. This is precisely the clash between the priority of negative and positive neutrality between persons. The negative framework that Nozick proposes would guarantee that people are left alone to do what they can with what they possess in the circumstances in which they find themselves. The positive framework that he opposes would guarantee that people have equal access to what they need to be full members of the community, and this could include the redistribution of resources from the most advantaged to the least advantaged through some kind of welfare principle. So does Nozick's critique of Rawls present a serious objection to the positive conception of neutrality?

Nozick objects to the view that accidental differences between persons must be neutralised because they are arbitrary from a moral point of view. He protests: "Why shouldn't holdings partially depend upon natural endowments? (They will also depend on how these are developed and on the uses to which they are put)" (Nozick, 1974, p.216). The assumption seems to be, says Nozick, that it is departures from equality that need justification; but: "Why ought people's holdings to be equal in the absence of special moral reason to deviate from equality?" (Ibid., p.222). And: "The legitimacy of altering social institutions to achieve greater equality of material condition is, though often assumed, rarely *argued* for" (Ibid., p.232).

Nozick proposes a counter argument (Ibid., p.224):

(1)   People deserve their natural assets.
(2)   If people deserve $X$, they deserve any $Y$ that flows from $X$.
(3)   People's holdings flow from their natural assets.
      Therefore:
(4)   People deserve their holdings.
(5)   If people deserve something, then they ought to have it (and this over-rides any presumption of equality there may be about that thing).

Nozick anticipates one objection, the infinite regress argument: that people only deserve $X$, and therefore any $Y$ that flows from $X$, if $X$ itself flows from some property that is also deserved: otherwise the argument has an arbitrary starting point. He therefore supplies two alternative premises to replace the original two (Ibid., p.225):

(1)   If people have $X$ and their having $X$ (whether or not they deserve to have it) does *not* violate anybody else's right or entitlement to $X$, and $Y$ flows from (arises out of, and so on) $X$ by a process that does not itself violate anyone's rights or entitlements then the person is entitled to $Y$.
(2)   People's having the natural assets they do does not violate anybody else's entitlements or rights.

Setting the infinite regress objection aside, and therefore also setting aside Nozick's revised premises, there are other problems concerning the original argument. Premise 2 as it stands is simply false, unless a pure anarchist 'anything goes' principle is adopted; but Nozick is not an anarchist and so it can be assumed that he would not adopt such a principle. To avoid the 'anything goes' implication, he must add a clause to premise 2 that sets limits to the ways in which people can use their natural assets to secure holdings: e.g., that they cannot be used in ways that violate the liberty of others.

Premise 3 is either a description or a prescription. If it is a description it is simply false, except within a specific social and economic system, something like a free market with a minimal state -- although it is still not obvious that it would be a complete description of how holdings flow within such a system. But clearly there are alternative social systems available in which different descriptions of how holdings flow would be true. If it is a prescription, then some argument is needed to establish it as the right rule for the distribution of holdings, but that argument is not supplied but rather stated as the conclusion of the overall argument. Therefore if it is a description, the argument only follows through for a very specific type of social system, and has no grip on alternative social arrangements; and if it is a prescription, the argument starts to look somewhat circular.

Another problem with premise 3 is that, if it is true that people's holdings flow from their natural assets, it would seem also true that people's holdings are affected by their natural disadvantages: if natural assets are allowed to determine outcomes, surely natural disadvantages must also be allowed to determine outcomes. Now, this seems harsh on those with natural disadvantages, such as the disabled, and the free market theorist may want to exclude them from the argument and maintain they should be treated separately. However this would entail intervention in the market process and the only argument that could justify such an intervention would be one based on positive neutrality between persons, which would bring with it much broader implications for intervention in the market process -- if intervention in the market process is justified in order to 'neutralize' these arbitrary differences, why not others?

In fact, Nozick abandons the notion of desert, and presents a parallel argument in terms of entitlement, largely, it seems, because of the problems posed by the infinite regress objection. The new argument now runs (Ibid., pp.225-226):

(1)   People are entitled to their natural assets.
(2)   If people are entitled to something, they are entitled to whatever flows from it (via specified types of processes).
(3)   People's holdings flow from their natural assets.
      Therefore:
(4)   People are entitled to their holdings.
(5)   If people are entitled to something, then they ought to have it (and this over-rides any presumption of equality there may be about holdings).

Nozick says: "Whether or not people's natural assets are arbitrary from a moral point of view, they are entitled to them, and to what flows from them" (Ibid., p.226).

Nozick certainly believes this solves the infinite regress objection, but surely he now faces an equivalent problem concerning the grounding of entitlement, a problem that he never deals with adequately. The other problems noted above still hold for this version of the argument. Premise 2 now suddenly has the rider clause that rules out the 'anything goes' implication, "via specified types of processes"; but still it should be noted that the rider clause remains open -- which processes are to be specified? Until that is known, nothing is ruled out -- the Rawlsian difference principle could certainly count as such a process. Nozick here has ruled out the pure anarchist 'anything goes' principle, but nothing else. The problems with premise 3 remain unsolved, unless the rider clause from premise 2 is carried forward -- but doing this renders the argument's conclusion empty. It now reads: If people are entitled to something they have received through the specified process, then they ought to have it. Who would argue with that? In the end, Nozick seems to be arguing that natural assets can be used to gain access to resources within specified limits, but this is uncontroversial: the difference principle can count as such a specified limit. The argument only rules out positive neutrality strategies if the rider clause is removed, but this transforms the argument into one for pure market anarchism, which is not a position Nozick would adopt. Nozick needs to specify the content of the rider clause, which he does not do.

Nozick's appeal to the notion of natural assets is problematic at a deeper level. The 'natural assets' argument goes something like this. People have unequal talents and resources, and if they are left free to use those talents and resources as they wish (as long as they do not use them to violate the freedom of others), then people will use or fail to use them in different ways, and unequal shares will arise. If equal shares are to be ensured, the freedom of people to use their talents and resources as they think fit must be taken away, and this is an unacceptable constraint upon freedom. Now, to a certain extent, this is a genuine problem: certain inequalities are natural -- some people are taller, stronger, fitter than others, and it would be highly problematic to try to prevent them using those advantages to pursue their life-plans (Kurt Vonnegut, in a short story "Harrison Bergeron", paints a nightmare picture of such a community (Vonnegut, 1950)).

However, at another level, the argument is based on a confusion. A distinction needs to be made between normative and empirical inequalities: that is, between inequalities that carry an implication of better/worse, and inequalities that do not. And a second distinction needs to be made between natural inequalities and artificial inequalities (inequalities that arise from economic, political and cultural features of society). The inequalities at the base of Vonnegut's nightmare -- that some are taller, stronger, fitter than others -- are not inequalities in a normative sense; they are empirical inequalities. The fact that one person is taller than another has no moral implications; it does not mean that the former is more valuable than the latter. Their heights are unequal in that their heights are different, but their heights are not unequal in that one is more valuable than another. These inequalities are also natural, not artificial, and there is something especially disturbing about suggestions that people's natural attributes should be controlled in some way by the state.

There is something far less disturbing about suggestions that artificial inequalities should be ironed out by the state through programmes of positive neutrality. However, the point of the argument is that artificial inequalities arise from the use of natural attributes, and therefore controlling the degree of artificial inequality in society precisely does mean controlling how people use their natural attributes. There are two replies to the argument. Firstly, it is not obvious that state control over the ways in which people use their natural attributes is necessarily wrong: and indeed any liberal political theory -- including Nozick's -- must allow some degree of such control. For example, a person should not use their greater strength to take the possessions of others against their will. Nozick's 'specified types of processes' are precisely for this purpose. Secondly, whether a natural attribute acts as an advantage or disadvantage leading to artificial inequalities is a matter of political and social policy -- there is no 'natural' connection between natural differences and the artificial inequalities that rest upon them. For example, in South Africa under the now defunct apartheid system difference in skin colour, a natural difference, gave rise to immense inequalities in political and social advantages -- but these advantages were obviously the artificial creations of a particular regime that chose to base the distribution of advantages on the basis of the difference in skin colour. In many societies, being male is an advantage and female a disadvantage when it comes to gaining access to certain resources and social positions. But again one's sex is a natural difference, and whether one's sex acts as an asset or disadvantage is a matter of policy not nature.

Therefore it is a matter of policy whether natural features act as assets or disadvantages, and this is the case for *any* natural feature. For example, it is possible to have a social system in which intelligence is a disadvantage for some: in Robert Graves' *I, Claudius*, Claudius' survival depends upon his pretence at being an idiot -- if his intelligence becomes known to certain parties, they will kill him (Graves, 1972) [3]. And there are many examples of societies in which 'intellectuals' have suffered immense disadvantages. It could be replied that under a free market regime, there *is* a natural connection between the differences in natural attributes and the artificial inequalities that would arise under that regime -- but this would only be true if the free market regime were itself 'natural' in some fundamental sense. Nozick, then, talks as though many of the advantages some would enjoy over others in a minimal state/free market regime are natural, when in fact they are artificial inequalities, resting on a choice of which 'natural' attributes should be rewarded. It is a society that determines whether natural differences are going to act as advantages or disadvantages, however 'society' is to be understood [4]. The free market theorist may reply that under their favoured regime that choice is made by 'free' individuals in the market place, rather than by the state; but even if this could be made sense of, it does not make the choice any more 'natural', nor necessarily any more benign.

Natural differences, therefore, do not have to give rise to political, social, economic or cultural inequalities: they will only do so in the context of a particular political, social, economic and cultural order. If it is decided that certain natural differences should not affect a person's access to the resources, opportunities and powers they need in order to enjoy equally valuable membership of their community, then it may be within the powers of the community to ensure that they have no such affect. This is the case even where the natural differences between people can be understood as natural inequalities: for example, the 'able bodied' and the 'physically disabled' can be naturally unequal when it comes to the power of movement, but it can be decided that this natural inequality should not give rise to unequal membership. Positive neutrality between persons which aims to iron out those artificial inequalities that rest upon natural differences or inequalities, is a legitimate aim of a programme of social justice: such a programme is called for where it is decided that it would violate the principle of equality of membership to allow those natural differences to play any role in determining the value of membership of the community -- that is, the ability of a person to be an equally active chooser, doer and participator in that community. Indeed, as has been pointed out, *any* version of a liberal political theory would recognise the legitimacy of this principle to some extent -- e.g., ruling out the use of superior

142

physical strength in determining the possession of property. Nozick's concession that there must be 'specified types of processes' governing the connection between natural advantages and what flows from them, concedes enough space within even his theory to justify positive neutrality as a legitimate goal, including Rawls' difference principle strategy.

## Section 5.4 -- Against Intervention?

The contrast between negative and positive neutrality between persons seems to amount to a contrast between a non-intervention principle and an intervention principle. However, both principles could have a common source. An extremely basic moral principle is that, on the face of it, one ought not to harm others -- a 'no harm' rule. This principle can be read in either a negative or positive way. The negative reading would be: "Perform no action that harms another person." This negative principle can be interpreted in a narrow or wide sense: the narrow sense would be that the principle only rules out actions that aim to harm others; the wide sense would be that the principle rules out any actions that have harmful consequences for others, whether those consequences are intended or not. The positive reading of the 'no harm' rule would be: "Prevent harm to others." This positive principle is at no great distance from the negative version: it can be arrived at simply by adding an "omissions" clause to the negative principle, so that it now reads: "Perform no action or omission that leads to harm to others." As one serious criticism of the purely negative principle is its refusal to take omissions seriously, the positive principle may well be the logical conclusion to reach. However, an objection to the positive principle is that it demands too much: if people must do whatever is in their power to prevent harm to others, or render assistance once harm has happened to them, then most, if not all their powers, will be spent performing this task. This is what might be called the "bottomless pit" objection. However, it seems reasonable to suppose that the "prevent harm" principle can be framed such that it avoids the bottomless pit objection. Negative neutrality demands only the purely negative 'no harm' principle (however, the question of the narrow or wide interpretation will be crucial). Positive neutrality demands the "prevent harm" principle.

So both negative and positive neutrality between persons could have a common moral source in the 'no harm' principle, as both the negative and positive versions of that principle can be deduced from it. Joseph Raz comments:

> Even though deontological and teleological considerations are distinct, they derive from a common moral core. Therefore, since the core moral concern should be politically promoted through the enforcement of some deontological constraints it seems plausible to hold that it should also be promoted by advancing the correct conception of the good as well. Since the two parts of morality are separate only at a superficial level, whereas at the fundamental level they both stem from a common source, there is a *prima facie* case for requiring political action to take notice of both. (Raz, 1986, p.137)

The position being argued here is one that recognises the need for a mixture of negative and positive strategies when it comes to securing the equal value of life chances, and places no theoretical priority upon either. However, two objections could be raised.

Firstly, this approach cannot be neutral on the question of the valuable life. The stress on positive neutrality between persons, the teleological aspect, necessitates a commitment to a position on what is good for people. This places it at odds with the entire liberal tradition, and gives grounds for treating it with a great deal of caution.

Secondly, this approach is highly interventionary. It sees a positive role for the state in securing the value of life chances, and this means granting the state extensive powers to intervene in people's lives. Entrusting the state with such power again is at odds with the entire liberal tradition, and gives additional grounds for treating it with a great deal of caution.

Both objections are true: the argument does necessitate a commitment to a position about what is good for people, and does grant the state powers to intervene in people's lives. But still, are these serious problems? Only, surely, if there is an alternative position available that is (i) genuinely neutral on the question of the valuable life; (ii) genuinely non-interventionary; and (iii) would deliver a community that people would believe to be worth living in. There are serious problems in outlining any such position, especially one that would actually be compatible with the liberal tradition. The two objections will be explored in more depth in the rest of the section.

The argument behind the first objection could be this. If one of the central principles of liberal theory is the moral equality of persons, then it follows that no conception of the valuable life can be imposed upon people. An essential element of moral equality must be that all people are regarded as equally capable of arriving at a legitimate conception of what makes life valuable -- to impose a conception upon them is to regard them as morally incapable of doing this, and therefore as morally inferior. Therefore it follows that the state must remain neutral on the question of the valuable life, because to actively intervene and impose such a conception on some members of the community is to single those members out as morally inferior to others. The approach developed here is both deontological and teleological, but the teleological element entails a commitment to a particular conception of the valuable life, and so would entail imposing that conception on certain members of the community, and so does entail seeing some members of the community as morally inferior to others. It is therefore incompatible with liberal theory's commitment to the moral equality of persons. A political theory that *is* neutral on the question of the valuable life is therefore to be preferred.

However, this objection fails, because it is perfectly coherent to accept the principle that the community should not impose a particular conception of the valuable life, and reject the principle that the community must remain neutral on what makes life valuable. The community can have a conception of what makes life valuable without imposing it upon members of that community -- it can employ it in other ways; and it may be essential for the community to have such a conception if it is going to fulfil its obligations to its members. The problem is usually presented in terms of a dilemma. Either the state imposes values on the community by deciding what sort of lives people should lead, and this involves the claim that the states knows best what makes lives valuable for individuals. Or the state leaves people 'free' to pursue their life chances in the market, which leads to the consequence that many people's life chances are determined by arbitrary market forces. Either option has the consequence that people do not choose their life chances in any acceptable sense.

The dilemma is, of course, a real one. There have been and still are states that dictate the valuable life of their members; and a great many people still have their life chances determined by market forces, rather than by any genuine choice they have made. The key to solving the dilemma lies in an approach which mixes the deontological and teleological considerations of the negative and positive strategies of neutrality between persons. A programme of social justice that has the achievement of freedom as one of its goals is just such a mixed strategy. Such a strategy will ensure that people are left alone to determine their life goals; that they have the capacity to make rational choices about their life goals; and that they have the powers and resources they need to enact those life goals. The positive elements of that strategy do not amount to forcing people to adopt a particular conception of the valuable life, but they do entail taking a position on the question of what makes life valuable. The argument is based on the assumption that being an equally active chooser, doer and participator in the community is of value, and is an important element of the value of life chances. Therefore the position is not neutral on the question of what makes life valuable. However, it does not involve imposing a particular conception of what makes life valuable upon people, and so remains neutral in that sense.

The first, defensive, reply to the objection is, then, that neutrality on the question of what makes life valuable is not a necessary condition for avoiding the imposition of such a conception upon members of a community -- the adoption of the conception could have other purposes. A second, more assertive, reply, is that it is not even sufficient: remaining neutral on the question of what makes life valuable may lead to the imposition of a particular form of life upon people by default -- failure to intervene may condemn many people to a particular form of life they have not chosen for themselves, but which they remain powerless to challenge. Therefore the imposition of a negatively neutral framework upon a community does not lead to the radical freedom for all to shape their lives as they wish; it could instead lead to the imposition of radically impoverished forms of life upon those members of the community who lack the power to challenge the arbitrary forces that threaten them. The objection to the mixed strategy fails to realise that one strong motivation for its adoption is the *prevention* of certain forms of life, rather than the imposition of them. The objection seems to be based upon the assumption that in a community where the state takes a thoroughly neutral stance on the question of the value of life, and therefore refuses to intervene in people's lives, the members of that community will be able to shape their lives in any way they wish within the limits of mutuality. A more realistic picture is that in societies where the state takes such a non-interventionary position, people are left to struggle *against* a particular form of life being imposed upon them by the capitalist market system; and particularly vulnerable members of the community will lose that struggle. Far from the minimal state/free market being a sphere of radical freedom to shape life chances, it becomes a sphere of struggle against economic oppression.

The conception of what gives value to life being appealed to in the theory developed here is that being an active chooser, doer and participator in one's community contributes to the value of one's life. Paradoxically, the purely negatively neutral position carries no such commitment to the value of choice, in that people are left to make the best of the circumstances in which they find themselves, and those circumstances may rule out choice when it comes to forms of life. Therefore the positive framework of intervention, that entails a commitment to a conception of the good, promotes choice; and the negative framework of non-interference constrains choice. There is an essential role for the teleological element of the theory: without it, there is no guarantee of the power of choice essential for liberty. Once more, we come to the conclusion that both the negative and positive aspects of the theory are needed, and that one without the other destroys freedom rather than creating it. A commitment to a conception of the good is therefore essential to the mixed strategy for two reasons: first, it supplies the goals of the theory, without which it loses its commitment to the value of freedom; secondly, some practical decisions will need to be made about the balance between the positive and negative strategies under particular circumstances, and this can only be done through a conception of the good [5].

However, the main ground for rejecting the objection from the perspective of the purely negatively neutral position, is the disbelief that any political theory could occupy that position -- certainly no *liberal* theory can be neutral in this radically negative way. All recognizably liberal theories have been impure. Even Nozick could not adopt a principle of pure market anarchism -- he added the rider clause that goods must flow via *specified* processes, and those processes could only be specified by appeal to a view of what is harmful and what is valuable to human life. The point is that if the 'anything goes' principle is to be rejected -- and liberal theory rejects it -- then a decision has to be taken about which human capacities and potentialities are going to be permitted to play a role in determining life chances. Nozick faces this question just as does any liberal theorist, and he cannot answer it and at the same time remain neutral on the question of the valuable life. Nozick acknowledges this in a sense when he suggests that the gaps in his theory can be answered by referring to "the meaning of life" (Nozick, 1974., p.50). The gap is the lack of a moral theory, which Nozick excuses by saying:

The completely accurate statement of the moral background, including the precise statement of the moral theory and its underlying basis, would require a full-scale presentation and is a task for another time. (A lifetime?) That task is so crucial, the gap left without its accomplishment so yawning, that it is only a minor comfort to note that we here are following the respectable tradition of Locke, who does not provide anything remotely resembling a satisfactory explanation of the status and the basis of the law of nature in his *Second Treatise*. (Ibid., p.9)

He promises that he will "grapple" with such issues "on another occasion" (Ibid., p.51).

No recognizably liberal theory is neutral on the question of the valuable life. An extreme minimum liberal position would be that people should be left do do whatever they like as long as they don't interfere with any body else's capacity to do the same -- but even this minimum position entails spelling out what is to count as an illegitimate interference, in that anything we do, however isolated it may appear, can interfere with what other people want to do. The only way to spell out the difference between benign and malign interference with others must be some conception of what can harm others, and that entails some conception of what is good for them. Most liberal theorists venture well beyond this extreme minimum position, and so entail a far richer conception of what is good for people.

William Galston rejects neutrality as a liberal concern. He says:

Liberalism cannot, as many contemporary theorists suppose, be understood as broadly neutral concerning the human good. It is rather committed to a distinctive conception of the human good, a conception that undergirds the liberal conception of social justice. (Galston, 1991, p.18)

Every society, including liberal ones, says Galston, rest upon a shared conception of the good which is achieved through collective endeavour; but in a liberal society this need not be a total good, because some parts of the human good, according to liberal theory, fall outside the scope of the political community (Ibid., p.70). He argues that every contemporary liberal theory relies upon a triadic theory of the good, the elements of which are:

(1)     The worth of human existence.
(2)     The value of fulfilment of human purposes.

(3)     Commitment to rationality as the chief guide to fulfilling human purposes.

Any liberal theory which claims to be neutral on the question of the human good:

> begins by promising to do without a substantive theory of the good; each ends by betraying that promise. All of them covertly rely on the same triadic theory of the good, which assumes the worth of human existence, the worth of human purposiveness, and the worth of rationality as the chief constraint on social principles and social actions. If we may call the beliefs in the worth of human existence and in the worth of purposes and their fulfilment the root assumptions of humanism, then the theory of the good presupposed by these neutralist liberals is the theory of rational humanism. (Ibid., p.92)

To conclude this section, two replies have been made to the objection that the position being developed here is not neutral on the question of the valuable life. The first was that any position that was genuinely neutral on that question would have to be radically negatively neutral between persons, taking no position on where they start or where they finish or what happens to them in between -- and this could be extremely destructive of people's freedom. The best strategy is one that mixes the deontological and teleological elements, and that strategy cannot be neutral on the question of the valuable life because (i) such a conception is needed to supply the teleological element of the theory, and (ii) it is also needed to decide what balance between the negative and positive elements is appropriate in particular circumstances.

The second reply was that no liberal position is neutral on the question of the valuable life, and so no liberal position could be so purely negatively neutral between persons. Even Nozick's position needs a conception of what is good for people, even though he does not supply one. Therefore the fact that the position being developed here involves a commitment to a conception of what makes life valuable is no ground for isolating it from the liberal tradition.

The second objection to the approach being developed here is that it would entail state intervention, which is anti-liberal. However, it is difficult to see how any liberal theory can be completely non-interventionary. The previous argument established that the liberal theorist must make a commitment to a conception of the good in that they must decide which human potentialities are going to be permitted to play a role in determining life chances. There are therefore two levels of intervention that could be called for: (i) intervention to ensure that all members of the community acquire these particular potentialities; and (ii) intervention to ensure that *only* these potentialities play a role in determining life chances.

Minimal state/free market theorists face this problem of intervention as much as any other position. In the first place, the model of the properly functioning market presupposes autonomous, fully informed agents, with specific levels of self-confidence and bargaining skills, etc. Therefore it is difficult to see why the free market position can decline the commitment to the provision of a positive framework that enables people to develop these capacities. The refusal to do so would mean that the market system would bring about distinct hierarchies, and the development of under-privileged groups who are excluded from educational opportunities to develop into full market agents. The free market theorist who wants to avoid the creation of an 'underclass' should therefore offer such a positive programme of education and training for all. The free market theorist could argue their way out of this commitment by claiming that the members of this 'underclass' are somehow 'naturally' incapable of benefiting from such education and training programmes -- their capacities are somehow 'naturally' fixed so that any such investment is a waste of resources. Disputes over the existence and nature of such an 'underclass' (Lister ed., 1996) are usually over whether its members are there due to their own behaviour and values (Murray, 1996), or because of social, economic and political factors beyond their control (Field, 1996). The position taken here is that any such class is largely due to social exclusion caused by the latter factors [6].

Even if the free market theorist does succeed in avoiding this first kind of commitment to intervention, it is difficult to see how they can avoid the second. Even if the free market system is regarded as, in some sense, more 'natural' than any other system, extensive interventionary strategies will be needed in order to create the conditions under which such a system could emerge and flourish. An analogy with gardening is enlightening here. The gardener aims to create conditions within which a particular plant will grow and flourish, but these may entail the brutal suppression of things the gardener considers to be weeds and pests, and extensive intervention in the soil with digging, fertilizers, etc. F.A.Hayek appeals to such an analogy:

> The attitude of the liberal towards society is like that of the gardener who tends a plant and, in order to create the conditions most favorable to its growth, must know as much as possible about its structure and the way it functions. (Hayek, 1944, p.18; taken from Heath, 1989, p.107)

The more delicate the plant, of course, the greater need for firm action to combat anything that interferes with its growth. This means the free market theorist must call for extensive intervention to establish the conditions needed for the free market to develop, including extensive interference with what people might want; e.g., workers may want to organize labour monopolies. Some free market theorists even regard democratic structures as problematic. Hayek comments:

> The successful politician owes his power to the fact that he moves within the accepted framework of thought, that he thinks and talks conventionally. It would be almost a contradiction in terms for a politician to be a leader in the field of ideas. His task in a democracy is to find out what the opinions held by the largest number are, not to give currency to new opinions which may becomes the majority view in some distant future. (Hayek, 1960, p.112)

And: "We can either have a free Parliament or a free people" (Ibid., p.102). John Gray, defending what he sees as classical liberalism, comments:

> ...an authoritarian type of government may sometimes do better from a liberal standpoint than a democratic regime, always provided that the governmental authorities are restricted in their activities by the rule of law. (Gray, 1986, p.74)

The institution of liberal limited government is compatible, he says, "with the restriction or absence of political democracy..." (Ibid.).

The free market theorist might accept this need for extensive, possibly repressive, state action, but argue that this need for intervention is temporary; once the correct conditions are in place, the state can withdraw to a more passive, non-interventionary role. This is, then, a two-stage theory like Rawls', and it is the second stage, as with Rawls, that is the ideal. But how plausible is this two-stage theory? It may be that the conditions needed for the free market to operate and flourish will need constant maintenance: the gardener cannot simply put the initial conditions in place, and then walk away and expect the plant to flourish in their absence! There will be a constant need to intervene to keep the weeds and pests at bay. The state, as gardener, may always be called upon to intervene in a repressive manner. For example, why should workers at some stage give up their preference for labour monopolies?

Perhaps the most the free market theorist can claim is that their approach would involve non-interference in the market -- the state would not interfere with what are private market choices. But this depends on what is regarded as a choice within the market: is the choice of workers to struggle for labour monopolies not a market choice? And this still allows for extensive interference outside the market: the social, political and cultural frameworks that would have to be in place to ensure that the free market flourishes may involve extensive interference with what people want. For example, they may want democratic procedures of decision-making.

The free market theorist may object that this equation of the free market with a repressive state is unfair -- a free market need not require a repressive state to enforce it. But equally, a welfare state need not require a repressive state to enforce *it*. Too often an equation is made between minimal state = benign state, and extensive state = repressive state, without that equation ever being historically or theoretically justified. All that is being suggested is that minimal states can be repressive and extensive states can be benign. Both the free market and the welfare state require state intervention to put them in place and maintain them. Whether or not such intervention will lead, in the shorter or longer term, to repressive state regimes, is a matter to be settled by the historical record. How many attempts to set up and maintain welfare state structures within liberal democracies have led to extensive state repression of what people want? How many attempts to set up and maintain free market economic systems have led to extensive state repression of what people want? The point is that the historical record shows that there is no necessary connection between

152

extensive states and state repression, and equally no necessary connection between minimal states and state benevolence.

To conclude this section, the objection that the approach being developed here should be opposed by liberal theory because it would entail state intervention has been rejected, on the grounds that all versions of liberal theory entail state intervention to some extent. It has also been argued that the sort of state intervention required by this approach is no more likely to lead to state repression of what people want than the sort of state intervention required by the minimal state/free market position.

## Section 5.5 -- Nozick and State Intervention

Robert Nozick's theory of justice represents perhaps the most serious attempt within the liberal tradition to spell out a completely non-interventionary theory; but in this section it is argued that even here the principle of non-intervention is compromised in an open-ended way. Nozick uses the idea of private property as the central objection to programmes of positive neutrality. According to the welfare liberal position, the best way to give life chances equal value is to bring about rough equality of socially important resources, and this entails redistribution of wealth. But, says Nozick, to redistribute wealth means taking things away from people when those things are their property -- and this is simply a Robin Hood theory of social justice, except this time the theft is performed by the state itself. If something belongs to someone, then they have control over its use and its disposal, and nobody else has any say in the matter. Then as long as the wealthy came by their resources by legitimate means, the less well off have no claims against them that can justify redistribution of that wealth. But for the idea of property to act as a fundamental block to redistribution, then people must have a right to their property which must carry considerable weight, outweighing, for example, any right to be in a particular material condition. How is such a right to be grounded? Nozick's answer is to ground the right to property upon the notion of entitlement. The wealthy are entitled to their resources, and once that entitlement has been established nothing can outweigh it. But this is merely postponing the problem: what grounds entitlement? At this point the idea of private property begins to look mysterious: what can it be that justifies someone in claiming that some item is their's to control as they see fit? Is it something about the objects? Or something about the owners? Or something about the social organization in which they live? Are such rights natural, or historical, or artificial constructs that can be deconstructed?

Nozick is aware that to make out a plausible case for private property he must answer questions concerning (i) the original acquisition of holdings: how things came to be owned in the first place; and (ii) the transfer of holdings: how objects can be transferred from one owner to another. He therefore proposes (i) a principle of justice in acquisition, and (ii) a principle of justice in transfer -- principles which can justify claims of ownership of resources. And that, according to Nozick, is almost all that is needed. Once these two principles are in place, then "If the world were wholly just..." (Nozick, 1974., p.151):

(1)     a person who acquires a holding in according with the principle of justice in acquisition is entitled to that holding;
(2)     a person who acquires a holding in accordance with the principle of justice in transfer, from someone else entitled to the holding, is entitled to the holding; and
(3)     no one is entitled to a holding except by (repeated) applications of these two principles.

These principle gives us an (almost) complete picture of distributive justice: "...a distribution is just if everyone is entitled to the holdings they possess under the distribution" (Ibid., p.151); or: "A distribution is just if it arises from another just distribution by legitimate means" (Ibid., p.151).

Now, Nozick has done nothing so far except to state the obvious: that the questions of initial appropriation and subsequent transfer have to be answered convincingly in order to make out a strong status for private property rights. His two principles are meant as answers to those questions, but as they stand Nozick has simply pointed out the need for such principles, he has not supplied the content. Nozick acknowledges that all he has supplied is a general framework -- the details of the principles need to be specified; but, he says, "I shall not attempt that task here" (Ibid., p.153). One might expect him to supply those details elsewhere in the book, but it is difficult to identify anything that could count as such a step. It may be that the argument he outlined concerning the connection between natural assets and market outcomes, discussed in section 5.3, performs this task -- but if that is the case the theory rests on extraordinary fragile foundations, if any foundations at all [7].

How does the Entitlement Theory rule out redistributive strategies of social justice? The important point for Nozick is that: "Justice in holdings is historical; it depends upon what actually has happened" (Ibid., p.152). But note Nozick's initial qualification, that the two principles only supply a complete theory of distributive justice "if the world were wholly just". The world is *not* like that, and so a third principle is needed to take into account the possible effects of past injustices. This is the principle of the Rectification of Injustices in Holdings. The complete theory now reads:

> ...the holdings of a person are just if he is entitled to them by the principles of justice in acquisition and transfer, or by the principle of rectification of injustice... If each person's holdings are just, then the total set (distribution) of holdings is just. (Ibid., p.153)

Once more, little detail of the principle of rectification is supplied, but the important point is that if each person's holdings satisfy the principles, then the total set of holdings must be just, whatever the overall pattern of distribution. What matters is how each individual comes to hold what they have: if they came about it by means that fall within the scope of the principles, then they are entitled to it; and if each person came about their holdings in this way, then the total distribution is just. What matters is how the distribution came about, not its shape. "No over-arching aim is needed, no distributional pattern is required" (Ibid., p.159).

There are two problems with Nozick's position here:

Firstly, Nozick concedes that the distribution of resources across society according to his theory will not be random with respect to any pattern -- unplanned strands of patterns will emerge (Ibid., p.157). The important point for Nozick is that the pattern will be random with respect to any *pre-designed* pattern. In other words, no particular pattern is aimed at. However, even on Nozick's principles, some patterns will emerge -- resources will flow along certain predictable lines towards specific groups and away from other groups. In a free market system, resources will flow to centres of purchasing power, away from groups with weaker purchasing power., These results will not be random, because they are the products of processes that are understandable and predictable. Nozick therefore ignores the possibility of intervening in the market process, not to *produce* a particular pattern, but to *prevent* one.

Secondly, Nozick's starting position is a situation of anarchy in a hypothetical state of nature. He aims to show, in the first part of the book, how a minimal state could emerge from that situation without violating individual rights. His purpose in the second part of the book is to show that any attempt to justify anything more than a minimal state must violate individual rights. According to the entitlement conception of justice, "there is no argument based upon the first two principles of distributive justice, the principles of acquisition and of transfer, for a more extensive state..." (Ibid., p.230). However, the third principle, of rectification, has yet to come into play. And even so, it cannot be known in advance that the first two principles will not lead to a more extensive state, because their details have not been supplied. Even more worrying, the principle of rectification may well demand a more extensive state. In an extraordinary passage, Nozick discusses the role of the third principle:

> Perhaps it is best to view some patterned principles of distributive justice as rough rules of thumb meant to approximate the general results of applying the principle of rectification of injustice...
> ...an important question for each society will be the following: given *its* particular history, what operable rule of thumb best approximate the results of a detailed application to that society of the principle of rectification? These issues are very complex, and are best left to a full treatment of the principle of rectification. In the absence of such a treatment applied to a particular society, one *cannot* use the analysis and theory presented here to condemn any particular scheme of transfer payments, unless it is clear that no considerations of rectification of injustice could apply to justify it. Although to introduce socialism as the punishment for our sins would be to go too far, past injustices might be so great as to make necessary in the short run a more extensive state in order to rectify them. (Ibid., pp.230-231)

Firstly, note that Nozick seems to promise a fuller treatment of the principle of rectification, but he nowhere supplies it. He allows that fully specified principles of acquisition, transfer and rectification, if applied to a particular society, could require sweeping redistribution of wealth towards radical equality. Nozick says his theory cannot be used to condemn *any* system of transfer payments, short of socialism -- although it is hard to see how he can justify even this limitation on the scope of the rectification principle. And so *any* positive programme of social justice could be compatible with his theory -- nothing has been ruled out.

Secondly, note that Nozick claims the extensive state would be short term. His position is therefore a two-stage version of free market theory, where the state must extensively interfere in the first stage to put into place the conditions needed for the free market to operate -- for Nozick, those conditions, dramatically, are to do with the question of justice, not efficiency. And so even Nozick's most minimal of liberal theories explicitly advocates the need for positive intervention by the state to secure what justice demands, however short term Nozick believes that need to be.

It may be replied that Nozick has, nonetheless, hit upon something crucial. A situation in which the state carries out a minimal and negative role is surely preferable to having an actively interfering state: minimal state intervention with what people want to do is surely an attractive model. Therefore a system of negative neutrality should be preferred over positive strategies. This is not to say that *only* negative strategies should be used; positive strategies have a role to play, but the mixed strategy should be such that they are kept to a minimum, and are always secondary to and limited by the priority of the negative framework.

However, while there are many good reasons not to take a romantic view of a benign state, positive programmes of social justice need not be equated with hostile state interference with what people want to do. As was argued in section 5.4.2, such programmes can be equated with a community working to enable all its members to be active choosers, doers and participants. Such a programme does not limit choice, it creates it. Certainly, if positive programmes of social justice always had a tendency to lead to state dictatorships, that would be a good reason for qualifying enthusiasm for them -- but there is no historical evidence for any such tendency. Therefore the slippery slope objection to state welfare provision has little substance; predictions of the road to serfdom have not been born out.

In a sense, a situation of complete negative neutrality, a minimally active state, is attractive, but only in the sense that such a situation is only conceivable and justifiable when all conditions that ensure the equal value of life chances are in place, and are guaranteed to remain in place. In such a situation, there is no more work for positive programmes of social justice to do, and the state may as well wither away from that point of view. This does make a two-stage theory look attractive: positive strategies of intervention are employed to achieve a certain level of well being, but once that level has been achieved and guaranteed to stay in place, interventionary programmes can be abandoned. But such a two-stage view is always going to be over-simplistic. To return once more to the garden, the conditions that ensure the equal value of life chances cannot be guaranteed to stay in place by themselves: they may need constant creation, renewal or protection. Therefore it is likely that positive programmes of social justice will not be temporary and short term: they may well be permanent features of a community committed to the equal value of life chances for all its members.

## Section 5.6 -- Conclusion

This chapter has argued that the value of neutrality does not constrain the interventionary role of the state called for by the impure theory of freedom -- indeed, the value of neutrality may call for a far wider interventionary programme of social justice. Liberal political theories are characterized by neutrality, and it is often argued that neutrality rules out the state carrying out any radically interventionary programme of social justice. This is because neutrality amounts to being neutral between conceptions of the good, and any programme of social justice involves a commitment to a conception of the good -- therefore, any strictly liberal political theory rules out *any* role for the state in securing social justice.

However, this is a mischaracterization of liberal theory. What characterizes liberal theory is not the lack of any commitment to a theory of the good, but a positive commitment to the equal moral value of persons: that is, neutrality between persons. Any liberal theory is grounded on some conception of the good -- they have to be in order to be coherent. Now the question is whether neutrality between persons rules out positive programmes of social justice?

It has been argued here that there are two forms of neutrality between persons: negative and positive. Negative neutrality between persons means leaving them alone to make the best of their circumstances: it is radically non-interventionary. Positive neutrality means that, because all members of the community are of equal value, all are entitled to equally valuable lives, and the community must take steps to ensure this neutrality of outcome. It is only if the first kind of neutrality has priority that state programmes of social justice are limited, if not ruled out altogether. The second kind of neutrality requires positive programmes of social justice.

The question then is, are there any good reasons to prefer the negative conception of neutrality between persons over the positive? And the answer supplied here is that, at the level of theory, there are not: both are *prima facie* of equal value. Therefore there is nothing about the value of neutrality that rules out the interventionary role of the state called for by the impure theory of freedom.

158

# Notes

[1]      For the distinction between the Right and the Good, see Rawls (1972), pp.528-532. For the distinction between the Reasonable and the Rational, see Rawls (1980), pp.515-572, especially pp.546-552.

[2]      This echoes Sir Isaiah Berlin's comments on the potential damage the priority of a non-interference principle can cause, including damage to the freedom of members of the community. See section 4.2.

[3]      Claudius receives the following advice (p.112):
"...exaggerate your limp, stammer deliberately, sham sickness frequently, let your wits wander, jerk your head, and twitch with your hands on all public or semi-public occasions. If you could see as much as I can see you would know that this was your only hope of safety and eventual glory."

[4]      Cf. Raphael (1980), especially pp.61-65.

[5]      This is similar to the point made against Rawls, that the transition point from the general to special conception of justice can only be decided through a conception of the Good, and therefore the Good is prior to the Right.

[6]      Ruth Lister argues that the term 'underclass' carries "such strong connotations of blame" that it is best avoided (Lister ed., 1996, p.12). She prefers the idea of social exclusion: "This is a more dynamic language which encourages a focus on the processes and institutions which create and maintain disadvantage rather than what can become a voyeuristic preoccupation with individual poor people and their behaviour" (p.11). The language of exclusion is used in this work.

[7]      Nozick does discuss Locke's theory of initial acquisition of private property, the mixing of labour with things, but he rejects this as incoherent and concludes: "No workable or coherent value-added property scheme has yet been devised..." (Nozick, 1974, p.175).

# 6  Freedom and Equality

## Section 6.1 -- Introduction

This chapter examines the connection between freedom and social justice. The argument has been that freedom and social justice have a positive, not merely negative, connection, in that as freedom has positive conditions, it makes positive demands on any programme of social justice. The connection between freedom and social justice is made through the idea of membership, that freedom within a community requires active membership of that community, and therefore, under the principle of equal membership, all are entitled to be equally active choosers, doers and participators in their community. This active membership requires particular social conditions, one of which is material equality. In other words, freedom requires equality of membership, but that equality must be substantive, not merely formal. The first half of this chapter examines an objection to this approach -- that equality of membership does not require equality of resources, and therefore freedom and social justice remain disconnected. Two of the political theorists that have been discussed in previous chapters have argued that some degree of inequality is compatible with equal membership and, therefore, with equal liberty. Robert Nozick complained that the value of equality is often assumed, but rarely argued for (section 5.3), and argued that there is nothing morally wrong with inequalities that arise from voluntary activity, even where they are affected by involuntary factors such as the possession of natural assets -- freedom gives rise to inequality. John Rawls argues for the application of the difference principle (section 6.5) which would allow inequalities in social primary goods apart from liberty, where those inequalities work for the good for the worst off in society -- freedom does not require inequality for Rawls, but remains disconnected from the distribution of other social primary goods. The first parts of this chapter (sections 6.2, 6.3 and 6.4) will supply one answer to Nozick's plea for justification of equality, by arguing that equality of resources and equality of membership are closely connected. They will also supply an answer to Rawls, by arguing that equality merits far greater priority over other goals than the operation of the difference principle, as he describes it, assumes; and that the distribution of other social primary goods is closely connected with the equality of liberty. Therefore equality of material resources and equal liberty are closely connected, and equal liberty within a community demands substantive, not merely formal, equality of membership.

In a sense, Rawls' difference principle states the obvious and so has great intuitive power. If it can be shown that everybody will be better off under a situation of inequality than they would be under a situation of equality, then surely they would move to the situation of inequality. However, inequality itself has costs that must be taken into account, and it may be that Rawls under-estimates these costs. Indeed, they may be so great that the difference principle, while theoretically plausible, would justify very little inequality in practice once the complexity and the costs of inequality are taken into account. Michael Walzer develops a theory of what he calls "complex equality" (Walzer, 1983, chapter 1). This chapter explores the complexity of inequality, a complexity that threatens to render the difference principle incoherent.

Section 6.3 will therefore examine the connection between the distribution of wealth and the distribution of health. Making this connection clear shows that inequality is highly complex and also carries a cost for people's life chances, not merely in terms of material resources but also in terms of fitness and health, and life expectancy. The second cost of inequality is to the value of membership of the community. In section 6.4 it will be argued that inequality of resources has a destructive effect on the opportunities for active participation in the community, and therefore damages membership. It develops a view of a particular kind of deprivation -- not deprivation of a particular kind of material resource, but deprivation of the opportunity to be a fully active chooser, doer and participator in the community. This form of deprivation can be characterized as exclusion, where particular groups are excluded from full participation within society's institutions and practices. The claim is that full participation is constitutive of freedom, and that therefore exclusion from participation is a violation of freedom.

The rest of the chapter examines one dominant response to social injustice within liberal political theory, that of compensation. Section 6.5 argues that this approach is in inadequate response to this form of deprivation, in that it compensates people for the loss of the opportunity to be an active member of their community, but does nothing to restore the value of that membership. It is argued that the only justifications for taking this option are either that the conditions that exclude people from the community are unpreventable or unpredictable, or that the cost of altering or preventing them is too high; and that while the first possibility imposes a genuine constraint on what can be done in the name of social justice, the second does not necessarily. Section 6.6 shows that the conditions of exclusion are not unpreventable or unpredictable, and therefore only the second, very limited and controversial, justification for compensation is available. Section 6.7 argues that there are good reasons to reject the compensation approach altogether, as it does nothing to solve the problem of exclusion, and so reduces the worst off in the community in a highly vulnerable position, beyond the limits of justice. They are excluded, not only from the community, but from the theory of justice itself.

## Section 6.2 -- Poverty and Inequality

An initial problem is the relationship between the concept of 'inequality' and the concept of 'poverty'. It could be argued that the two are very different, and that what harms people is poverty, not inequality: therefore welfare programmes should aim to eliminate poverty, but not inequality. The difference between the two is that inequality is a relative measure, while poverty is in some sense an objective measure: it can only be judged that someone is in an unequal position if that position is compared with that of others; someone can be judged to be in poverty without making any such comparison. However, it could be argued that poverty is a *form* of inequality, and therefore *is* essentially relational: not all inequality constitutes poverty, but poverty is nevertheless a type of inequality. There is a dispute here between the absolute and relative conceptions of poverty. The approach being developed here rests on the relative conception.

Robert Holman describes the two conceptions of poverty (Holman, 1978, chapter 1). Absolute or subsistence poverty has three elements:

> ...the poverty line is set at just that level which allows people to be physically efficient. Enjoyment of life or the development of intellectual capacities are not involved. (Ibid., p.7)
> ...the concept involves the utmost stringency both in its calculations and in the mode of life it implies. (Ibid.)
> ...the subsistence concept is not related to the incomes of society as a whole. (Ibid., p.8)

The conception of relative poverty has four elements:

(1)     it involves comparisons with other people;

(2)    it is concerned with standards within a contemporary social environment;

(3)    it talks of a gap or distance or inequality between sections of the community; and

(4)    it depends upon value judgments about what is morally right and wrong. (Ibid., pp.13-20)

Holman attacks the subsistence conception of poverty for its inflexibility: the impoverishment of people's lives can take many forms. This absolute conception of poverty is based only on physical subsistence, and therefore disregards "social, psychological and cultural needs" (Ibid., p.13). Holman complains that:

> The subsistence concept rested on the assumption that poverty means simply a lack of money to meet physical needs. It crumbles under the discovery that humans are as strongly motivated to meet other needs of a more social nature. (Ibid., p.13)

Therefore the subsistence conception of poverty is not objective or absolute, and does not fix upon an objective set of universal basic needs, but is "littered with subjective, even arbitrary judgments..." (Ibid., p.10). For example, what is to count as 'physical efficiency'?

Nicholas Barr is equally cautious about the absolute conception of poverty:

> With an *absolute* definition a person is poor if his income is too low to keep him alive and healthy. Early studies attempted to define poverty 'objectively' by reference to basic nutritional requirements. There are serious objections to this approach. People have different nutritional requirements even in the absence of special medical diets, so that no universally applicable standard is possible; nor is it reasonable to expect people to fulfil their requirements at minimum cost. Philosophically, the idea of an absolute poverty line stems from times when it was natural to think in subsistence terms, but this can be argued to be out of place (at least in developed countries) when people live well above subsistence, and where the concept of deprivation is applied to emotional and cultural standards as well as physical ones. (Barr, 1987, pp.133-134)

Barr describes the concept of relative poverty as:

...a person is poor if he or she cannot participate in 'normal' life, i.e., poverty is related to social stratification. Thus a person without access to television is culturally deprived, and a poverty budget should include at any rate a black-and-white television set. (Ibid., p.134)

Holman argues that such a relative conception of poverty is superior in that it is openly normative, and is "adaptable to changing social standards and expectations" (Holman, 1978, p.20).

Peter Townsend is another commentator who favours the relative conception:

...needs which are unmet can be defined satisfactorily only in terms relative to the society in which they are found or expressed... Poverty must be regarded as a general form of relative deprivation which is the effect of the maldistribution of resources. (Townsend, 1970, p.2; also see Townsend, 1979, especially chapter 1)

Martin Rein suggests three conceptions of poverty:

(1)     subsistence: the minimum needed to maintain health and working capacity;
(2)     inequality: relative position of income groups; and
(3)     externality: the social consequences of poverty for the whole society -- its overall disutility. (Rein, 1970, p. 46)

He argues that the subsistence definition is "arbitrary, circular and relative" (Ibid., p. 60), and that the latter two conceptions "deserve more attention and development" (Ibid., p. 62).

There is, therefore, a link between poverty and inequality, in that poverty is type of inequality, and is therefore to that extent a relational concept. If poverty does cause harm to members of the community, then this is a problem to do with the injustice of inequality.


## Section 6.3 -- Inequality and Health [1]

Rawls' difference principle strategy justifies any inequality that benefits the worst off in society. However, before it can be put into

165

effect, the worst off must be identified, and so must what counts as improving their situation. Rawls identifies the worst off by appealing to the notion of "representative men" (Rawls, 1972, pp.97-100). When the principles of justice refer to persons, they do not refer to particular persons, but to representative persons holding the various social positions established by the basic structure of society.

Rawls describes two ways of identifying the worst off representative person (Ibid., p.98):

(1) By choosing a particular social position, for example the unskilled worker, and counting all those with the average income and wealth of this group as the least advantaged. The expectation of the lowest representative person is taken to be the average of this group.

(2) By defining the worst off position purely in terms of relative income and wealth, with no reference to social position. All persons with less than half the median income and wealth can be taken as the least advantaged. This focusses attention on the gap between the average person and the worst off person.

Rawls does not decide between the two alternatives: "I suppose that either of these definitions, or some combination of them, will serve well enough" (Ibid.). He says that it may be "that a more exact definition of the least favored proves unecessary" (Ibid.).

There are good reasons to doubt this strategy -- inequality seems to be more complex than Rawls allows. For example, Nicholas Barr -- while not directly addressing Rawls' difference principle -- comments:

Money income is a flawed measure of individual welfare, and is one of the major causes of the somewhat unhappy intellectual state of analytical definitions of poverty. (Barr, 1987, p.133)

The difference principle strategy might work where the utility of the best off and worst off rests on their income alone. However, where that utility also rests on other factors, the situation becomes more complex. Barr suggests two possible societies (Ibid.7, p.136)[2]:

| | |
|---|---|
| *Society 1* | |
| Average income of poor | 4 |
| Average income of rich | 10 |
| Average income | 7 |
| *Society 2* | |
| Average income of poor | 6 |
| Average income of rich | 14 |
| Average income | 10 |

Society 2 could arise from an application of the difference principle --
and indeed the difference principle logic seems to apply: why not move
to the situation where, despite the greater inequality, everybody is
better off? So which society should the worst off person prefer? The
answer is in fact very complex. Where their utility rests on their
income alone, then the rational choice is Society 2; but where utility
depends on externalities, then their utility may decrease as the income
of the representative person rises. If that externality is sufficiently
strong, then Society 1 is the rational choice.

Barr gives the following examples to illustrate the problem. As
incomes rise, the demand for inferior goods falls, and they may
disappear from the market. For example, the more people have cars,
then public transport is cut and gets more expensive; or the more
people have washing machines, so public launderettes become scarce
and more expensive. Therefore an increase in affluence can create
poverty as a by-product, even where the worst off have more income
as a result (Ibid., p.134).

Brian Barry describes Rawls' treatment of the identification of the
worst off as "off-hand" (Barry, 1973, p.49):

> ...it is now widely accepted that in the advanced industrial
> societies the problem of poverty cannot be tackled by raising the
> average income of all unskilled workers or increasing any broadly
> based average. It is now thought that the chief sources of poverty
> are such things as having children or being sick or unemployed
> for a long period, being old or disabled. There are certain pockets
> of low pay as (in many countries, including industrial ones)
> agricultural and jobs done almost exclusively by women. These
> causes of poverty would remain untackled while either of Rawls'
> indices for the 'worst-off representative man' were maximised.
> Indeed, in the absence of specially directed and vigorous efforts
> by the state there seems to be a tendency for those hit by these
> sources of poverty to fall ever behind as society's average wealth
> increases. (Ibid., pp.50-51)

Vinit Haksar draws attention to the possibility of being worst off in
terms of mental health:

> It is arguable that in very poor societies the worst off are the
> economically poor rather than the mentally distressed; but as
> societies get less and less poor a point is reached when, from the
> contractarian standpoint, the prevention of mental distress gets

priority over the good of economic advancement of the worst off. (Haksar, 1979, p.174)

Rawls draws a clear line between wealth and health when he describes primary goods, those essential requirements for any life-goal which can be pursued within the limits of the well-ordered society. He makes a distinction between *social* primary goods -- liberty and opportunity, income and wealth, and the bases of self-respect (Rawls, 1972, p.303); and *natural* primary goods: "...primary goods such as health and vigor, intelligence and imagination, are natural goods; although their possession is influenced by the basic structure, they are not so directly under its control" (Ibid., p.62). Therefore these natural primary goods fall under the principles of justice only indirectly.

Samuel Scheffler (1982) also argues that health itself is not a suitable subject for a theory of social justice. Social justice is concerned with the question of fair distribution of resources, and health is not a commodity that can be distributed. But, says Scheffler, the things people need for a healthy life *are* distributable commodities, and so do fall under the theory: "...people are not said to have a natural right to a good health or a good life, for these are not distributable goods. Rather, each person is said to have a right to adequate food, clothing, shelter, and medical care" (Ibid., p.153).

However, neither point is convincing. Rawls concedes that natural primary goods are influenced by the basic structure of society -- his position is that they are not so directly under its influence as social primary goods, and therefore social primary goods are the more appropriate focus for a theory of social justice. The difference could be put like this: social primary goods can be directly redistributed; natural primary goods can only be indirectly redistributed, through the redistribution of social primary goods. Julian Le Grand comments:

> Although in one sense it is true that it is impossible to redistribute health, this does not mean that the distribution of health is insensitive to public policy. For it is obviously possible to influence by policy many of the factors that *affect* health, such as nutrition, housing and work conditions, and, of course, medical care itself. (Le Grand, 1991, p.113)

Therefore it does not follow that the social primary goods are the more appropriate focus for the theory of social justice. It may be the case that the redistribution of natural primary goods is such an important issue that it provides one of the main justifications for the redistribution of social primary goods -- the fact that one can be directly, the other only indirectly, redistributed, does not establish which must be the primary focus for a theory of social justice.

Scheffler's point is equally dubious. His position is that a healthy life is not a distributable commodity and so cannot be included within a theory of social justice, but the resources needed as the basis for a healthy life *are* distributable, and so can be included in such a theory. However, if the focus of a theory of social justice is the value of life chances, it has to be conceded that valuable life chances are not a distributable commodity, while the resources needed to act as their basis are: but it does not follow that the value of life chances should be excluded from the theory of social justice. Rather, they act as the focus of that theory in that they provide the basis and the logic for the patterns of distribution of resources identified as the most just. Similarly, the resources needed for good health can only be justly distributed if the idea of a just conception of good health is fixed, however roughly. Le Grand comments that as public policies influence the distribution of health:

> ...any evaluation of the relevant policies must involve an evaluation of their health outcomes; and, if part of that evaluation concerns equity, then it is essential to have a conception of what constitutes an equitable health outcome. (Ibid., p.113)

Therefore the ideas of the valuable life and of the healthy life enter theories of social justice as their focus, and therefore are an indispensable element of them. There is, then, nothing incoherent in claiming that natural primary goods, health chances, should be a primary focus for theories of social justice.

However, the argument so far has only established that they *could* be such a focus, not that they *should* be. To show that they *should* be, the connection between the distribution of social primary goods, such as income and wealth, and the distribution of natural primary goods, such as health and vigour, needs to be established. This can be done by demonstrating a connection between people's social position and their health. There is overwhelming evidence from the United Kingdom that there is such a connection. Three reports -- the Black Report in 1980, *The Health Divide* in 1987, and the King's Trust Report *Tackling Inequalities* in 1997 [3] -- all display the connection between the distribution of wealth and the distribution of health.

The evidence shows that the health gap displays itself in three ways:

(1)     If a current-time slice is taken, there is a clear gap in life
        chances between the best off and worst off in terms of health,
        fitness and longevity.
(2)     If life-times are taken, then this gap widens from birth
        onwards.
(3)     If a longer time period is taken, then while the health of people
        in the United Kingdom has improved during the 20th century,
        the gap between the best off and the worst off has widened. It
        is this widening gap which represents "one of the biggest
        possible challenges" to any programme of social justice.
        (Townsend, Davidson and Whitehead eds., 1988, p.1)

The Black Report's data covered the period from 1931 to 1971,
and led it to conclude that men and women in Social Class V have a
two and a half times greater chance of dying before they reach
retirement age than those in Social Class I [4]. According to the
Report:

If we break it down by age we find that class differences in
mortality are a consistent feature of the entire human life-span.
They are found at birth, during the first year of life, in childhood,
adolescence and adult life. At *any* age people in occupational
Class V have a higher rate of death than their better-off
counterparts. (Ibid., p.43)

And:

At birth and in the first month of life twice as many babies of
unskilled manual parents as of professional parents die, and in the
next eleven months of life nearly three times as many boys and
more than three times as many girls, respectively, die. In later
years of childhood the ratio of deaths in the poorest class falls to
between one and a half and two times that of the wealthiest class,
but increases again in early adulthood before falling again in
middle and old age. (Ibid., p.55-56)

Among the Report's conclusions is the statement:

We do not believe there to be any single and *simple explanation* of
the complex data we have assembled. While there are a number of
quite distinct theoretical approaches to explanation, we wish to
stress the importance of differences in material conditions of life.

170

*In our view much of the evidence on social inequalities in health can be adequately understood in terms of specific features of the socio-economic environment*: features...which are strongly class-related in Britain and also have clear causal significance. (Ibid., p.199)

*The Health Divide* examined data made available after the Black Report, and concluded that the evidence:

...confirms that serious social inequalities in health have persisted into the 1980s. Whether social position is measured by occupational class, or by assets such as house and car ownership, or by employment status, a similar picture emerges. Those at the bottom of the social scale have much higher death rates than those at the top. This applies at every stage of life from birth through to adulthood and well into old age.

Neither is it just a few specific conditions which account for these higher death rates. All the major killer diseases now effect the poor more than the rich (and so do most of the less common ones). The less favoured occupational classes also experience higher rates of chronic illness and their children tend to have lower birth-weights, shorter stature and other indicators suggesting poorer health status.

The unemployed and their families have considerably worse physical and mental health than those in work. Until recently, however, direct evidence that unemployment *caused* this poorer health was not available. Now there is substantial evidence of unemployment causing a deterioration in mental health, with improvements observed on re-employment. (Ibid., pp.351-352)

The reports also looked at evidence of "significant social inequalities in the availability and use of health services" provided by the State, despite the principle of treatment free at the point of delivery (Ibid., p.68). The Black Report concluded that:

Inequalities exist...in the utilization of health services, particularly and most worryingly of the preventative services. Here, severe under-utilization by the working classes is a complex result of under-provision in working class areas and of costs (financial and psychological) of attendance which are not, in this case, outweighed by disruption of normal activities by sickness. (Ibid., p.198)

This zero-sum aspect of public health provision has been described as the Inverse Care Law:

> In areas with most sickness and death, general practitioners have more work, larger lists, less hospital support, and inherit more clinically ineffective traditions of consultation than in the healthiest areas; and hospital doctors shoulder heavier case loads with less staff and equipment, more obsolete buildings, and suffer recurrent crises in the availability of beds and replacement staff. These trends can be summed up as the inverse care law: that the availability of good medical care tends to vary inversely with the need of the population served. (Hart, 1971)

Although health resources are, largely, provided free at the point of use, secondary costs, both financial and psychological, determine unequal access. In order to to gain access to the public service, the individual must have access to a range of other resources: transport, clothing, time off from the workplace or from the family, etc. Those best able to gain access to *those* resources will find it easiest to exploit the publicly provided service: and those are usually the better off in society. The worst off will be least able to afford transport, suitable clothing, time off from work or from family care, etc; and so they will make least use of the public health resources.

The most recent studies are making it clear that it is relative poverty, not absolute poverty, that is having the greatest impact on health in developed countries -- inequality in itself damages people's health prospects. Andrew Haines and Richard Smith comment:

> We are beginning to understand that, for developed countries, relative poverty (having an income substantially below the mean for that society) is a more important influence on health than absolute poverty (lacking the basic means to live). (Haines and Smith, 1997, p.529) [5]

Inequality in the United Kingdom has grown, and according to the United Nations Development programme report in 1996 was one of the most unequal industrialized nations (Ibid.). Haines and Smith comment:

> Unskilled men now have a mortality three times that of professional men. This is a widening from a twofold differential in the early 1970s. In the 1980s this was equivalent to a five year

differential in life expectancy for men aged 20. Now it will be wider. (Ibid., p.529)

There is, then, overwhelming evidence in the United Kingdom that inequality of social primary goods such as income and wealth is a major factor in the distribution of natural primary goods, such as health, fitness and longevity. There is therefore every reason to have natural primary goods as one of the primary subjects of the theory of social justice: one of the major reasons for the redistribution of social primary goods is to bring about a redistribution of natural primary goods.

This reflects on Rawls' use of the difference principle in two ways:

Firstly, the principle depends on an over-simplistic conception of inequality. Inequality in modern western societies is far more complex than Rawls allows. This makes it very difficult identify who the worst off are and how to calculate an improvement in their position. And this makes it far more difficult to *calculate* the operation of the difference principle.

Secondly, if one of the costs of inequality is in terms of health, fitness and longevity, this makes it far more difficult to *justify* the operation of the difference principle -- the scope for justifiable departures from equality may be far narrower than Rawls' theory envisaged.

## Section 6.4 -- Inequality and Participation

The argument of this chapter is that inequalities can carry costs which must be taken into account when weighing up their benefits, and the previous section presented evidence of one of those costs: the connection between inequalities of wealth and inequalities of health, damage to the value of life chances in a very literal sense. This section presents evidence of another cost of inequality: the damage it causes to the value of one's membership of the community. If membership is as valuable as was suggested in section 6.1, and is as closely connected to freedom as has been argued throughout this book, then this is a very heavy price to pay for whatever benefits inequalities might bring.

In a publication entitled *Excluding the Poor*, issued by the Child Poverty Action Group in 1986, writers describe the ways in which poverty excludes people from society. Peter Golding, the editor of the publication, comments: "Poverty excludes, and not least it excludes from power and influence" (Golding ed., 1986, p.x). Peter Townsend argues that poverty has a dual nature: material deprivation and political powerlessness. It therefore calls for a twin attack, both on systems of distribution of resources that marginalize certain groups, and upon the social and political institutions that deprive those groups of the power to fight their marginalization. People need levels of resources which not merely allow them to meet their basic needs, but which also allow them to "fulfil what is expected of them at the workplace, in the home, the family and the community, and as local as well as national citizens" (Ibid., pp.v-vi). And in a paper entitled "Drawing the Line: on Defining the Poverty Threshold", Megnhad Desai states: "...economic entitlement to an adequate standard of living should be such that citizens can take full part in the political community. Not to give this is tantamount to a denial of political rights" (Ibid., 1986, p.3).

The worst off in the community are excluded, to a lesser or greater extent, from many of its values: health and fitness, work, transport, leisure, culture, information, political and community activity, etc. These are all ways of actively participating in the community, and inequality of resources makes access to them problematic. As Sir Isaiah Berlin comments: "The extent of a man's negative liberty is, as it were, a function of what doors, and how many, are open to him; upon what prospect they open; and how open they are" (Berlin, 1969, p.xlviii). A door can be firmly locked to prevent access; or, if it unlocked, people may lack the power to push it open. Political repression may firmly lock doors, poverty drains the power to open them. In *Excluding the Poor* writers look at the ways in which the worst off are generally excluded from dimensions of active participation, such as leisure, culture, communication, information, and political and community activity.


*6.4.1 -- Leisure and Culture*

Alan Tomlinson writes: "...it is the accessibility of different groups to commodity culture which is the major dividing line between the privileged and the poor" (Golding ed., 1986, p.46). If leisure and culture are commodified, then they must respond primarily to purchasing power in the market, and loss of purchasing power means loss of access to leisure and culture. Access to sports facilities, cinemas, theatres, musical events, museums, art galleries, etc., becomes restricted, both in terms of the primary costs of entrance fees, but also in terms of the secondary costs such as transport, time from

174

work or from the family, equipment, and clothing. To the extent that these leisure and cultural activities and centres are an important aspect of the community, the loss of access to them constitutes a loss of access to the community itself.

## 6.4.2 -- Information

Graham Murdock writes: "...because adequate information is a basic precondition for real choice and effective political participation, ensuring its diversity and accessibility to all groups in society has to be a core concern of social and cultural policy" (Ibid., p.83). However, access to information is becoming increasingly reliant on access to technology, and there is a division between the information technology available in the market, and public and voluntary supply of information. Most can choose either to depend upon the public sector or buy access to the latest information technology in the market, or depend on a mixture of the two. The worst off do not have that choice: they are dependent on public and voluntary provision of information, and even then much of that information may be issued through technology to which they have little access. Equally problematic, as there is a movement to greater market provision of information, support is withdrawn from the public and voluntary sectors: public libraries and voluntary information centres become more scarce. Therefore the worst off are excluded twice over: "They are priced out of the markets for the new commercial information services and left with an impoverished and overstretched system of public provision which is increasingly unable to meet either their demands or their needs" (Ibid., p.70). [This is another illustration of Nicholas Barr's argument that the value of one's income is affected by the value of the income of others -- that the value of one's income can decrease if everybody's income increases.]

For example the television has become a fundamental source of information in the community -- but here there is the dual information system Murdock describes (Ibid., p.82). The poor are priced out of the technology market and "left with a structure of public provision that is increasingly unable or unwilling to deliver the range of general information required for full citizenship" (Ibid., p.82). If information is one of the basic requirements if someone is to be an active chooser, doer and participator in the community, then to be deprived of access to that information through market forces may injure one's ability to be a full member of the community as much as political censorship.

### 6.4.3 -- Communication

The telephone now plays a fundamental role in communication within the community, so much so that major organizations assume that people have access to one, and build their services around that assumption. Access to a telephone can save precious time in getting hold of information and advice: someone without access to a phone will often face a long trip simply to make an appointment, let alone to have access to the information. The telephone also provides a vital link to family and friends for those isolated through disability, poverty, ill health or old age. In 1984, 78% of all households had a telephone, but only 48% of single pensioners possessed one.

### 6.4.4 -- Political and Community Activity

All the factors listed so far can undermine one's capacity to be an active member of the community, but poverty can more undermine attempts to be politically or communally active more directly. Sue Ward writes:

> The methods by which policy is made and fought for, individuals selected for office, essential political work carried out, all presuppose a fair amount of money at one's independent command, over and above the amount needed simply for survival. (Ibid., p.33)

Being politically active costs money: there are costs of membership, transport to meetings, child care, costs of literature, of participating in social and fund raising events. Of course, one does not have to do many of these things in order to be a member of a political or community group, but the extent to which one is thought of as a full member of the group will depend upon this kind of participation.

One of the most precious resources for any activity is time. As Sue Ward points out:

> Being poor takes up an enormous amount of time and energy. You must walk to your meeting, or take three buses, rather than even the occasional taxi. You must buy cheaper, less convenient, food, or else less nourishing 'junk food' that is going to sap your energy in the long run. The food must cook slowly, and then you have to wash the dishes, rather than just switching on first the micro wave and then the dishwasher. You must tramp around

jumble sales and junk shops for your clothes and household equipment. You certainly can't afford someone to clean for you.

If you have children, they will be underfoot constantly, because getting them out of the way costs money...

Nor does the affluent person have an exhausting tramp around council offices and DHSS waiting rooms hunting for means- and stamina-tested benefits. The more financial trouble you get into, the more it eats into your time. Being taken to court for non-payment of rent must be the ultimate time-wasting occupation. All this is compounded by cuts in public services that might otherwise compensate the poor -- and save them time -- like public transport, school meals and libraries. (Ibid., pp.37-38)

Lack of these resources means lack of the ability to be an active member of the community, such that the loss of access to them constitutes a loss of access to the community itself. Michael Walzer comments: "The community is itself a good -- conceivably the most important good -- that gets distributed" (Walzer, 1983, p.29).

## Section 6.5 -- Social Justice as Compensation

The first half of this chapter has shown that material inequality damages membership of the community, and therefore undermines liberty: it excludes people from being equally active choosers, doers and participators of their community, therefore bringing about a particular form of deprivation. Equality of membership therefore demands *substantive* equality. The second half of the chapter examines a particular response to this form of deprivation that can be found through liberal political theory and informs theories of social justice, the idea of compensation. The problem here is the relationship between liberal political theory and the capitalist market, and how liberal theory attempts to reconcile its commitment to the moral equality of persons with the economic and social inequalities produced and required by the capitalist market system -- this is, of course, the problem of social justice as defined within contemporary liberal political theory.

One way to deal with this seeming contradiction is to set up a distinction between the political sphere and the economic sphere, between the public world and the private world, and to insist that what is required in order to respect equality of membership is equality as 'citizens' within the political sphere, not equality in the economic sphere: members are public equals, but in private there can be no enforcement of such an order. However, this distinction does not work: few would seriously argue that equal political citizenship can be maintained in the face of the radical economic inequalities to be found in liberal-capitalist states -- and so the original problem returns; how can liberal theory reconcile loss of equality as citizens with its commitment to moral equality of persons? But it should be noted that even if the public/private distinction did make sense here, it does not solve the problem: if the commitment to equal moral worth of persons entails political equality, why does it not entail social and economic equality, the equality of life-chances? How can a line be drawn between the value of a person's life in the political sphere and the value of their life in the social and economic sphere, such that the former must be equal with others, while the latter need not be? What can justify this difference in commitment?

An alternative response is to claim that the primary political value is liberty, and that the capitalist market is the best regime of equal liberty -- equal liberty is not compatible with social or economic equality. However, this response only ensures equal liberty by appeal to the purely negative definition of liberty; and, more importantly, it is a distortion of the essentials of liberal political philosophy -- the fundamental commitment of liberal theory is to the moral equality of persons, not liberty.

Rather, the characteristic response of liberal theory is the recognition that moral equality, and equality of membership, are undermined by economic and social inequality; and the claim that equality is respected by compensating those whose equality has been undermined through no fault of their own within the capitalist market place, by redistributive welfare strategies. More weakly, the equal moral value of persons is *acknowledged* through such compensation, in that it is recognized that something is owed people for the loss of their equality through capitalism: but it is conceded that their equality cannot be completely restored -- rather, the compensation is an acknowledgement for the loss. Whether liberal compensatory redistribution can deliver the stronger thesis or only the weaker version is, of course, a crucially important question.

This emphasis upon achieving the demands of social justice through compensatory redistribution re-occurs throughout contemporary liberal texts. John Gray, as self-appointed spokesperson for what he calls the classical liberal tradition, says: "...the moral defence of liberty requires rectification of past injustices..." (Gray, 1986, p.89). The aim of policy should be to "compensate for past departures from equal liberty" (Ibid., p.88). Robert Nozick,

178

representing the minimal state position, concedes that "past injustices might be so great as to make necessary in the short run a more extensive state in order to rectify them" (Nozick, 1974, p.231). John Rawls, representing the welfare liberal position, says his theory of justice is about the "basic structure" of society, that is "the institutions that define the social background and includes as well those operations that continually adjust and compensate for the inevitable tendencies away from background fairness..." (Rawls, 1978, p.54). Ronald Dworkin talks in terms of insurance, suggesting "a tax scheme constructed as a practical translation of a hypothetical insurance market, which assumes equal initial assets and equal risk..." (Dworkin, 1981, pp.326-327); but insurance is a compensation scheme, and Dworkin does use the language of compensation, especially when discussing those suffering physical handicap (Ibid., pp.296-304).

It should be noted, though, that there is an important difference between the accounts of compensatory redistribution given by 'classical' or 'libertarian' liberals like Gray and Nozick, and by 'welfare' liberals like Rawls and Dworkin. For the former, there is a one-off, large scale redistribution to compensate for all the past injustices that have occured, and then the free market is left to run unimpeded from this situation of initial fairness. For the latter, there is the same large scale compensatory redistribution at the start, but it is followed by an ongoing programme of redistribution, on a much smaller scale, in order to maintain fairness.

This emphasis upon achieving the demands of social justice through compensation tends to tie liberal theory down to an after-the-event view of social justice, an essentially backward-looking view. One response is to claim that justice *is* essentially backward-looking, and therefore any programme of social justice must itself be backward-looking. Any programme that aims to secure people's *future* welfare without reference to their past may be justifiable in some other terms, but it has nothing to do with justice. Genuine theories of social justice are therefore purely backward-looking: one example is Nozick's entitlement theory (Nozick, 1974, pp.149-182). According to Antony Flew, this is all justice amounts to: "...the notion of justice is necessarily backward-looking" (Flew, 1985, p.193); and he contrasts this with the "ideal of equality of outcome, equality of welfare", which "is by contrast essentially forward-looking" (Ibid., p.193).

However, the situation is more complex than this: three different perspectives on social justice can be distinguished -- backward-looking, present-looking and forward-looking views:

(1)     Backward-looking views see social justice as a matter of compensation for past departures from justice -- welfare strategies are methods of compensation aiming to repair the damage caused to life chances by those past departures.

(2)     Present-looking views see social justice as a matter of distributing resources so that they fit some ideal pattern, e.g. equality -- welfare strategies aim to restore the ideal pattern after departures from it.

(3)     Forward-looking views see social justice as a matter of securing future welfare -- the object of welfare strategies is to lay the ground for that future welfare.

The weakness of Flew's claim is that the forward-looking view is to an important extent the corollary of the backward-looking view. Nani L. Ranken points out that: "since the reparation presupposes the *recognition* of the wrong, that very recognition entails a duty to take steps to prevent the repetition of the wrong" (Ranken, 1986, p.113). And: "...any sincere efforts to compensate for the wrongs caused by such practices must include efforts to change the conditions that perpetuate the practices" (Ibid.). This severely undermines the position of those like Flew, Nozick and Gray who urge a one-dimensional view of social justice as purely after-the-event compensation. Also, the backward-looking view they endorse is extremely thin. As we have seen, Gray concedes the need for the rectification of past injustices -- the actual distribution of resources in the community has come about through many factors, "including previous acts of injustice in the form of violations of property rights, restrictions on contractual liberty, and inequitable uses of economic power". Rectification of these past injustices can take place "by a renegotiation of established rights" (Gray, 1986, p.89). Note that Gray limits such claims to compensation by stating that the only past injustices which count are violations of classical liberal rights, such as private property rights -- but the past injustice may lie in the inadequacy of these rights in ensuring the equal value of membership and protecting against "inequitable uses of economic power". An adequate conception of social justice will, therefore, consist of more than only the backward-looking view, and will also take a more comprehensive view of what counts as injustice.

In the end, the backward-looking view is concerned with past unfairnesses, and is restricted to compensation or redress for what happened. But the present and future-looking views are not so restricted: present conditions can be altered and future conditions can be prevented or created. Liberal theory is usually willing to take all three perspectives, and yet the emphasis is still on social justice as compensation. The implication of this is that misfortunes are allowed to befall people rather than altered or prevented. The only justifications for taking this option are either that the present conditions are inalterable and the future conditions are unpreventable or unpredictable; or that the cost of alteration or prevention or creation is too high -- it is cheaper to compensate. While the first possibility would impose a genuine constraint on what can be done in the name of social justice, the second possibility creates a much weaker constraint: the most expensive option may also be the most just, and, all things considered, the one that ought to be taken.

Why the emphasis on social justice as compensation in welfare-liberal writings? The answer lies partly in the liberal view of capitalist markets, and why some people do well in them while others do badly (Kymlicka, 1990, pp.85-86). For the liberal, people's life chances should be shaped by their free choices, rather than determined by the circumstances in which they find themselves: an ideal market allows life chances to be shaped by free choices made by fully rational agents under conditions of full information, and in equal political, social and economic starting positions. But, of course, the real-world market is not like this at all -- it allows circumstances to play a significant role in determining life prospects. The differences in circumstances between people are largely the product of natural, social and historical accident, and are therefore arbitrary from a moral point of view: people do not deserve them and so do not deserve the social position they determine. It would therefore be unjust to allow arbitrary circumstances to determine the value of life chances. John Rawls says:

> What the theory of justice must regulate is the inequalities in life-prospects between citizens that arise from social starting-positions, natural advantages and historical contingencies.

These, for Rawls, are the "fundamental" inequalities (Rawls, 1978, p.56): there is a moral obligation to prevent them from undermining the value of people's life chances. However, the best way to deal with these inequalities is not to limit the market freedom of those who have been arbitrarily advantaged: this would entail heavy-handed start intervention in the market, and interference with individual liberty. Rather, there should be a system of welfare through which those who do badly because of their arbitrary disadvantages are compensated by those who do well. For example, John Rawls says:

No one deserves his greater natural capacity nor merits a more favorable starting position in society. But it does not follow that one should eliminate these distinctions. There is another way to deal with them. The basic structure can be arranged so that these contingencies work for the good of the least fortunate. (Rawls, 1972, pp.101-102)

Of his difference principle strategy, he says that it sets up a:

...social system so that no one gains or loses from his arbitrary place in the distribution of natural assets or his initial position in society without giving or receiving compensating advantages in return. (Ibid., p.102)

He wants a system:

...which does not weight men's share in the benefits and burdens of social cooperation according to their social fortune or their luck in the natural lottery... (Ibid., p.75)

And so welfare liberal theory takes a distinctly benevolent view of the worst off in capitalist societies: by and large their position is not their fault -- it is a matter of bad luck. And, as people do not deserve bad luck (neither do they deserve good luck), it is appropriate to compensate them for their misfortune. Of course, there is still an extent to which people earn their position in capitalist markets, and therefore deserve the market outcomes they aim for: indeed, Dworkin distinguishes between what he calls option luck, "a matter of how deliberate and calculated gambles turn out..." (Dworkin, 1981, p.293), and brute bad luck, which is unpredictable misfortune. What is important, though, is the claim that market outcomes are significantly determined by luck, brutely bad or otherwise, and therefore are not, to that extent, deserved. Julian Le Grand comments: "...it seems to be regarded as inequitable if individuals receive less than others because of factors *beyond their control*" (Le Grand, 1981, p.86). And:

Distributions that are the outcome of factors beyond individual control are generally considered inequitable; distributions that are the outcome of individual choices are not. (Ibid., p.87)

This view of the worst off and the compensatory role of welfare can be contrasted with a much harsher view of the worst off in capitalist markets. Their situation can be seen as the result of their own shortcomings: they lack the qualities needed to succeed in the competitive market system and this makes them failures in a normative sense. Provided there is freedom to compete for scarce resources in the market, people will deserve what they get, whatever it is. It could be said that this position holds a view the 'virtuous person': the person who has the qualities needed to succeed in the market. The free rider problem seen from this perspective is a matter of "...the virtuous citizenry...robbed by the few who prefer a parasitic life to one of hard work"; the issue of welfare becomes "a confrontation between parasitism and the work ethic..." (Wolin, 1987, p.475) [6]. If this view of the worst off is taken, then there seems no reason of justice to have a welfare system at all. The worst off have no *claim* to welfare: they deserve what they have got -- they can have no *rights* against those who have succeeded. Any welfare the successful provide will be equivalent to charity. In fact, because from this perspective welfare is charity, its provision can be left to charity organizations, and the state need only step in where private charity cannot cope. State welfare systems can even be made to operate like private charities -- with a specific amount of money in a 'social fund', such that once all the money has been claimed and the fund is empty, subsequent claimants have no claims.

There could be other motives for having a welfare system from this point of view. For example, it could be argued that if people are allowed to fall into the depths of deprivation, then social conditions for unrest and disorder will be created. To avoid these threats to social order, a welfare system is provided to act as a safety net, specifying a minimum level below which people should not fall. That level can be calculated by reference to the level of poverty the social system can tolerate before destabilizing or losing its legitimacy. This is to see the welfare system as a pay-off to the worst off to ensure that they do not disrupt an economic system that is working in the interests of the most powerful -- a pay-off which the worst off are in no position to refuse.

Another argument for a welfare system could be this: A framework of welfare can be used as a system of discipline, exerting power and control over the worst off. If it is made particularly difficult to obtain welfare payments, either through bureaucracy or through long delays in entitlement, then people can be forced back into the labour market at lower wages; only the most hopeless and helpless will persist in claiming. Such a welfare system gives close economic and social control over people's lives: they can be made to attend particular places at particular times; forced to live in certain areas; their private lives can be spied on to detect fraudulent claims; information can be kept on them; they can be kept in a state of uncertainty and anxiety so that they are rendered powerless to make long term plans or to have long term commitments. This kind of welfare system can operate as a system of power, control and discipline over certain sections of the community. A practical example of this is how the social security system in Britain has been increasingly used as a reinforcement of immigration control, such that:

> ...entitlement to education, social security and other benefits and services has become increasingly dependent upon immigration status and in which it has become legitimate for a range of officials to question claimants and others about their status and thus act as agents of immigration control. (Gordon, 1989, pp.7-8)

If this less benevolent view of the worst off is taken, then the welfare framework emerges as a mixture of a system of charity, a one-sided pay-off for the sake of social stability, and an system of discipline and control. Therefore there are three models of welfare at work here: the Charity Model; the Stability Model; and the Power/Control Model. In contrast, the Compensation Model characteristic of liberal theory takes a very different and more benevolent view of the worst off under capitalism: it is, by and large, not their fault, and it is appropriate to compensate such people through a redistributive welfare system.

## Section 6.6 -- Two Forms of Bad Luck

What is so objectionable about the compensatory approach to social justice? It seems a reasonable alternative to the more harsh approach described above. There are at least two problems: (i) Are the 'fundamental inequalities' Rawls talks of really the result of bad luck? (ii) What are the consequences of treating these fundamental inequalities as if they were the result of bad luck?

The first problem, then, is whether the situation of the worst off in capitalist societies is actually the result of anything that could coherently be described as bad luck or misfortune. When assessing a distribution of outcomes, there are two variables that must be kept in mind: firstly the extent to which those outcomes were determined by the agent's own choices; and secondly, the extent to which they were determined by factors beyond the agent's control. As Le Grand pointed out (section 6.5), the question of justice only arises for the second variable. However, if this aspect of capitalist market outcomes is going to be characterized in terms of good or bad luck, then are are two levels of market misfortune that must be distinguished. The first is where the market agent can normally be expected to secure the conditions for a valuable life, whatever it is, under her own powers; but she is thwarted by market forces beyond her control and comprehension -- she cannot be blamed for her market failure. This is the person who has no problem in finding reasonable employment in the market, but is made redundant, for example as the result of some crisis striking the company she works for that she could not have foreseen. The second level of market misfortune is where the market agent lacks the powers needed to secure the conditions for a valuable life: full market agency is out of the question, but again this is not her fault in any sense. A example would be the person who is so physically disabled that they cannot gain access to work.

These two forms of market misfortune are obviously different, so different that it may not be appropriate to deal with them in the same way. In the first kind of case, where the market agent possesses the powers needed to compete for the conditions she needs for the valuable life, but has been struck down by market forces, it can be assumed that her crisis is temporary, and that she will be able to re-establish herself in the market system. The function of the welfare system in this case is to offer the market agent basic support until she can re-establish herself in the market -- it becomes a system of temporary crisis-management. It is not, nor should it be, the task of such a welfare system to provide the conditions for human flourishing; that, in this kind of case, can be left to the market. The most appropriate way to deal with such market misfortune is to set up a system whereby everybody contributes to a central fund from which they can claim whenever a crisis hits them -- a national insurance system. The assumption, then, is that this kind of misfortune can hit anybody at any time, and that market agents, once they are over such misfortune, can once more gain the conditions for their life prospects within the capitalist market. Such a system of compulsory insurance may also be appropriate for cases of what Dworkin called "option luck" -- "a matter of how deliberate and calculated gambles turn out" (see section 6.5), to the extent that employment is a gamble. Julian Le Grand discusses the example of an economic situation where there is a five per cent risk of involuntary long-term unemployment (Le Grand, 1991, pp.98-100). The state offers a voluntary unemployment insurance scheme, which offers full compensation for unemployment. Some workers join the scheme and some do not, and five per cent of those that do are hit by unemployment, as are five per cent of those that do not. The five per cent who did not take out the scheme receive no compensation and so are close to starvation. However, Le Grand points out that those who did not join the scheme and became unemployed "are the victims not solely of their own choices, but, at least in one sense, of bad luck. Hence, their situation is in large part an outcome of factors beyond their control" (Ibid., p.99). They could not have predicted that they would be within the five per cent of non-contributers who became unemployed rather part of the 95 per cent who did not. The solution, argues Le Grand, is to use the economic conception of 'expected value', "the value of the outcome itself multiplied by the probability of the outcome actually occurring" (Le Grand, 1991, p.99). If the total loss of being unemployed is £10,000, then the expected value of the loss is five per cent of £10,000, which is £500. Le Grand's conclusion is:

> ...it seems reasonable to hold people responsible for the expected value of an uncertain outcome, *whether or not* the outcome actually occurs. In the situation described in our example, this could be achieved by compelling all individuals to join the state insurance scheme and charging a premium equal to the expected value. In that case, everyone would simply bear the financial cost of being unemployed, not only the five per cent unemployed themselves: an outcome that seems fair, given the fact that the unemployment is involuntary. (Ibid., p.99)

So even where employment and the risks of losing it are seen as an issue of option luck rather than brute bad luck, a compulsory state insurance scheme for all seems the fairest option. And as Le Grand's example shows, the boundary between option luck and brute bad luck is not clear here: it may be an option to gamble on a certain kind of employment, but whether or not one loses that employment seems down to brute luck.

The second kind of bad luck is more difficult to deal with, and looks more clearly like brute bad luck. The most obvious problem here is that the fundamental inequalities for certain groups are not temporary crises through which they can be expected to pass -- such people are excluded from the capitalist market as such. Their crisis is therefore permanent, and unless the welfare system does supply them with the conditions required for human flourishing, these agents will be unable to secure them elsewhere, except perhaps through charity. This is a serious problem: to fail to supply the conditions for valuable life prospects through a welfare system is in effect to write such groups off altogether. Their status as equally valued persons is therefore questionable.

However, notice that this problem effectively undermines the fairness of the national insurance scheme designed to deal with the first level of bad luck. The 'fundamental inequalities' will have varying effects on the market performance of people, and therefore upon their capacity to contribute to the insurance scheme. This kind of insurance system connects welfare with the power to contribute to such schemes through employment, and this disadvantages certain groups whose employment record is interrupted through no fault of their own. This leads Hermione Parker to comment that:

> Social insurance is a system of exclusion, because those who are not insured, or who have not paid sufficient contributions, or who fail any of the other manifold requirements, are ineligible or receive substandard amounts. (Parker, 1989, p.89)

And Ruth Lister says: "...social insurance serves to mirror the inequalities of the labour market to the advantage of the strong and the detriment of the weak" (Lister, 1990, p.53). And so the national compulsory insurance scheme, designed to deal with the ethical problems of the capitalist market, actually reflects one of the fundamental problems of that market -- that those in most need are in the weakest position and so least able to contribute, and therefore receive the least benefits; while those in least need are in the strongest position to contribute, and so receive the most benefits.

Another difficulty is that the fundamental inequalities arise from natural advantages and historical processes, but these are very broad and ill-defined notions, and it is questionable whether their effects on social starting positions should be seen in terms of bad luck at all. For example, one's health is a natural feature that can act as an advantage or disadvantage in the capitalist market. Rawls writes of these natural features as distributed through the "natural lottery", thus implying that they are distributed throughout the population at random. But as was seen in section 6.3, the overwhelming evidence is that levels of wealth and levels of health are linked. The problem, therefore, is not simply that one's health can undermine one's ability to compete in the capitalist market, but that the capitalist market undermines the health of certain groups within it. That evidence makes it implausible to see the issue of health and its effects on life chances as a matter of luck, and the same problem applies to the other 'fundamental' inequalities -- it is not that they strike the population at random; capitalism creates such problems, and it constructs them as problems, and it does so on the basis of class.

There are two possible replies here. Firstly, although it may be shown that a particular disease strikes at a particular section of the community systematically and predictably, and its causes are well known and documented, the fact that one is a member of that section of the community, and the fact that one is a member of it that does get struck by the disease, are both dimensions of bad luck. Therefore it does make sense to talk of bad luck here. However, the argument taking place is whether the restriction of strategies of social justice to after-the-event compensation can be justified: in section 6.5 it was argued that the only justifications for taking this option are either that the present conditions are inalterable and the future conditions are unpreventable or unpredictable; or that the cost of alteration or prevention or creation is too high; and that while the first possibility imposes a genuine constraint on what can be done in the name of social justice, the second possibility does not necessarily. The point of characterizing these outcomes as bad luck is to justify the strategy of compensation by appeal to the first justification: bad luck is unpredictable, and therefore can *only* be compensated for. But while there are dimensions of bad luck here, these are not dimensions that can justifiably limit the state to after-the-event compensation: there *are* at least two other options -- either one can be removed from that group, and therefore removed from risk; or the causes of the disease can be tackled, and the whole group removed from risk. The only argument for preferring after-the-event compensation over the removal from or prevention of risk strategies must be that it is less expensive, and this is a very limited and controversial justification.

The second possible reply is that the argument from bad luck has been misunderstood. Clearly, Rawls does talk of "social misfortune" and of people's "luck in the natural lottery" (Rawls, 1972, p.100); but this can be set aside. Rather, while it is obviously wrong to characterize these fundamental inequalities as accidental or the outcomes of bad luck, rather than as the outcomes of planned and/or predictable processes, it may not be wrong to deal with them as though they were. Clearly, this is the procedure Rawls in particular follows with his device of the original position and the veil of ignorance (Ibid., pp.136-142): people are placed in a position where they cannot know what their social position or plan of life will be, and must choose the most appropriate principles on that basis. This is, in effect, to treat one's social position and the inequalities attached to it as a matter of brute bad luck.

The question is then, not whether these fundamental inequalities *are* the outcomes of brute bad luck, but whether they should be treated as though they were. One obvious difficulty is that this perspective does limit social justice to after-the-event compensation, rather than alteration and prevention. It is to treat the conditions of injustice as though they were inalterable, unpreventable or unpredictable. Indeed, it is to treat social justice as misfortune, when the two are very different: people have claims of right against injustice, but have no claims of right against misfortune, only claims of insurance or benevolence. As Nicholas Barr comments: "Bad luck may require remedial action, but does not imply that society is unfair" (Barr, 1987, p.141). So there are at least two distortions: (a) seeing injustice as misfortune; and (b) seeing the conditions of injustice as inalterable, unpreventable or unpredictable. Such distortions are unacceptable, as they place the recipients of welfare under capitalism in a very precarious position: they are left only with claims of benevolence, not with claims of right. To be reliant upon benevolence is a much more precarious position than to be reliant upon rightful welfare, in that claims of benevolence are hardly *claims* at all: benevolence cannot be demanded, only requested, and such requests do not give rise to duties in any significant sense. This is, in effect, to leave the worst off outside the boundaries of social justice altogether.


## Section 6.7 -- Conclusion

This chapter has identified a certain form of deprivation: the exclusion of certain groups from full participation within society's institutions and practices -- in other words, the deprivation of the opportunity to be an active member of the community. As freedom within a community requires active participation, this form of deprivation includes the absence of liberty. However, it has been shown that such groups are not only excluded from participation in certain institutions and practices, they are also excluded at the level of theory. In Part 1 of this book, the reluctance to include the issue of physical disability within the boundaries of freedom-talk was noted: this is allegedly not an issue of freedom, but of social justice. It was argued that this is a mistake, and that groups like the physically disabled can coherently be included within the theory of freedom. But even if the point is conceded and the issue is seen as one of social justice, the same problem remains -- for such groups are excluded from theories of social justice too. Such groups exist in the margins of society and in the footnotes of texts. This is John Rawls' position, described in a footnote:

> ...since the fundamental problem of justice concerns the relations among those who are full and active participants in society, and directly or indirectly associated together over the course of a whole life, it is reasonable to assume that every one has physical needs and physiological capacities within some normal range. Thus the problem of special health care and how to treat the mentally defective are laid aside. If we can work out a viable theory for the normal range, we can attempt to handle these other cases later. (Rawls, 1978, p.70 note 9)

Elsewhere he describes the subjects of his theory as "being full participants in social cooperation throughout their lives" (Rawls, 1980, p.546).

Rawls' position is reflected in the social contract tradition, which sees the need for a social compact only between equally powerful parties -- the need arises, not because of the good people can do for each other, but because of the danger we oppose to each other. Thomas Hobbes states:

> Nature hath made men so equall, in the faculties of body and mind; as that though there bee found one man sometimes manifestly stronger in body, or of quicker mind than another; ... the difference between man, and man, is not so considerable as that one man can thereupon claim to himselfe any benefit, to which another man may not pretend, as well as he. For as to strength of body, the weakest has strength to kill the strongest, either by secret machination, or by confederacy with others, that are in the same danger with himselfe. (Hobbes, 1968, p.183)

Of mental faculties, Hobbes says: "I find greater equality amongst men, than that of strength" (Ibid.). And John Locke observes that when God made the world, "He gave it to the use of the industrious and rational (and *labour* was to be *his title* to it)" (Locke, 1924, p.132). So the earth was given by God to the 'normal range'.

David Hume clearly expresses the point that the contract is required because of the threat people pose to each other -- where there is no threat, there is no need for contract, and indeed no need for justice:

Were there a species of creatures intermingled with men, which, though rational, were possessed of such inferior strength, both of body and mind, that they were incapable of all resistance, and could never, upon the highest provocation, make us feel the effects of their resentment; the necessary consequence, I think, is that we should be bound by the laws of humanity to give gentle usage to these creatures, but should not, properly speaking, lie under any restraint of justice with regard to them... (Hume, 1975, p.190)

Therefore there can be no relationship of justice towards such people -- the able-bodied can do whatever they like to the mentally ill or handicapped, for example, as long as it is done in the name of giving 'gentle usage' to them; but they can be under no constraints of justice.

Of course, Rawls claims to have simply set the problem aside for now, with every intention of dealing with it later. However, there are two problems with such a response. Firstly, the very dynamic of social contract theory works against taking such persons into account -- the contract can only be between members of the specified normal range. Secondly, if the problem is laid aside when the theory of social justice is constructed, what guarantee is there that there will be any space in the theory to deal with it at some later stage -- such groups have, in effect, been excluded from the theory altogether. William Galston (Galston, 1991, note 7, pp.317-318) offers such a diagnosis of Rawls' position:

For more than a decade, critics such as A.K. Sen have argued that Rawls' theory is in principle incapable of dealing with the problem of special needs. To the best of my knowledge, Rawls has never offered a full response. The Dewey Lectures simply rule the question out of court. Rawls stipulates that no party in the original position 'suffers from unusual needs that are especially difficult to fulfil... [T]he fundamental problem of social justice arises between those who are full and active...participants in society' (Dewey Lectures, p.546). He goes on to talk vaguely about extending the theory, so conceived, to hard cases. But he never does so, and it is difficult to see how he could do so in a manner consistent with his basic approach. Unusual and costly needs present difficulties that simply cannot be addressed by an index of primary goods.

191

For Rawls, the normal range seems to consist of those who are able to be full and active participants, directly or indirectly associated with each other over the course of a whole life. This is an extraordinary way of dealing with the issue, for it is the ability to be a full and active participant in society which is at stake in the first place. Whether the physically disabled, for example, are able to take an active part in social cooperation depends on how that cooperation is organized. It must be arbitrary to take social cooperation as we find it, and specify that only those who are full and active participants in *this* form of social cooperation constitute the normal range for a theory of justice. Rawls seems to take the normal range as given: but it is not given -- it is socially, politically and culturally determined. Who is able to be an active and full participant in the community is the fundamental question of social justice.

For Rawls it seems that the question of who can take part fully in social cooperation is taken as settled by current practice -- the problem of social justice concerns the fair terms of cooperation in society, and the only persons entitled to participate in the choosing of those terms are those who are able to take an active part in that cooperation. But that issue, so far, is arbitrary from a moral point of view: it is the constitution of the normal range itself which must be subjected to critical attack. Certainly, at first sight, it might seem fair to claim that only those who participate in a cooperative enterprise ought to be allowed to choose its terms -- it would surely be unfair to allow outsiders who have no stake in the enterprise to have a say in laying down the rules for the participators. But this at-first-sight fairness is surely illusory. For the groups excluded are not *literally* outsiders -- they fall *within* the boundaries of community: and so the enterprise is arbitrarily excluding members of the community who want to participate and have a stake. The constitution of the normal range is therefore the fundamental question for the fair terms of social cooperation. For Rawls, those limits are arbitrarily given before the terms of social cooperation are negotiated. Therefore certain groups are excluded, not only from participation in social cooperation, but also from participation in the negotiation of the terms of that cooperation. The principles chosen will, therefore, reflect the interests of specific groups and will ignore the interests of excluded groups. Or, while the included may feel that have some obligations to the excluded, this will be to give them 'gentle usage', perhaps in terms of charitable care: they will not be "under any restraint of justice with regard to them." They are, therefore, placed beyond the limits of the theory of justice, just as they were placed beyond the limits of the theory of freedom.

192

Rawls has taken the step of demanding that all who take part in a cooperative enterprise should have the right to take part as equal negotiators in determining the terms of that practice, and this is in itself a radical step. However, he does not take the further step of demanding that all should have the right to be active participators. For Rawls, the *right* of negotiation comes with the *fact* of participation, but there is no *right* of participation [7].

The groups most vulnerable to exclusion from the community are the old, the unemployed, the sick and disabled, single parent families, the low paid, single women with aged parents, the poor in institutions, the mentally ill and handicapped, and racial minorities (Field, 1981, pp.49-60). These groups are handicapped in their struggle to gain access to social cooperation and its benefits and responsibilities -- they are excluded, more or less or absolutely, from work, from structures of community and political power and authority, from systems of resources such as health, housing and transport, and from values such as culture, leisure and communication. Far from enjoying the benefits of society without contributing, they bear a disproportionate burden of society's failures and inefficiencies. People deprived of active membership of their community are not simply deprived of access to systems of material resources, but of much else besides -- dignity, self-respect, the respect of others, independence, power, work, creativity, friendship, pleasure: values that go together to make up even a minimal conception of what makes life worth living. Their life chances are impoverished, not only in terms of material resources, but in terms of all these values and others. These values can be as scarce as material resources, and cannot be redistributed by a welfare system. And, of fundamental importance for the view of social justice as compensation that dominates liberal theory, their loss cannot be compensated for.

This chapter has established the connection between freedom and social justice through the idea of active membership of the community -- being an equally active chooser, doer and participator. It has established that there is a particular form of deprivation, through which people are deprived of the opportunity to be such active members, and are therefore excluded from participation in their community. It argued that the compensation approach to social justice cannot adequately address this form of deprivation, as it fails to restore the value of membership for those deprived of it, it merely attempts to compensate them for its loss. They are therefore placed beyond the limits of justice, and so in a highly vulnerable position in the community. The system of welfare cannot, therefore, merely be a system of compensation, but must be an expression of membership. And an essential component of that expression must be the provision of the conditions of liberty.


# Notes

[1]     Much of this section is spent, not in philosophical discussion, but in the presentation of empirical evidence for the connection between the distribution of wealth and the distribution of health in the United Kingdom. The justification for this is the importance of the evidence for understanding the true costs of inequality, and the lack of any serious acknowledgment of this connection in contemporary political philosophy.

[2]     I have simplified the example, hopefully without distorting its point.

[3]     The Black Report and *The Health Divide* were published as Townsend, Davidson and Whitehead eds. (1988) .

[4]     The social classes referred to are the Registrar General's categories:
I.      Professional (eg, accountant, doctor, lawyer).
II.     Intermediate (eg, manager, nurse, schoolteacher).
IIIN.   Skilled non-manual (eg, clerical worker, secretary, shop assistant).
IIIM.   Skilled manual (eg, bus driver, butcher, carpenter, coalface worker).
IV.     Partly skilled (eg, agricultural worker, bus conductor, postman).
V.      Unskilled (eg, cleaner, dockworker, labourer).

[5]     This special issue of the *British Medical Journal* contains a range of papers providing evidence for the claim made by Haines and Smith. See also R.G.Wilkinson (1996).

[6]     It should be made clear that Wolin is simply reporting the prevalence of such a view in the United States during a specific period, not endorsing it.

[7]     Rawls' position seems to be that only those who have a *stake* in the enterprise can have a say. This perhaps reflects arguments about the extension of the franchise that took place in England in the 17th century following the Civil War, when it was considered that only those who possessed a certain level property were entitled to the franchise, because only such people had a stake in the community. C. B. Macpherson argues that this was in fact the position of even the Levellers, the 'radical' wing of the debate:
"...the right to a voice in elections did not inhere in everyone, for not everyone had retained that part of his human freedom which consisted in his property and his own labour. The franchise was needed and could be claimed only by those who had retained that property, and whose economic life was consequently one of active enterprise..." (Macpherson, 1962, pp.145-146).

# 7 Freedom and Welfare

## Section 7.1 -- Introduction

The claim being made here is that there is a positive connection between freedom and social justice, such that it must be part of any programme of social justice to secure the conditions of freedom. Liberty within a community consists of being an active chooser, doer and participator in that community, and therefore any programme of social justice must, amongst other goals, aim at establishing the conditions of such active membership. The previous chapter defended this claim against two objections: first, that equal membership does not require substantive equality, that is, equality of resources; and second, that freedom and substantive equality are disconnected, such that former can be enjoyed without the latter. There is a particular form of deprivation, the exclusion from participation in central frameworks and institutions of the community -- and this form of deprivation can be understood as lack of liberty. The chapter also characterized the liberal response to this form of deprivation as after-the-event compensation, and argued that such an approach was deeply problematic, in that while people can be compensated for the loss of the opportunity to be active members of their community, no form of compensation could enable them to become active members -- they remained excluded. This chapter pursues this criticism further, by arguing that the compensation approach reduces the worst off in the community to the status of 'unfree riders', and so places them beyond the limits of justice itself; and it criticizes another aspect of the compensation approach, the restriction of compensation to meeting only the 'basic' needs of the excluded (section 7.2).

The chapter then outlines the more positive approach to social justice required by the impure conception of freedom. That which programmes of social justice provides, frameworks of welfare, must be seen not as frameworks of compensation, but as frameworks of membership (section 7.3). The chapter then develops these frameworks of membership into what can be termed the Civil, Democratic and Social frameworks (section 7.4). And finally the chapter reconnects the problem of welfare with the problem of freedom in two ways: firstly, it makes clear how active membership of the community and freedom are connected, such that a concern for freedom must lead to the kind of positive welfare framework outlined here. Secondly, it translates the three conditions of liberty -- the negative, autonomy and power conditions -- into conditions of active membership, and shows how these conditions connect with the three frameworks of membership developed in section 7.2.

## Section 7.2 -- The Unfree Rider and Basic Needs

The previous chapter showed how certain groups are excluded from active membership of the community -- they are excluded from the cooperative enterprise of society, not only in terms of the activity of producing social goods and other resources, but also in terms of the activity of producing decisions. This is to exclude them from systems of production of social goods and decisions, and also from dignity, self-respect, the respect of others, independence, power, work, creativity, friendship, pleasure -- values that make life worth living. The welfare liberal response of compensating for the loss of the value of membership has been criticized on two grounds: (i) it is difficult to see how the value of membership can be restored through compensation; (ii) the strategy of compensation places welfare recipients beyond justice.

The latter issue can be posed in terms of the free rider problem. If certain people are excluded from active participation in the production of social goods, why should they have any access to those goods? One obvious answer is that their exclusion is not their fault, so why should they lose out? But neither is it the fault of those who do actively participate, so why should *they* lose out by having to share the rewards of cooperation with non-participants? The non-participants are free riders, and the active contributors could put forward the following complaints:

(1)     If the non-participants do not contribute any input to the productive process, they have no entitlement to any share of the output. Any goods the active participants grant them is equivalent to charity, and must depend on the charitable impulses of the producers.

(2)     If it is replied that the needs of the excluded ground an entitlement to some share of social output, it cannot be the the same share as the active producers. It can only be an entitlement to *basic* needs, and no more.

(3)     If it is replied that the excluded have an equal entitlement to flourish as human beings, and therefore an entitlement to

196

resources that goes beyond meeting basic needs, they still have no entitlement to participate in the decision-making processes of the cooperative -- they have no right to any say in the organisation of production.

The active participants surely have a point -- the excluded *are* free riders, to the extent that they receive *any* share of social goods without contributing to their production. However, the fundamental point remains that the non-participants are excluded against their wishes, and are therefore *un*free riders, and so have a justifiable ground for complaint themselves. Why should their fate rest on the charitable impulses of others? Why, if their entitlement to resources is established, should only their 'basic' needs be met -- why should their chances of human flourishing be constrained to a basic level? Why should they be denied participation in the negotiation of the organization of cooperation, when it is that organization that excludes them in the first place? Antony Skillen comments on the precariousness of the "situation of one forced to 'free-ride' because he or she cannot get a job, cannot *be* an active contributor... Here we seem to have an injustice that excludes people from the very sphere of reciprocal justice" (Skillen, 1985, p.11). What is also obvious is that an argument based on needs only moves the debate towards the limited position (c), unless the need to participate is recognized. An argument based on membership seems to be preferable, as it gives rise to a much fuller entitlement than an argument based upon needs.

The more severe power/control model of welfare discussed in section 6.5 conferred no bargaining rights upon the worst off in society, but it is equally difficult to see them as holding any bargaining rights under the compensation model. Raymond Plant (Plant, 1991, p.62) observes that in practice:

> Conferring social rights outside of economic performances is not compatible with either the prevailing ideology or, more importantly, the self-understanding of those who are most likely to claim the rights. They are unlikely to see themselves as independent citizens claiming what is theirs by right, rather than essentially the recipients of charity.

And so, in effect, the compensation strategy of social justice places the worst off outside the boundaries of reciprocal justice, as dependents upon benevolence and recipients of charity.

The compensation strategy therefore places the worst off in liberal capitalist societies in a very vulnerable position, with little, if any, bargaining power, and few, if any, entitlements: they must rely on the benevolence of those who have benefited from the system. By treating the situation of the worst off as though it were the result of bad luck, the welfare liberal portrays their position as not an issue of justice at all -- because nobody has acted unjustly to place them in this situation. The position of the worst off therefore becomes that of recipients of charity rather than rightful welfare.

What is at stake here is a power relationship in which compensation has a role to play. The welfare liberal has acknowledged that the power relationships that make up the capitalist market are harmful for certain groups in society, and has decided either that the harm being caused is insufficiently worrying that it ought to be prevented (compensation will do -- being worst off under capitalism is not so bad that anything as rash as significantly interfering with the capitalist system need be considered); or that the power relationship that is causing the harm to some is so valuable to others that this outweighs the evil of the harm, and so must be preserved -- the most that can be done is to compensate those harmed.

Whichever view the welfare liberal takes, the harm suffered by certain groups under capitalism is seen as a price worth paying for its benefits -- the damage caused to the life-prospects of such people is written-off through compensation. The advantage of the compensation approach is, in the end, that it can be enacted without interfering with the existing power relationships -- compensation is linked with maintaining or restoring the status quo; at the very least it does not seek to challenge that status quo. What is at issue here, then, is not social justice, but a pay-off the most powerful believe they can impose upon the rest -- a pay-off that has not been fairly negotiated, even hypothetically. The status of the worst off as equally valued persons is hardly being respected here, and cannot be respected if their inequality is regarded as the result of bad luck rather than as the predictable and preventable product of a social and economic system that generates this sort of injustice through its very nature.

Another problem with the compensation approach is that it seems to restrict the excluded to the level of 'basic' needs. The move of making a distinction between 'basic' needs which a welfare system must provide, and 'other' needs that the individual can secure for themselves through the market, is problematic at the level of both theory and practice. William Galston makes this sort of distinction at the theoretical level when he argues that the cooperative endeavour that

198

is a liberal polity gives rise to three kinds of claims for resources (i) claims based upon the "bare fact" of membership (need); (ii) claims based upon contribution to the community (merit); and (iii) claims arising from voluntary individual disposition of resources (choice) (Galston, 1991, pp.182-184). The position being developed here is that the "bare fact" of membership gives rise to wide-ranging entitlements to whatever is required in order to be a fully active member of the community, able to make contributions to the community, and able to make voluntary individual dispositions of resources. Galston's position, in contrast, allows that some will be restricted to "bare" membership, and so unable to contribute to the community or make individual choices. He does allow that claims based on membership have *some* priority: "...because all individuals are equally members, needs claims are imperative demands for equal access to the liberal good, or the means to it" (Ibid., p.184). However, such claims must be based upon a conception of the human good, and this must be kept minimal -- it must be an account of certain human goods which are prudential values for any life, but which do not constitute or define a preferred way of life. Galston says:

> One widely shared conjecture is that the liberal account represents something like the minimal conditions for, or ingredients of, a human life that can be regarded as normal, tolerable, or worthwhile. (Ibid., p.167)

Galston states that what is required is a "limited but nonetheless objective account of well-being" (Galston, 1991, p.168), based upon "broad generalizations -- propositions rooted in basic commonalities of human nature, experience, and circumstances..." (Ibid., p.169). Here, there is an equation of 'basic' or 'core' values with some kind of minimum condition. Galston says that in the United States of America, this would be cashed out in terms of sufficient food to prevent starvation, primary medical attention, and basic education need to function as a competent citizen and contributory worker (Ibid., p.184). There are three possible objections to this approach. Firstly, it seems vulnerable to some of the objections made to the concept of absolute poverty in section 6.2, although it does not strictly amount to an absolute poverty view. That it does not amount to such a view is perhaps a consequence of its own internal confusions, as there does seem to be a basic contradiction in supplying food sufficient to prevent starvation, and at the same time supplying education sufficient to function as a contributory worker -- there seems no point in supplying education to the latter level for people whose nutritionary requirements are restricted to the former level; they would not be able to contribute work on such a diet, nor perhaps even benefit from the educational opportunities. Secondly, as has been argued above, those restricted to this level of 'basic' needs have a valid objection: why should their activity be restricted to this 'basic' level when they are excluded from the opportunities for fuller activity through no fault of their own? Surely the only justification for restricting them to 'basic' needs can be on the grounds of efficiency, and it is important that efficiency arguments can always be over-ridden by justice arguments. Thirdly, the argument seems to justify the restriction of membership-based claims to basic needs because of the requirement for some core or common needs which do not define a preferred way of life. However, this looks like some version of a neutrality requirement, a requirement Galston explicitly rejects:

> Liberalism cannot, as many contemporary theorists suppose, be understood as broadly neutral concerning the human good. It is rather committed to a distinctive conception of the human good, a conception that undergirds the liberal conception of social justice. (Ibid., p.18)

A position based on the 'bare fact' of membership cannot be one that declines to define a preferred way of life -- it must identify a *basic* preferred way of life; and Galston, with his rejection of neutrality, would have no problem with this requirement. He therefore needs to make a distinction between a *basic* preferred way of life, as opposed to the variety of preferred forms of life individuals may pursue within the liberal polity. But there seems to be absolutely no reason, within the terms of Galston's non-neutral approach, why the *basic* preferred way of life, the basic form of life the community wishes *all* of its members to enjoy, should be based upon minimum conditions. There is no reason why the basic level of activity the community expects all members to have access to should be cast at the lowest possible level of activity the community can tolerate.

An illustration of the practice of the 'basic' needs approach can be seen in the proposals of the Commission on Social Justice (The Commission on Social Justice, 1994), which issued its report on the future of the welfare state in the United Kingdom in 1994, after being commissioned by the late leader of the British Labour Party, John Smith. The philosophical basis of the Report is the equal value of all citizens. One of its fundamental principles is "that the foundation of a free society is the equal worth of all citizens..." (Ibid., p.18). In a preliminary document the Commission states: "For 'equal worth' to be meaningful, people must be able to meet their needs, or at least their basic needs" (The Commission on Social Justice, 1993, p.ii). It is important to note this shift from talking of the needs of citizens to the *basic* needs of *people*. Again, in the same document: "...it is the natural application of the idea that everyone is of equal worth that they should have access to what they need, or at least what they basically need" (Ibid., p.8). No explanation of this move from people having access to what they need, to having access only to what they basically need, is given. There are, therefore, two distinct positions within the Commission's thinking: (1) That for equal worth to be meaningful, people must be able to meet their needs, and that the idea of everyone being of equal value means that they should have access to what they need. And: (2) That for equal worth to be meaningful people must be able to meet their *basic* needs, and that the idea of everyone being of equal value means that they should have access to what they *basically* need. This move from 'needs' to 'basic needs' involves a radical shift in position. By isolating a conception of the basic needs of people from a conception of the needs of the citizen, the Commission has opened a gap between those who are restricted to the basic needs of people, and those who go beyond such limits and enjoy the needs of citizens. Therefore the equal worth of members of the community cannot be ensured by restricting welfare provision to some conception of basic needs.

It is highly significant that in the final report of the Commission no such shift is made, because the basic needs of people and the needs of the citizen are united into one conception of the basic needs of citizens:

> ...everyone is entitled, as a right of citizenship, to be able to meet their basic needs for income, shelter and other necessities. Basic needs can be met by providing resources or services, or helping people acquire them: either way, the ability to meet basic needs is the foundation of a substantive commitment to the equal worth of all citizens. (The Commission on Social Justice, 1994, p.18)

One might reply that a commitment to basic needs may be the *foundation* of a substantive commitment to the equal worth of all citizens, but does not in itself amount to such a commitment; more harshly, one might judge that it is difficult to see how it can even amount to the foundation of such a commitment, as one could quite coherently be committed to meeting the basic needs of all without aiming at the equal worth of all citizens -- a hierarchical society could have the same commitment to meeting the *basic* needs of all its members as an egalitarian society, and even set basic needs at the same level. Egalitarianism requires a commitment beyond basic needs.

An egalitarian commitment to welfare would see it as the provision of the conditions necessary for equally active membership of the community. This is to move from a discourse of compensation to a discourse of participation; from the welfare state to what Antony Skillen terms the welfare society (Skillen, 1985), or what Ralf Dahrendorf describes as the social state: "The social state (as I prefer to call it) is about guaranteeing social citizenship rights for all" (Dahrendorf, 1987). And Raymond Plant argues for a society based on democratic citizenship, which is based on "policies that enable every citizen to lead a full and autonomous life shaped by their own values and purposes". This requires a "framework of education, health care, income and law that underpins such citizenship" (Plant, 1988). This connection of welfare with citizenship takes the debate beyond frameworks of welfare that aim to compensate, towards frameworks of membership that aim to enable, empower and liberate -- frameworks that aim to provide all with the political, social and economic conditions they need if they are to be equal members of their own community. Equal participation is the primary signifier of equal value, and so members of a community can only be equally valued if they are able to participate equally and on an equal basis with all other members. The loss of that ability to participate cannot be compensated for in any way that can respect or restore the equal value of membership, unless the ability is itself restored. The only liberal justifications for 'writing off' those who cannot participate in the capitalist market are either that their exclusion is inalterable, or that their inclusion is too costly. The first claim cannot stand up to critical scrutiny. The second is a claim of efficiency, and is therefore open to be over-ridden by principles of justice; and it exposes welfare liberal theory to the charge of leaving the power relationships between the 'haves' and 'have nots' under capitalism more or less intact. William Connolly comments that welfare liberal theory "is neither at home in the civilization of productivity nor prepared to challenge its hegemony" (Connolly, 1984, p.234). And Will Kymlicka says of Rawls and Dworkin that:

Neither has challenged the 'civilization of productivity' whose maintenance has involved the perpetuation and often exaggeration of entrenched inequalities of race, class, and gender. (Kymlicka, 1991, p.87)

## Section 7.3 -- The Idea of Citizenship

The movement towards seeing frameworks of welfare as frameworks of membership has moved the discussion towards the idea of "citizenship", and a connection between welfare and citizenship. Before exploring that connection further, the notion of citizenship itself needs development. The idea of citizenship has undergone a revival in western political theory. In particular, many thinkers on the left have focussed on it as a key to reviving socialist theory, possibly constituting an area of reconciliation with liberal political philosophy. For example, Geoff Andrews comments: "Citizenship appears -- in the dimensions of constitutional reform -- as a historic compromise between socialists and liberals" (Andrews ed., 1991, p.13). He believes that "citizenship should provide a focus for a wider engagement between socialists and liberals. An assessment of the relationship between the collective and the individual, liberty and equality, and (critically) the community and the environment is now beginning to emerge" (Ibid., p.14). Will Kymlicka and Wayne Norman comment that the "explosion of interest" in the concept is

> ...a natural evolution in political discourse because the concept of citizenship seems to integrate the demands of justice and community membership -- the central concepts of political philosophy in the 1970s and 1980s, respectively. (Kymlicka and Norman, 1994, p.352)

The concept of citizenship at the heart of the revival is one of activity, and so draws from the tradition of republicanism. For example, Maurizio Passerin D'Entreves characterizes Hannah Arendt as seeking to revive the idea of a politics based on the idea of active citizenship: "on the value and importance of civic engagement and collective deliberation about all matters affecting the political community" (D'Entreves, 1994, p.2). As such she was writing in the tradition of civic republicanism, the tradition of Aristotle, Machiavelli, Montesquieu, Jefferson and Tocqueville, in claiming that:

> Political activity is valued not because it may lead to agreement or to a shared conception of the good, but because it enables each

citizen to exercise his or her powers of agency, to develop the capacities for judgment, and to attain by concerted action some measure of political efficiency. (Ibid., p.2)

Part of Arendt's project is to articulate "the conditions for the exercise of active citizenship and democratic self-determination" (Ibid., p.2).

Adrian Oldfield makes a distinction between two conceptions of citizenship: liberal individualist and civic republican (Oldfield, 1990). The first sees citizenship as essentially a status; the second see it as essentially an activity or practice (Ibid., p.177). The most important contrast is that under the liberal individualist approach the social bonds of citizenship are purely contractual (Ibid., p.178). There is no obligation to participate in the public, political realm:

> Taken on its own, this conception of citizenship creates no social bond, beyond that of contract. It neither creates nor sustains any social solidarity or cohesion, or any sense of common purpose. (Ibid., p.180)

The basic problem with this conception, then, is that citizenship can be totally passive: it draws boundaries against others rather than makes connections with others. It therefore has the potential of offering citizenship in a purely formal, rather than substantive sense -- in that the excluded are included within the boundaries of citizenship, formally, but remain excluded from any serious level of participation in the community.

In contrast, the civic republican conception is public and communally based: citizenship here is a practice or activity: "...what it is necessary for citizens to do in order to define, establish, and sustain a political community of fellow-citizens" (Ibid., p.180). This activity is not a contractual obligation, entered into in exchange for some other good: it is identified with citizenship, what citizenship is: "...a shared responsibility for the identity and continuity of a particular political community" (Ibid.). Importantly, then, citizenship is nor a contractual arrangement between individuals and community or each other, in exchange for something; it is an obligatory activity one has simply by being a citizen, such that neglect of that activity is a significant omission. This conception of citizenship is therefore essentially public and active, and has the implication that people must be empowered to be citizens. Oldfield comments:

Citizens have to be empowered to act. They *require* many of the civic, political, and legal freedoms, and many of the entitlements to health, education, and income, which appear as 'rights' in the liberal-individualist conception. What thus are rights in one conception of citizenship are necessary conditions in the other. (Ibid., p.183)

This notion of citizenship therefore requires frameworks of empowerment, the frameworks of membership developed in section 7.2.

The liberal individualist conception of citizenship allows for passive citizenship, in the sense that individuals are not obliged to engage in any activity that constitutes citizenship. The implication of this approach is that the community is not obliged to empower its members to engage in any activity that constitutes citizenship. Therefore while some may choose to be passive citizens, others will be forced to be passive citizens, forced to take the unfree ride. The civic republican approach requires active citizenship, in that simply being a citizen of the community means that a certain kind of activity is needed, that activity which is needed to sustain the political community. The implication of this approach is that if this activity is required, the community must ensure that all have the ability to engage in it. There is now no room for frameworks of welfare that compensate people for the loss of their ability to be an actively participating member of the community. An egalitarian society that embodies the civic republican conception of citizenship will connect welfare and citizenship in a very different way.

## Section 7.4 -- Empowerment and Liberation

It does seem, then, that the civic-republican conception of citizenship lies at the core of the approach to liberty being developed here. The argument has been that freedom, welfare and social justice are connected through and centred upon the idea of the active member of the community -- the free agent is an equally active chooser, doer and participator in their community; frameworks of welfare must aim at establishing the conditions for such membership; and the failure to establish those conditions is an issue of social justice. There is clearly a connection between the active member that connects all these ideas, the the conception of the active civic-republican citizen. However, that connection needs to be carefully examined, and the move from the impure theory of freedom to the civic-republican citizen might be being made too quickly and uncritically, such that the central theme of this book, the connection between freedom and social justice, may be lost.

Four models of welfare were identified in section 6.5:

(1) *The Charity Model*: there is no function for a welfare system beyond systems of charity, through which those citizens who have prospered through their own efforts or good fortune can make voluntary transfer payments to those who have failed to prosper for whatever reason.

(2) *The Stability Model*: the function of the welfare system is to ensure overall social stability, by avoiding potential unrest caused by excess poverty and inequality in the population.

(3) *The Power/Control Model*: the function of welfare is to enable the state to exert control over certain sections of the population, and to render certain sections of the population powerless.

(4) *The Compensation Model*: the function of welfare is to compensate those who are unable to meet their basic needs through normal market participation, where this is no fault of their own.

It might seem that a fifth model of welfare has emerged in this chapter, based around the idea of active membership of the community:

(5) *The Empowerment Model*: the function of welfare is to empower people to be active citizens.

However, this model of welfare is incomplete, and a sixth alternative is closer to what is required by the impure theory of freedom:

(6) *The Liberation Model*: the function of welfare is to liberate people to become autonomous members of the community.

These two models need to be distinguished, because while both involve empowering people to fulfil certain goals and activities, the Liberation Model empowers them to fulfil goals which they, to some extent, have chosen for themselves. The Empowerment Model has no such implication: one can empower people to fulfil goals and activities which one has chosen for them. For example, military training can involve empowering conscript soldiers to fulfil goals and activities, but those goals and activities are not chosen by them, but imposed upon them. It must be kept in mind that while a welfare programme may aim to empower people, it may aim to empower them to fulfil certain activities that the state values, rather than activities people have chosen for themselves.

The ideal that lies behind the idea of active membership of the community is that of the autonomous chooser, and what is lacking from the Empowerment model is this aspect of choice, allowing the possibility of the equally active *conscript* member of the community, rather than the equally active autonomous member. What is worrying about the civic republican conception of active citizenship is this conscript element. In the end, the function of welfare may well be described as empowerment to be an active citizen, as long as active citizenship includes being, not only and active doer and participator in the community, but also an active chooser and participator in the choices of the community.

The impure theory of freedom has stressed that the free person is not independent of the community, but is embedded within it, but embedded in a particular way. The free person has a range of options from which to choose, and those options must be part of the structure of the community in order to be meaningful. The exclusion of people from membership deprives them of the opportunity to make meaningful choices, and so deprives them of their autonomy. However, inclusion may also deprive them of the opportunity to make meaningful choices, if the community structure does not allow for such an opportunity. And so while freedom is not the absence of social context, it is the presence of a certain kind of social context. That context must ensure the three conditions of freedom, which can also now be understood as conditions of membership:

(1)   *The Non-Interference Condition* -- being left alone to make choices about which options to pursue; the right to individual freedom from interference, in the form of rights to privacy and equality before the law.

(2)   *The Autonomy Condition* -- the possession of the ability to make rational choices concerning the best options open to one; the right to make choices and participate in choices concerning the community; this includes the right to the information needed to make such choices.

(3)   *The Power Condition* -- the possession of or access to the powers and resources needed to pursue those options, the power of enactment; the right to a level of welfare and security required to be an active member of the community.

A theory of freedom that recognized only the Non-Interference Condition would most likely see compensation as the most appropriate response to freedom violation. Nozick talks in terms of after-the-event compensation for "border crossings" (Nozick, 1974, pp.57-59, and pp.71-73). And Rawls also talks in terms of compensating people for the lesser worth of their liberty (Rawls, 1972, pp.204-205). A theory of freedom that recognizes the need for the Power Condition would require empowerment as a condition of freedom, and as an appropriate response for violations of freedom; but, as has been pointed out, empowerment need make no reference to the choices or preferences of the 'free' agent. The impure theory of freedom recognizes the need for all three conditions, and it is the Autonomy Condition that gives it a distinctive response to violations of freedom -- that what is required is not merely compensation, or only empowerment, but something that can be understood as liberation. And at the heart of liberation is the notion of autonomy.

A welfare system that aims to ensure, amongst other things, the conditions for freedom, would therefore have to provide frameworks that express, protect and develop the conditions for *autonomous* membership of the community. These are not so much frameworks of welfare, as frameworks of membership, and even though such a vision of welfare is not spelt out in detail here, three elements can be identified:

(1)     *The Civil Framework*: a framework of rights to non-interference; the defining of a space within which one is free from non-interference and scrutiny by others and by the state, and where one is left free to shape one's life.

(2)     *The Democratic Framework*: a framework of rights to participation in the decision-making processes of the community, through which individuals can play an active role in the way the community arrives at decisions and enacts them.

(3)     *The Social Framework*: a framework of resources and powers people need in order to play a full and active role in the community, and to make full use of their civil and democratic rights.

These three frameworks are obviously connected to and ensure the three conditions of freedom/membership. And just as the Autonomy Condition was the crucial element of liberty that ensured that what was needed was not only empowerment, but liberation, the Democratic Framework ensures that members of this community are

208

not merely empowered to act as the community determines, but are active and autonomous participators in determining the choices of the community.

Now, while the three frameworks are connected with the three conditions of freedom/membership, the connection is not straightforward. Participation in the Civil Framework, for example, calls for all three conditions of freedom; it would be a mistake to suppose that the Civil Framework was essentially negative, and therefore only demands the negative condition for freedom -- in order to define a space within which one is to determine one's own life plan, and in order to determine it and pursue it, all three conditions of freedom are required. Therefore, within each separate framework, freedom remains impure. It is, therefore, impossible to prioritize any of the conditions of liberty by prioritizing any of the frameworks of membership. For example, one could accept the claim that the Civil Framework was the most important, without having the accept the addition claim that the Non-Interference Condition was therefore the most important element of liberty.

This three-fold distinction is not original. John A. Hall claims that such a distinction is part of the liberal idea of liberty: "There are three components to liberty. The first component is that of the secure provision of the basic necessities of food and health, the absence of which makes life miserable" (Hall, 1988, p.184). However, this provision must go beyond mere sufficiency -- it must supply the power required to enable the individual to choose from a significant range of opportunities, rather than simply fulfil 'basic' needs. The second element, says Hall, is "negative liberty" -- equality before the law and the right to free opinion (Ibid.). The third component is "the right of the people to control political power by democratic means" (Ibid.). Hall remarks: "A coherent liberal view of liberty demands that all three elements be present" (Ibid., p.185). It is also, of course, very close to T. H. Marshall's three-fold distinction of civil, political and social rights:

The civil element is composed of the rights necessary for individual freedom...and the right to justice. The last is of a different order from the others, because it is the right to defend and assert all one's rights on terms of equality with others and by due process of law.

By the political element I mean the right to participate in the exercise of political power, as a member of a body invested with political authority or as an elector of the members of such a body.

209

By the social element I mean the whole range from the right to a modicum of economic welfare and security to the right to share to the full in the social heritage and to live the life of a civilised being, according to the standard prevailing in the society. (Marshall, 1952, p.11)

However, there is a distinction to be made between Hall's three elements of liberty and Marshall's three spheres of rights of the citizen, a distinction that corresponds to that between the three conditions of freedom/membership and the three frameworks of membership. The importance of this distinction is that all three of the conditions of freedom are needed to ensure equal participation in all three frameworks of membership.

## Section 7.5 -- Conclusion

This chapter has demonstrated the connection between freedom and welfare, through the idea of membership. The chapter has argued for a particular conception of active membership, where the individual is an equally active chooser, doer and participator in the community. But the basis of this participation is autonomy, so that there is a clear distinction between the equally active conscript member, who acts out choices made for them, and the equally active autonomous member, who acts out their own choices and choices they have participated in formulating. This connection between freedom and membership means that the conditions for freedom have to be ensured at the level of membership, and therefore the Frameworks of Membership developed in this chapter have to reflect those conditions -- otherwise the connection between freedom and membership is lost.

The three conditions for freedom are the negative, autonomy and power conditions, and these are embodied at the level of membership through the Civil, Democratic and Social frameworks of membership. These three frameworks seek to ensure the conditions, both negative and positive, required for all to be equally active choosers, doers and participators in the community. This shows how certain issues of freedom are also issues of social justice, in that particular forms of deprivation can injure the freedom of members of the community. These groups are then excluded from full membership, and this is a *prima facie* injustice. There is a specific family of issues of social justice which, it is claimed, can be best understood as problems of freedom. These issues can be characterized as problems of exclusion, where particular groups are excluded from full participation within society's institutions and practices. The claim is that full participation is constitutive of freedom, and that therefore exclusion from participation is a violation of freedom. Seeing these issues of exclusion as problems of freedom leads to a distinctive approach to how they should be understood within the context of social justice, and a distinctive view of what social justice demands in these cases. Part of the programme of social justice is concerned with the conditions needed to be an active chooser, doer and participator in the community: that is, an actively participating citizen. Social injustice arises when people are deprived of that opportunity, when they are excluded from the community, when their citizenship is rendered empty. Therefore programmes of social justice cannot be restricted to compensating people for the effects of exclusion, but must aim at the ending of that exclusion. People are excluded from active participation in the community, not by their nature, but by alterable social, political, cultural and economic practices.

In those cases where it is considered that those practices can be altered, so that people can become active participants, then the failure to alter those practices is both a violation of liberty *and* a social injustice. It is a violation of liberty because it constitutes the failure to provide the positive conditions for freedom to which all members of the community are entitled. It is a social injustice because it deprives people of the equal opportunity to be active participants in their own community, an opportunity to which all are equally entitled. And so the close connection between freedom and social justice can be seen.

Once this connection has been established, a distinctive approach to problems of freedom and social justice emerges: and approach that seeks both empowerment and liberation. It leads to the rejection of any approach to freedom that seeks to divorce the issue of liberty from empowerment; but equally it leads to the rejection of any approach to social justice that fails to connect empowerment with liberation.

211

# Conclusion:
# Freedom and Membership

A distinction which runs through many discussions of freedom is that between freedom and its worth. If an agent lacks the resources to do $x$, they are nonetheless free do do it, but that freedom is of no worth to them. They are as free to do $x$ as the person who does have the necessary resources: the difference between them is not that one is free to do $x$ while the other is not, but that the freedom to do $x$ is of worth to the one agent, and of no worth to the other. John Rawls uses this distinction in his theory of social justice, and it has a central role to play (see section 2.1, pp.31-32). The lesser worth of a person's liberty is something for which she can be compensated. "But compensating for the lesser worth of freedom is not to be confused with making good an unequal liberty" (Rawls, 1972, pp.204-205).

W. A. Parent makes the same distinction: "...providing goods like education and fair opportunity is a demand, not of liberty as such, but of justice. These goods are valuable, not because they increase liberty, but because they render its use more valuable" (Parent, 1974A, p.162). Of aids to help the disabled, he claims that these do not increase their freedom: "What we ought to say...is that such aids are indispensable to the creation of social and economic opportunities for the less fortunate and therefore are necessary for the meaningful exercise of their freedom" (Ibid., p.163).

According to this picture, then, freedom is equal for all -- only the worth of that freedom can differ. For Rawls, this means we can insist that freedom be equal, but allow that the worth of freedom be unequal, as long as this inequality has some benefit for the worst off under the difference principle. Therefore his first principle of justice, that of equal liberty, is not undermined by the inequalities allowed under the second principle -- these inequalities in social primary goods do result in inequalities in the worth of freedom, but not in inequalities in freedom itself; and such inequalities can be compensated for under the difference principle.

An alternative is to make a distinction, not between freedom and its worth, but between freedom and its conditions. H.J. McCloskey states:

...we have liberty to enjoy our rights only when the conditions are such that it is possible for us to do so; and this does entail special aids to the needy and less fortunate. These aids are not part of liberty but rather conditions for its existence... (McCloskey, 1965, p.504)

Note that these aids are not conditions for the enjoyment of an already existing freedom, but for the very existence of that freedom, such that the absence of such conditions means the absence of freedom itself.

Sir Isaiah Berlin also makes a distinction between freedom and its conditions, but for him the distinction operates in the same way as Rawls' distinction between liberty and its worth. He says:

It is important to discriminate between liberty and the conditions of its exercise. If a man is too poor or too ignorant or too feeble to make use of his legal rights, the liberty that these rights confer upon him is nothing to him, but it is not thereby annihilated. (Berlin, 1969 p.liii)

And: "Useless freedoms should be made usable, but they are not identical with the conditions indispensable for their utility" (Ibid., p.liv).

Both the McCloskey version and the Rawls/Berlin version make perfectly good sense, but at very different levels of application. The McCloskey liberty/conditions of liberty distinction applies at the level of freedom, as described in the impure theory of freedom. The Rawls/Berlin liberty/worth of liberty distinction applies at the level of membership of the community, as described in terms of the Frameworks of Membership in the previous section. The impure theory of freedom makes a distinction between freedom and its conditions, and argues that freedom needs both negative and positive conditions. This mixture of conditions makes the liberty/worth of liberty distinction inapplicable at this level: it no longer makes sense to argue that, in the absence of its conditions, freedom remains behind like the Cheshire Cat's grin. The impure theory of freedom makes a strong connection between freedom and ability -- the free person has both the space and power to choose, and this power to *enact* choices is essential. A person who cannot choose because of the lack of the positive conditions of freedom is simply *not* free to choose -- beggars cannot be choosers. This is made clearer when it is realized that the negative and positive conditions of freedom depend upon each other if they are to ensure freedom -- the free person requires the space to make use of their powers to choose, and needs those powers in order to maintain their space to choose. In the absence of the space to choose, those powers are no longer *their* powers; in the absence of the power to choose, that space is not *their* space, if it exists at all.

According to Berlin, negative freedom is "a field (ideally) without obstacles, a vacuum in which nothing obstructs me..." (Ibid., p.144). The rationale for setting up this space is to ensure that "some portion of human existence must remain independent of the sphere of social control" (Ibid., p.126). The problem is, of course, that in order for the agent to have effective control over that area of their life, it is not sufficient that others do not interfere with it; it is also necessary that they have practical powers that ensure *their* control over it. That others do not actively exercise control over that area does not ensure that the agent has control over it; if the agent has no power, then others may still retain control over that space, even though they do not actively exercise that power and interfere within it. Therefore the absence of the agent's powers of control mean that this area -- in which they must "remain independent of the sphere of social control" -- disappears.

Therefore, at this level, in the absence of the conditions of freedom nothing that can be recognized as freedom remains. The liberty/worth of liberty distinction cannot be applied here. This has serious implications for Rawls' position, because it means that the inequalities in social primary goods permitted by the second principle of justice undermine the equality of freedom supposedly guaranteed by the first principle; equality of freedom at this level requires equality of the conditions of freedom. However, Rawls may avoid this implication, because he is using the liberty/worth of liberty distinction at another level. He identifies freedom with the "complete system of liberties of equal citizenship", by which he means something at the same level as what has been described here as the Frameworks of Membership (although by no means the same shape as those frameworks). The Frameworks of Membership can be formally in place, and therefore formally equally available to all, but people can lack the resources needed to make full use of them -- those frameworks remain of little value to them. Therefore the value or worth of membership in this formal sense can be undermined, even though people remain formally equal members of society -- they hold the same rights as all other members of the society, but lack the power to use those rights. This is the distinction Rawls, Parent and Berlin are making, and it is an important one. However, while it makes sense when applied to the framework of rights that constitute membership, there are at least two problems concerning its scope.

Firstly, it is difficult to apply the distinction to the Social Framework -- that framework is a system of powers and resources all must enjoy in order to make use of their other rights: in a sense, it acts as the foundation of the worth of the Civil and Democratic frameworks, by ensuring that all have the power to use them. However, the distinction might still make sense here, if there are ways in which people can be prevented from gaining access to those systems of resources and powers provided by the Social Framework, such that although they formally have equal rights of access to them, they are unable to make use of them, and therefore their formal right of access is of little worth to them. Such problems were examined in section 6.3.

The second problem is connected with the distinction between formal and active membership. While the liberty/worth of liberty distinction applies to formal membership, it does not apply to active membership. Active membership consists in being an active chooser, doer and participator within the community. This is a practical, not formal, capacity, and it requires practical, positive conditions in order to be enjoyed. Here, the freedom/conditions of freedom distinction returns -- for in the absence of the conditions for active membership, that membership itself is absent. While formal membership is equal for all whatever their material condition, the capacity for active membership is not. And, of course, the notion of membership at the centre of this account of freedom, welfare and social justice is active, not formal. That is why participation in all three Frameworks of Membership requires all three of the conditions of freedom: the freedom required for participation in any of the three frameworks remains impure.

What follows is that if all are equally entitled to the freedom to participate in this sense, then all are entitled to equality of the conditions needed for that freedom. Therefore equality of freedom in this sense requires equality of relevant conditions. This refutes the kind of claim made by Antony Flew, who makes a clear distinction between the "equal liberty for all to pursue whatever each individual holds to be good...", and "equality of condition"; and who claims that these two forms of equality are "ultimately incompatible" (Flew, 1981, p.11) with each other. Rather, they are seen to be essential to each other: freedom requires both the space and the power to choose, and equal freedom requires equal space and power.

In that sense, the argument has come full circle, because the notion of active membership takes us back to the notion of freedom the argument began with. It also displays once more the connection between freedom and social justice: that there are some issues of freedom that are also issues of social justice, but issues of a particular type. That is, they are issues where the positive conditions of freedom are not in place: it is at least part of any programme of social justice to ensure that the positive conditions of freedom are equally in place for all. This means they are not issues of social justice where compensation is appropriate, if it is in the powers of the community to provide those positive conditions. The claim has been that the community can and should play an active role in providing those positive conditions; and that there is a danger of regarding the exclusion of groups from active participation as a natural fact about them. It may be that that these cases of exclusion are due, not to inalterable nature, but to alterable social, political and economic practices, such that the failure to alter those practices may constitute a violation of freedom -- the violation of the freedom to be an active chooser, doer and participator in the community.

The Alterability Thesis (section 3.2) can now be seen to have a wide application when applied to the question of exclusion from active membership. Here, the thesis states that a person is unjustly excluded from society if:

(1)     they lack the power to participate as an active member; or
(2)     they are prevented from participating as an active member by some external obstacle; and
(3)     there is some other practically possible political, social and economic order in which neither (1) nor (2) would hold; and
(4)     there is some agent or agency that can be identified as morally responsible for bringing about such a change.

The radical element of the thesis is proposition (1), that an individual's lack of power to participate is both a violation of their freedom and a social injustice, if propositions (3) and (4) hold; because under the interpretation of proposition (1) developed in chapter 3, this includes those who seem to lack power because of some internal disability, such as the physically disabled. This may initially sound implausible -- what if such people have, for example, permanently lost the power to use their legs, such that it lies beyond the limits of medical technology to restore that power? Surely now their situation is inalterable and so falls outside the scope of the Alterability Thesis. However, this is a mistake. Firstly, while medical technology may be insufficient to enable them to walk by restoring their power to use their legs, it may be sufficient to enable them to walk by making some other power available to them -- artificial limbs, for example. Secondly, and

217

more radically, it is not the power to walk which is at stake here; rather it is the power to get from *A* to *B*. The point is that the loss of the power to walk need not mean the loss of the power to get from *A* to *B* -- the disabled are not immobilized by their disability: they could get from *A* to *B* by the use of some alternative power. Therefore, even though the loss of their power to walk may be inalterable, the loss of the power to get from place to place is not -- alternative powers are available, and the community can enable the disabled by giving them access to those powers and/or by altering facilities so that they can gain access to them under the powers they do have. There is no good reason why access to facilities should be restricted to those who can use their legs. The disabled are not immobilized by their disability, but by the way the community is organized; they are not excluded from active membership by their nature, but by social, political and economic practices.

Therefore the Alterability Thesis has wide scope. Even if a person inalterably lacks a particular power to do *x*, this does not render them inalterably unable to do *x* -- they can still be enabled to do *x* through alternative powers. If this understanding of unfreedom is plausible, then those unable to participate as active members of the community because of the lack of the powers to do so are unfree to do so -- their freedom is being violated. The community should either supply them with the powers needed to participate, or alter its shape so that they can participate under their own powers. The latter strategy is more radical, in that it recognizes that the excluded are not powerless as such, but that the way society is structured prevents them from using the powers they do have.

In section 2.4 the point was made that it is not simply true that these are issues of freedom *and* social justice, it is *importantly* true. It is important to see that they are issues of freedom, because only then can it be seen that they are issues of social justice of a particular kind. They are issues of freedom because they are issues where the positive powers and capacities needed to be free are missing when they need not be. They are issues of social justice because this deprivation excludes such groups from membership of their own community. It is crucial to recognize that these are issues of social justice of a particular kind -- issues of freedom -- because it is crucial to recognize that they are *not* issues where after-the-event compensation is sufficient to meet the demands of justice. If the equal value of membership is the benchmark, then it is inappropriate to compensate people for the loss of the equal value of that membership, where compensation does nothing to restore that value. If the concern is equal freedom, then it is inappropriate to compensate people for the loss of their freedom in terms of some other primary good. This is why the rejection of the freedom/worth of freedom distinction is important. It rules out permitting the unequal worth of freedom as long as there is compensation for that unequal worth in terms of some other primary good, an approach Rawls seems to permit under the difference principle. He says:

> The lesser worth of liberty is...compensated for, since the capacity of the less fortunate members of society to achieve their aims would be even less were they not to accept the existing inequalities whenever the difference principle is satisfied. (Rawls, 1972, p.204)

Rawls seems to be committed to equal liberty without being committed to the equal worth of liberty. Just how this can amount to a commitment to equal liberty at all is hard to see, and so the liberty/worth of liberty distinction seems worth rejecting if it allows this possibility.

This point holds at the level of membership of the community too. Commitment to equal membership should entail a commitment to the equal value of membership, otherwise it is difficult to see what the commitment to equal membership amounts to. This requires radical alterations to society to ensure that nobody is deprived of the conditions for active participation. The compensatory moves envisaged under the Rawlsian difference principle are severely limited, because the difference principle is a strategy of compensation -- and here is a range of issues of social justice where the aim is not to compensate people for the loss of their equality, but to ensure their equality.

What of the concern that an emphasis on the positive conditions of freedom and membership renders the theory vulnerable to the charge that it would allow the state to force people to be free? At the level of the theory of freedom, this concern was met in section 4.3, where it was pointed out that forcing somebody to act as though they were rational does not empower them to act rationally. If part of freedom is the capacity to act rationally, then the use of force does not bring about such freedom, it is more likely to destroy it. And at the level of membership, in section 7.4 a clear distinction was made between the equally active conscript member of the community, who acts out choices made for them, and the equally active autonomous member of the community, who acts out their own choices and choices they have participated in formulating. It should also be remembered that the impure theory of freedom identifies three conditions for liberty, one of which is the negative condition of non-interference, and refuses to prioritize any of the conditions at the level of theory. Therefore the state should seek to ensure the positive conditions of freedom in ways that do not undermine or destroy the negative conditions for that freedom, and vice versa. Of course, the problem is that such a harmonious approach is not going to be possible all the time, nor even very often. The negative and positive conditions will often clash, such that one must take priority over the other. How should it be decided which takes priority? It seems to a dichotomy expressed by B.M. Leiser:

> In essence, the question resolves itself as follows: Will adult citizens of a democratic state be treated as children who are considered by their guardians to be too immature, too lacking in judgment, to make their own decisions; or will they be treated as free men and women, sovereigns in their own country and over their own lives, capable of making their own choices, for good or ill. (Leiser, 1973, p.188)

Certainly, in the case of children, most would accept that here is a good case for giving the positive conditions of their freedom priority over the negative conditions. The conditions for their future freedom are ensured by laying the groundwork form their power of rational choice. But of course, as Leiser objects, adults are not children, and it would be utterly inappropriate to equate the excluded, such as the physically disabled, with children. But neither are they sovereigns in their own country and over their own lives. There is a third possibility which is often overlooked, in which people are neither sovereigns in their own country nor children: they are excluded from being active members of their own country through no fault of their own -- they are impoverished, powerless, excluded from participation in their own society, pushed into the margins, rendered silent, at the extreme rendered invisible, precisely because they lack the positive conditions of freedom, the *power* to be free.

All people arc *prima facie* entitled to the equal value of their membership of the community, and this entitlement gives rise to an equal entitlement to what is required to ground such membership. The entitlement to the equal opportunity to be active choosers, doers and participators in the community is grounded in the fact of membership of the community. The exclusion of groups like the physically disabled from certain institutions and practices undermines their equal membership of the community, and therefore constitutes a *prima facie* injustice. Unless some compelling reason can be found to justify the exclusion of such groups from these institutions and practices, then this exclusion becomes, in fact, a social injustice which society must address.

The problem is not simply that deprivation of active participation in society deprives a person of access to material social goods: those goods can be distributed by other means. The problem is that there are social goods such as autonomy, power, self respect, that cannot be distributed by other means, but which seem to depend upon active participation in society's institutions and practices. And, more important, active participation is not only the foundation of other social goods, but is a social good itself: it is the power to shape, expand and pursue one's own life plans in a free and creative way, rather than having simply to make the best of whatever options happen to be left open to one; and it is the power to contribute to the shaping of the community itself, rather than having to fit within the mould that society has left for one, however narrow and constraining it turns out to be.

It should now be clear how the issues of freedom and social justice meet. That someone is deprived of the conditions of active participation in the community is an issue both of freedom and of social justice -- they are not distinct problems. The welfare strategy of compensation is inadequate and incomplete precisely because it fails to realize that a crucial aspect of the problem of exclusion is that the freedom of the excluded is destroyed. A broader understanding of the problem of exclusion is demanded, and leads to the demand for strategies of social justice that take the idea of welfare beyond compensation, towards empowerment and, most importantly, towards liberation.

# Bibliography

Ackerman, Bruce (1980) *Social Justice in the Liberal State* (Yale University Press, New Haven and London).

Andrews, Geoff ed. (1991) *Citizenship* (Lawrence and Wishart Ltd, London).

Arendt, Hannah (1953) "Understanding Politics", *Partisan Review*, 20, 1953.

Arendt, Hannah (1958) *The Human Condition* (Chicago University Press, Chicago).

Arendt, Hannah (1976) *Eichmann in Jerusalem: A Report on the Banality of Evil* (Penguin Books, New York).

Arendt, Hannah (1978) *The Life of the Mind, Volume 1: Thinking* (Secker and Warburg, London).

Barr, Nicholas (1987) *The Economics of the Welfare State* (Weidenfeld and Nicholson, London).

Barry, Brian (1973) *The Liberal Theory of Justice* (Clarendon Press, Oxford).

Bauman, Zygmunt (1988) *Freedom* (Open University Press, Milton Keynes).

Benn, S. I. (1967) "Freedom and Persuasion", *Australasian Journal of Philosophy* Volume 45, pp.259-275.

Benn, S. I. (1975/76) "Freedom, Autonomy and the Concept of a Person", *Proceedings of the Aristotelian Society* LXXVI, pp.109-130.

Benn, S. I. and Weinstein, W. L. (1971) "Being Free To Act, and Being a Free Man", *Mind* Volume 80, pp.194-211

Benn, S. I. and Weinstein, W. L. (1974) "Freedom as the Non-restriction of Options: A Rejoinder", *Mind* Volume 83, pp.435-438.

Berlin Isaiah (1962), "Does Political Theory Still Exist?" in P.Laslett and W.G.Runciman, eds. *Philosophy, Politics and Society* Second Series (Basil Blackwell, Oxford).

Berlin, Isaiah (1969) *Four Essays on Liberty* (Oxford University Press, Oxford).

Brown, Alan (1986) *Modern Political Philosophy: Theories of the Just Society* (Penguin Books, Harmondsworth).

Browning, Christopher R. (1993) *Ordinary Men: Reserve Police Battalion 101 and the Final Solution in Poland* (HarperCollins, New York).

Cane, Norman S. "On Fixing Social Concepts", *Ethics* Volume 84 Number 1, pp.10-21.

Clarke, Barry (1980) "Beyond 'The Banality of Evil'", *British Journal of Political Science*, Volume 10 Part 4, pp.417-439.

Cole, Phillip (1987) "Social Liberty and the Physically Disabled", *The Journal of Applied Philosophy* Volume 4 Number 1, pp.29-39.

Commission on Social Justice (1993) *The Justice Gap* (Institute for Public Policy Research).

Commission on Social Justice (1994) *Social Justice: Strategies for National Renewal* (Vintage, London).

Connolly, William (1983) *The Terms of Political Discourse* Second Edition (Martin Robertson, Oxford).

Connolly, William (1984) "The Dilemma of Legitimacy", in William Connolly, ed. *Legitimacy and the State* (Blackwell, Oxford).

Crocker, Lawrence (1980) *Positive Liberty: An Essay in Normative Political Philosophy* (Martinus Nijhoff, The Hague).

D'Entreves, Maurizio Passerin (1994) *The Political Philosophy of Hannah Arendt* (Routledge, London).

Dahrendorf, Ralf (1975) *The New Liberty* (Routledge and Kegan Paul, London).

Dahrendorf, Ralf (1979) *Life Chances: Approaches to Social and Political Theory* (Weidenfeld and Nicholson, London).

Dahrendorf, Ralf (1987), *Times Higher Education Supplement*, September 14th.

Day, J. P. (1977) "Threats, Offers, Law, Opinion, and Liberty", *American Philosophical Quarterly* Volume 14 Number 4, pp.257-272.

Day, J. P. (1986) "Is the Concept of Freedom Essentially Contestable", *Philosophy* Volume 6, pp.116-123.

Day, J. P. (1987) *Liberty and Justice* (Croom Helm, London).

Dworkin, Ronald (1977) *Taking Rights Seriously* (Duckworth, London).

Dworkin, Ronald (1978) "Liberalism", in Hampshire, S. ed. *Public and Private Morality* (Cambridge University Press, Cambridge).

Dworkin, Ronald (1981) "What is Equality? Part II: Equality of Resources", *Philosophy and Public Affairs* Volume 10 Number 4, pp.283-345.

Dworkin, Ronald (1986) *Law's Empire* (Harvard University Press, Cambridge Mass.).

Dworkin, Ronald (1987) "What is Equality? Part III: The Place of Liberty", *Iowa Law Review*, 73/1, pp 1-54.

Feinberg, Joel (1973) *Social Philosophy* (Prentice Hall Inc., Englewood Cliffs, New Jersey).

Field, Frank "Britain's Underclass: Countering the Growth", in Lister, Ruth ed. (1996) *Charles Murray and the Underclass: the Developing Debate*, the IEA Health and Welfare Unit, Choice in Welfare Number 33, November 1996.

Field, Frank (1981) *Inequality in Britain: Freedom, Welfare and the State* (Fontana, Glasgow).

Flathman, Richard (1987) *The Philosophy and Politics of Freedom* (Chicago University Press, Chicago).

Flew, Antony (1981) *The Politics of Procrustes* (Temple Smith, London).

Flew, Antony (1985) "The Concept, and Conceptions of Justice", *Journal of Applied Philosophy* Volume 2 Number 2, pp.191-196.

Gallie, W. B. (1955/56) "Essentially Contested Concepts", *Aristotelian Society Proceedings* LVI, pp.167-198.

Galston, William (1991) *Liberal Purposes: Goods, Virtues and Diversity in the Liberal State*, (Cambridge University Press).

Golding, R.G. ed. (1986) *Excluding the Poor* (Child Poverty Action Group, London).

Gordon, P. (1989) *Citizenship for some? Race and Government policy 1979-1989*, (Runnymede Trust).

Graves, Robert (1972) *I, Claudius* (Penguin, Harmondsworth).
Gray, John (1983) "Political Power, Social Theory, and Essential Contestability", in Miller, D. and Siedentop, L. eds. *The Nature of Political Theory* (Clarendon Press, Oxford).
Gray, John (1984) "On Negative and Positive Liberty", in Gray, J. and Pelczynski, Z. eds. *Conceptions of Liberty in Political Philosophy* (Athlone Press, London).
Gray, John (1986) *Liberalism* (Open University Press, Milton Keynes).
Grimshaw, Jean (1986) *Feminist Philosophers: Women's Perspectives on Philosophical Traditions* (Harvester Wheatsheaf, London).
Gutmann, Amy (1980) *Liberal Equality* (Cambridge University Press, Cambridge).
Hahn, Frank and Hollis, Martin eds. (1979) *Philosophy and Economic Theory* (Oxford University Press, Oxford).
Haines, Andrew and Smith, Richard (1997) "Working together to reduce poverty's damage", *British Medical Journal*, Volume 314, February 22nd, pp.529-531.
Haksar, Vinit (1979) *Equality, Liberty and Perfectionism* (Oxford University Press, Oxford).
Hall, John A. (1988) *Liberalism* (Paladin, London).
Hampshire, Stuart (1989) *Innocence and Experience* (Harvard University Press, Cambridge, Mass.).
Hart, J. H. (1971) "The Inverse Care Law", *Lancet* 1, February 26th.
Hayek, F. A. (1944) *The Road to Serfdom* (Chicago, Chicago University Press).
Hayek, F. A. (1960) *The Constitution of Liberty* (University of Chicago Press, Chicago).
Hayek, F. A. (1973-1979) *Rules and Order*, Volume 1 of *Law, Legislation and Liberty* (Routledge and Kegan Paul, London).
Hayek, F.A. (1973-1979) *The Mirage of Social Justice Volume 2 of Law, Legislation and Liberty* (Routledge and Kegan Paul, London).
Heath, Eugene (1989) "How to Understand Liberalism as Gardening: Galeotti on Hayek", *Political Theory*, Volume 17 Number 1, February, pp.107-113.
Hobbes, Thomas (1968) *Leviathan*, ed. Macpherson, C.B. (Penguin, Harmondsworth).
Holman, Robert (1978) *Poverty: Explanations of Social Deprivation* (Martin Robertson, London).
Hume, David (1975) *Enquiries Concerning Human Understanding and the Principles of Morals* Third Edition, Nidditch, P. N. ed. (Oxford University Press, Oxford).
Kant, Immanuel (1960) *Religion Within the Limits of Reason Alone*, Green, T. M. and Hudson, H. H. trans. (Harper and Row, New York).
Kymlicka, Will (1990) *Contemporary Political Philosophy: An Introduction* (Clarendon Press, Oxford).
Kymlicka, Will and Norman, Wayne (1994) "Return of the Citizen: a Survey of Recent Work on Citizenship Theory", in *Ethics* 104 (January), pp.352-381.
Laslett, Peter ed. (1956) *Philosophy, Politics and Society* First Series (Basil Blackwell, Oxford).
Le Grand, Julian (1982) *The Strategy of Equality* (HarperCollins, London).

Le Grand, Julian (1991) *Equality and Choice: an Essay in Economics and Applied Philosophy* (HarperCollins, London).

Leiser, B. M. (1973) *Liberty, Justice and Morals* Second Edition (Macmillan, New York).

Lister, Ruth (1990) *The Exclusive Society -- Citizenship and the Poor* (Child Poverty Action Group).

Lister, Ruth ed. (1996) *Charles Murray and the Underclass: the Developing Debate*, the IEA Health and Welfare Unit, Choice in Welfare Number 33, November 1996.

Locke, John (1924) *Two Treatises of Government* (Dent, London).

Macpherson, C. B. (1962) *The Political Theory of Possessive Individualism* (Oxford University Press, Oxford).

Marshall, T. H. (1952) *Citizenship and Social Class* (Cambridge University Press, Cambridge).

Maser, Werner (1979) *Nuremberg: a Nation on Trial*, translated from the German by Barry, Richard (Allen Lane, London).

McCloskey, H. J. (1965) "A Critique of the Ideals of Liberty", *Mind*, Volume 74, pp.483-508.

McIntyre, Alistair (1973) "The Essential Contestability of Some Social Concepts", *Ethics* Volume 84 Number 1, pp.1-9.

Miller, David (1976) *Social Justice* (Clarendon Press, Oxford).

Miller, David (1983) "Constraints on Freedom", *Ethics* Volume 94 Number 1, pp.66-86.

Miller, David (1985) "Reply to Oppenheim", *Ethics* Volume 95 Number 2, pp.310-314.

Miller, David (1991) ed. *Liberty* (Oxford University Press).

Muller, H. J. (1961) *Freedom in the Ancient World* (Secker and Warburg, London).

Murray, Charles "The Emerging British Underclass", in Lister, Ruth ed. (1996) *Charles Murray and the Underclass: the Developing Debate*, the IEA Health and Welfare Unit, Choice in Welfare Number 33, November 1996.

Nozick, Robert (1974) *Anarchy, State and Utopia* (Basil Blackwell, Oxford).

Oldfield, Adrian (1990) "Citizenship: an unnatural practice", *Political Quarterly* Vol 61 No 2, April-June, pp.177-187.

Oppenheim, Felix (1961) *Dimensions of Freedom* (St Martin's Press, New York).

Oppenheim, Felix (1985) "'Constraints on Freedom' as a Descriptive Concept", *Ethics* Volume 95 Number 2, pp.305-309.

Padfield, Peter (1984) *Donitz: the Last Fuhrer -- Portrait of a Nazi War Leader* (Victor Gollancz Ltd, London).

Parent, W. A. (1974A) "Some Recent Work on the Concept of Liberty", *American Philosophical Quarterly*, Volume 11 Number 3, pp.149-167.

Parent, W. A. (1974B) "Freedom as the Non-restriction of Options", *Mind* Volume 83, pp.432-434.

Parker, Hermione (1989) *Instead of the Dole* (Routledge).

Parkinson, Geoffrey (1984) "Spinoza on the Freedom of Man and the Freedom of the Citizen," in Gray, J. and Pelczynski, Z. eds. *Conceptions of Liberty in Political Philosophy* (Athlone Press, London).

Pateman, Carole (1988) "The Patriarchal Welfare State" in Gutmann, Amy ed. *Democracy and the Welfare State* (Princeton University Press, Princeton).

Plant, Raymond (1988) *Citizenship, Rights and Socialist*, Fabian Society Number 531, October.

Plant, Raymond (1991) "Social Rights and the Reconstruction of Welfare", in Andrews, Geoff ed. *Citizenship* (Lawrence and Wishart, London).

Pocock, David (1985) "Unruly Evil", in Parkin, David ed. *The Anthropology of Evil* (Basil Blackwell, Oxford).

Ranken, Nani L. (1986) "Compensation vs. Fair Equality of Opportunity", *Journal of Applied Philosophy* Volume 3 Number 1, pp.111-122.

Raphael D. D (1980), "Tensions Between Equality and Freedom", in Raphael, D. D. *Justice and Liberty* (The Athlone Press, London).

Rawls, John (1972) *A Theory of Justice* (Oxford University Press, Oxford).

Rawls, John (1978) "The Basic Structure as Subject" in Goldman, A. and Kim, J. eds. *Values and Morals*, (Reidel, Dordrecht).

Rawls, John (1980) "Kantian Constructivism in Moral Theory", *Journal of Philosophy* Volume LXXVII Number 9, pp.515-572.

Rawls, John (1982) "The Basic Liberties and Their Priority", in McMurrin, S. ed. *The Tanner Lectures on Human Values: Volume 3* (Utah University Press, Salt Lake City).

Raz, Joseph (1986) *The Morality of Freedom* (Clarendon Press, Oxford.

Rein, Martin (1970) "Problems in the Definition and Measurement of Poverty", in Townsend, Peter ed. *The Poverty Debate* (Heinemann, London).

Scheffler, Samuel (1982) "Natural Rights, Equality, and the Minimal State", in Paul, Jeffrey ed. *Reading Nozick* (Basil Blackwell, Oxford).

Skillen, Antony (1985) "Welfare State versus Welfare Society", *Journal of Applied Philosophy*, Volume 2 Number 1, pp.3-18.

Staub, Ervin (1989) *The Roots of Evil: the Origins of Genocide and Other Group Violence* (Cambridge University Press, Cambridge).

Swanton, Christine (1985) "On the 'Essential Contestedness' of Political Concepts", *Ethics*, Volume 95 Number 4, pp.811-827.

Taylor, Charles (1985) "What's Wrong with Negative Liberty", in Taylor, Charles *Philosophy and Human Sciences: Philosophical Papers Volume 2* (Cambridge University Press, Cambridge).

Townsend, Peter (1979) *Poverty in the United Kingdom* (Allen Lane, London).

Townsend, Peter ed. (1970) *The Poverty Debate* (Heinemann, London).

Townsend, Peter, Davidson, Nick and Whitehead, Margaret eds. (1988) *Inequalities of Health* (Penguin, Harmondsworth).

United Nations Development Programme (1996) *Human development report 1996* (Oxford University Press, New York).

Vonnegut, Kurt (1950) "Harrison Bergeron", in *Welcome to the Monkey House* (Dell, New York).

Walzer, Michael (1983) *Spheres of Justice: a Defence of Pluralism and Equality* (Martin Robertson, Oxford).

Wilkinson, R. G. (1996) *Unhealthy Societies: the Afflictions of Inequality* (Routledge, London).

227

Wolin, Sheldon (1987) "Democracy and the Welfare State: The Political and Theoretical Connections between Staatsrason and Wohlfahrtstaatsrason", *Political Theory* Volume 15 Number 4, pp.467-500.

Young, Robert (1986) *Personal Autonomy: Beyond Negative and Positive Liberty* (Croom Helm, Beckenham).

# Index

230

Intentionality thesis 63-65, 73-76, 86n
Internal/external distinction 67-68
Intervention 123-125, 133-134, 136, 139, 143, 150-153

Kant, Immanuel
  and equality 16
  on evil 105-106
Kymlicka, Will on equality 16-17
Kymlicka, Will and Norman, Wayne
    on citizenship 203

Laslett, Peter on the linguistic turn 27n
Le Grand, Julian
  on health 168, 169
  on luck 185-186
Liberal theory 13-15
Liberation 208, 211, 221
Liberation model of welfare 206
Liberty (see also freedom) 14
  negative 1, 5, 57-58
  positive 1, 89-90, 90-91, 92, 94
Life chances 113-115, 116, 117
Ligatures 114-115, 116
Limited government 14
Linguistic turn 20, 27n
Lister, Ruth on the underclass 159n
Locke, John
  and equality 16
  on private property 159n

Marshall, T. H. on rights 209-210
McCloskey, H. J. on conditions of freedom 213-214
Membership 3, 4, 15, 17-18, 115-116, 118, 123, 124, 142, 161-162, 173, 177-178, 193, 195-196, 199, 202, 206, 207, 210, 214, 216, 217, 218-219, 220-221
  civil framework of 208, 209

conditions of 207, 209
  democratic framework of 208-209
  and equality 177-178
  frameworks of 195, 208-209, 210, 215, 216
  social framework of 208, 216
Mentally handicapped and freedom 70
Mill, John Stuart and equality 16
Miller, David
  on constraints on freedom 42-43
  and essential contestability 28n
  and the linguistic turn 20, 23, 25
  on moral responsibility 53n
  on positive liberty 89-90
Moral equality 4, 13, 15, 49-50, 145, 124-125
Moral reasoning 104-105

Natural/social distinction 62-63, 78, 82
Negative aspects of freedom 2
Negative conditions of freedom 2, 6, 52, 87, 102, 124-125, 135
Negative freedom 30-31
Negative liberty 1, 5, 57-58
Negative neutrality between persons 125-126, 133-135, 143, 158
Neutrality 7, 13, 124-125
  negative 125, 133, 135, 136, 157-158
  between persons 125-126, 131-136
  positive 126, 135, 136, 142, 158
  on the valuable life 133, 144, 145-149
No-harm principle 143-144
Non-interference condition of freedom 3, 7, 59, 89, 118-123
Nozick, Robert
  on border crossings 208
  on compensation 178-179
  on the difference principle 136-137
  on entitlement 153
  and the Entitlement Theory 154-155, 179

on equality 20, 137-142, 161
and liberal theory 15, 27n
on moral theory 147-148
on positive neutrality 136
on property 153, 159n
and rectification 156
Nuremberg trials 107

Oldfield, Adrian on citizenship 204-205
Oppenheim, Felix
on constraints on freedom 42-43
on essential contestability 27-28n
Options 18, 80-81, 112-113, 113-115, 116-117

Parent, W. A.
on freedom and opportunity 69
on the intentionality thesis 71-72
and the internal external distinction 68
on liberty/worth of liberty distinction 89
on the physically disabled and freedom 71
and the pure negative theory of freedom 66
on social freedom and freedom of choice 69
on the value of freedom 213
Participation 3-4, 49-50, 52, 162, 174, 189, 190, 193, 202, 204, 211, 216, 221
Physically disabled
and exclusion 30, 31-32, 44, 46, 49, 52, 65-66, 217
and freedom 39, 42, 70, 77, 81-84
and social justice 45-46
Pluralism 13, 126
Pocock, John on evil 106
Political theories 13, 26
Positive aspects of freedom 2

Positive conditions of freedom 2, 4, 6, 47-48, 49, 52, 87, 102, 125, 135, 211
Positive liberty 1, 89-90, 90-91, 92, 94
Positive neutrality between persons 126, 135, 136, 142, 158
Poverty 163-165
absolute 163-165
relative 163-165
Power 25, 48, 80, 198, 214-215, 220
Power/control model of welfare 197, 206
Power condition of freedom 3, 7, 59, 88, 123, 207-208
Private property 14
Public order 14
Pure negative theory of freedom 31, 34, 37, 84-85

Quality of the will 88

Rational choice 80, 89, 95-96, 101, 102-104, 118
Rationality 95-96, 101, 104
Rawls, John
on the basic liberties 127-128
on compensation 179, 208
on the difference principle 136-137, 161, 179
on equal liberty 53n
on equality 161-162
on inequality 181-182
and liberal theory 15
on liberty 29-30
on the moral powers 128-129
on the 'natural lottery' 182, 187-188
on natural and social primary goods 168
on pluralism 126
and political theory 20

233